# Building B2B Applications with XML

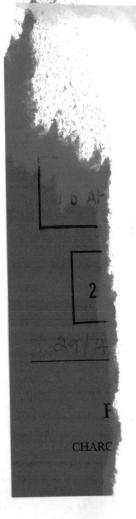

# Building B2B Applications with XML

## A Resource Guide

Michael Fitzgerald

**Wiley Computer Publishing**

**John Wiley & Sons,** Inc.

NEW YORK · CHICHESTER · WEINHEIM · BRISBANE · SINGAPORE · TORONTO

Publisher: Robert Ipsen
Editor: Cary Sullivan
Assistant Editor: Christina Berry
Managing Editor: Marnie Wielage
Associate New Media Editor: Brian Snapp
Text Design & Composition: Publishers' Design and Production Services, Inc.

This book is printed on acid-free paper. ♾

Published by John Wiley & Sons, Inc.

Published simultaneously in Canada.

This publication is designed to provide accurate and authoritative information in regard to the subject matter covered. It is sold with the understanding that the publisher is not engaged in professional services. If professional advice or other expert assistance is required, the services of a competent professional person should be sought.

*Library of Congress Cataloging-in-Publication Data:*

Fitzgerald, Michael.
    Building B2B applications with XML : a resource guide / Michael Fitzgerald.
      p. cm.
    Includes index.
    ISBN 0-471-40401-2 (pbk. : alk. paper)
    1. Electronic commerce.  2. XML (Document markup language)  3. Internet marketing.  I. Title
    HF5548.32 .F575  2001
    005.7'2—dc21                        2001017670

Printed in the United States of America.

10 9 8 7 6 5 4 3 2 1

For Cristi, Melissa, Amy, and Aubrey:

"While we look not at the things which are seen,
but at the things which are not seen: for the
things which are seen are temporal; but the
things which are not seen are eternal."

—2 Corinthians 4:18

# Contents

# Notes                                                           285

# Acknowledgments

I want to thank Robert J. Brunner for his many helpful comments and timely arrival on the scene. Thanks also to Christina Berry for her much needed guidance on this project, from beginning to end. And thanks to Cary Sullivan who, hope against hope, continued to believe in this book, even in its darkest hour. Finally, thank you, Cristi, for everything. None of this would be any fun without you.

# Introduction

With the huge potential of business-to-business (B2B) commerce over the Internet, reaching perhaps into the trillions of dollars in the first few years of the twenty-first century, it is no surprise that a lot of companies are offering B2B software solutions, all under-girded by Extensible Markup Language (XML), for the exchange of trading partner agreements, purchase orders, catalog data, and other business documents. This book is about how you can get a B2B system up and running yourself. It's not about how to select and purchase a ready-made system, however: It's about how you can build your own B2B system using freely available resources.

Maybe you're like me: I'm not satisfied to just drive the car, I want to know and understand what's going on under the hood as well. I could purchase an off-the-shelf B2B system, but why let everyone else have all the fun?

This is a book for software mechanics, folks who want see how and why all the parts and pieces of a B2B system fit together. You won't find a single, monolithic software solution between the covers of this book, but what you will find is a wide variety of resources—technologies, standards, and example programs—from which you can create your own, tailor-made B2B system to suit your needs.

I'll also help you understand why XML is the foundation upon which the B2B world rests. Does all the hype about XML and B2B make your stomach churn? It makes me queasy, too, but the nice thing about all the hype is that, by and large, it is warranted. XML won't become the be-all and end-all solution behind every software application, but it is a very important development in data exchange that cannot be ignored. Likewise, B2B may not be for everyone right now, just like the telephone wasn't for everyone in 1900, but it is a trend you and I must watch if we don't want to be left out or left behind.

As B2B technology gets into the hands of people, and into all the far reaches of the world, I predict that it will become ubiquitous. Like the telephone, not everyone will understand how it works, but a small company in Amsterdam will be able to send, with just a few keystrokes or mouse clicks, a digitally signed purchase order to a supplier in Hong Kong, and receive an immediate confirmation for that order, all in a matter of seconds over the Internet. That's what I think B2B is all about.

The potential gains for commerce in speed and efficiency cannot be lightly passed over. This book will help you get your bearings on B2B, bearings on what is happening in the B2B field, and how you can make it happen at your own company without spending a cool million.

## Who Should Read This Book

This book is for software developers and software managers—for anyone, really, who has the desire to begin, or responsibility for beginning a B2B project, whether it's just getting up to speed on the subject, preparing to oversee a B2B venture, or building a software framework for a B2B implementation.

If you are a manager and decision-maker, this book will give you a broad overview of how B2B systems work together and talk to each other. A software developer will find the resources, including sample Java code, to piece together solid programs that support B2B activities. Web developers, especially those serving up XML on business Web sites, will be interested to see the coverage of XML vocabularies and protocols, and how XML documents can be moved, stored, and retrieved.

## Technology Overview

This book broadly covers the technology behind B2B. It takes a logical approach, starting with XML as the ground floor technology of B2B, then progressing through transport mechanisms such as Hypertext Transfer Protocol (HTTP), Simple Mail Transfer Protocol (SMTP), and File Transfer

Protocol (FTP). A wide array of security technologies are introduced, including public and private keys, digital signatures, digital certificates, XML Signature, and Pretty Good Privacy (PGP). Also covered are XML vocabularies such as Electronic Business XML (ebXML), Commerce XML (cXML), and XML Common Business Language (xCBL), plus protocols such as Simple Object Access Protocol (SOAP) and BizTalk.

**NOTE** I have made a great effort to provide wide-ranging coverage of technologies related to B2B. Nevertheless, I was not able to cover every topic in agonizing detail. What this book will do is provide you with a general and somewhat detailed background of each of the areas covered, enough to help you make decisions if you are a manager, and to get your coding underway if you are a software engineer. Much of the detail is referenced in the notes at the end of this book.

## How This Book Is Organized

The book is divided into two parts. After an introductory chapter, Part One, "Foundation Technologies for B2B," covers the technological groundwork for a B2B system.

**Chapter 2, "The XML Foundation"** Covers XML, the underlying foundation for the universal exchange of data and documents.

**Chapter 3, "Transport"** Considers standard mechanisms for transport, such as HTTP, SMTP, and FTP.

**Chapter 4, "Security"** Explores many options for transporting B2B documents securely, including encryption, public and private keys, digital signatures, and authentication schemes. You will also learn about an XML Signature implementation called XML Security Suite (XSS) and PGP.

Part Two, "Vocabularies, Frameworks, and Protocols," is devoted to XML vocabularies and protocols that you can use to create and package B2B documents.

**Chapter 5, " ebXML"** Discusses the Oasis-UN/CEFACT joint effort to create a global B2B standard, Electronic Business XML (ebXML).

**Chapter 6, "xCBL"** Covers Commerce One's vocabulary XML Common Business Library or xCBL.

**Chapter 7, "cXML"** Reviews Ariba's Commerce XML (cXML) vocabulary.

Chapter 8, "Simple Object Access Protocol" Examines SOAP, a messaging protocol for packaging B2B and other XML documents.

Chapter 9, "BizTalk" Investigates BizTalk, Microsoft's SOAP implementation and B2B Web engine.

Chapter 10, "Putting It All Together" Summarizes the book and provides a checklist for using the technologies explored to build a simple B2B system. Endnotes at the end of the book provide numerous references for the resources mentioned throughout the chapters.

**NOTE** Unfortunately, RosettaNet is not discussed because the book had to go into production just before version 2.0 of the RosettaNet Implementation Framework (RNIF v2.0) was released. The book's companion Web site provides some RosettaNet resources.

## What's on the Companion Web Site

To access resources related to this book, check out the companion Web site at www.wiley.com/compbooks/fitzgerald. Here you will find a code archive for the programs presented in the book, links to online resources, plus book and technology updates. Because things can change quickly, it's a good idea to regularly check the companion site for breaking information on these rapidly evolving technologies.

## A Little Dream

The overwhelming thing about a book like this—one that covers a vast subject and fast-growing trend—is that you can't capture it all. For example, I have provided a handful of sample programs written in Java to help model the behavior of a B2B system. I wish I could have provided more programs, and to have written versions of them in C or C++, too, but I couldn't with my schedule. The thought occurred to me while developing this book, "Wouldn't it be great to get some help?"

So that's what I am asking for: Your help. You can take the ten programs provided with the book and do what you will with them, and here's my plea: If you can figure out better ways to do things, or you have written new and improved versions of these programs, then by all means share your ideas with me and the other folks who will read this book. I will be happy to credit you properly for any resources, programs, or otherwise, that you bring to the table. My little dream-come-true would be to create a repository of robust programs, free for the taking, that will evolve into an open source library of B2B software.

I hope you enjoy this book. It was a lot of fun to write—well, it was mostly fun to write. Even when it wasn't fun, I always knew it would be worthwhile. I hope you think it's worthwhile, too.

# Building B2B
# Applications with XML

# PART
# One

# Foundation
# Technologies for B2B

Part One covers the technological groundwork for a B2B system. After Chapter 1 introduces basic B2B concepts, Chapter 2, "The XML Solution," covers Extensible Markup Language (XML), the underlying foundation for the universal exchange of data and documents. Chapter 3, "Transport," considers standard mechanisms for transport, such as Hypertext Transfer Protocol. Lastly, Chapter 4, "Security," explores many options for transporting B2B documents securely, including encryption, digital signatures, and authentication schemes.

# Getting Down to Business-to-Business

On June 17, 1812, the United States Senate passed by just six votes a resolution declaring war on Great Britain. Unknown to the American Congress, however, an English act called the Orders in Council, which had curtailed American shipping and commerce and was an incentive to war, had been repealed by the British on June 16, only the day before. Nonetheless, on June 18, United States president James Madison signed an official declaration of war against Great Britain. So began the second American revolutionary war, or what later became known as the War of 1812.

That's not the whole story, either. Slow, faulty communication was not unusual for the early nineteenth century, and it was the first and last tyrant of the war. A treaty of peace formally ending the conflict had been signed by American and British delegations in Ghent, Belgium, on Christmas Eve, 1814. Unwittingly, the American "dirty shirts" and British redcoats fought on in the Battle of New Orleans and other skirmishes until word of the peace treaty finally arrived in February 1815.

The War of 1812 might never have began, nor ended months *after* the signing of the Treaty of Ghent, if someone could have picked up a telephone, sent a fax or an email, updated a Web site, or pushed a document across the Internet. Technology has not put an end to war, but I wonder if things would have turned out differently if at the beginning of the nineteenth century the United States and Great Britain had the technology that we have at the dawn of the twenty-first.

That's what this book is about: using the Internet to speed communication and to reduce or even eliminate the obstacles to commerce. I'm talking about business-to-business (B2B) communication.

## What Is Business-to-Business?

The meaning of the acronym *B2B* seems to be expanding daily, but we can nail down a couple of definitions for now. First of all, I think B2B means businesses doing business with each other, not just in traditional ways, but across the Internet and using virtually instant communication to make their enterprises not only increase sales but run more smoothly, quickly, and cheaply.

B2B, then, is about businesses working with other businesses to increase their profits and about organizations and governments communicating rapidly and efficiently. It means exchanging documents, such as orders, invoices, prices lists, scientific papers, legislation—you name it—not by fax or ground mail, but over the Net. Instead of heaps of paper jammed into filing cabinets, it's electronic documents stored on disk drives, still available to be printed at will. It's a year of transactions written onto a single optical disk and tucked away in your desk drawer. B2B is about legal agreements signed digitally by parties on different continents, executing them in minutes rather than weeks. It's about increasing the velocity and volume of commerce between remote systems running on incompatible platforms, now bridged via a mutually agreed-upon B2B interchange.

B2B is about sharing ideas, software, secrets, services, products, plans, goals, deals, and customers, all as fast as the Internet can carry them, which, if you have a decent network connection, might amount to only a second or two. It's about doing business faster, more efficiently, more accurately, and far less expensively so that you win, your organization wins, your government agency wins, your trading partners win, your customers win, everybody wins.

One of the most important technologies relating to B2B commerce is Extensible Markup Language, or XML. XML undergirds most, if not all, the technology that will support the new B2B commerce model. This book's main focus is how XML and other Internet technologies will make B2B as common as the desktop computer.

## B2B, B2C, C2C, A2A, and All That Jazz

Well, you know what B2B means by now, and you've probably seen the terms *B2C* and *C2C*. B2C stands for *business-to-consumer*. This refers to a direct business-consumer connection via the Internet, such as when you order a product from an Internet-based vendor. That business might be a product manufacturer, such as Dell, which markets directly to buyers, or it could be a vendor that takes on the traditional role of wholesaler, hawking an array of goods from disparate sources, such as Amazon.com.

C2C stands for *consumer-to-consumer*. This arrangement makes it possible to purchase items in single units or small quantities person-to-person such as through an online auction house—eBay.com, of course, comes immediately to mind, or auctions.yahoo.com. These sites, as well as portals to them like biddersedge.com, let individuals purchase from individuals somewhat efficiently. Buying one-on-one has been possible in the past by national print publications, but never before the Internet could you search for, find, and pay for your purchase so fast.

B2C and C2C are important components in the Internet marketplace, and they sometimes even share space, such as at JCPenney.com. This book, though, deals with B2B space almost exclusively.

A2A stands for *application-to-application*. What this means is that an application can communicate directly with another application, usually across a network. As the name implies, this process is automatic and requires no human intervention. Even though it can also require human interaction, one of the obvious goals of B2B is to set systems up so that they can communicate with one another automatically.

## What about EDI?

Electronic Data Interchange, or EDI, is a format for electronic trade and commerce that has evolved into national and international standards (ANSI X12, ISO 9735, and UN/EDIFACT). A number of major corporations have adopted EDI, but it has not made its way down to smaller companies because of cost and other barriers. While a larger company can benefit from reducing transaction costs through EDI, it must also be able to foot the bill for consulting, infrastructure, and maintenance. Even the cost of EDI specifications alone, amounting to hundreds of dollars, might be enough of a hurdle to keep the little guy out of the race.

If you take a close look at EDI, you will see that many of its concepts have been incorporated into the B2B model, and efforts are underway to wrap EDI in XML vocabularies, such as Open Buying on the Internet (OBI).

EDI will be around for a while, and it won't be replaced by XML anytime soon. Just as the simplicity and minimal cost of HyperText Markup Language (HTML) opened the doors for the small operator to get on the Web, so B2B will make it possible for just about anybody to automate and quicken the pace of business transactions.

## Tired of the Hype?

Is all this blather about B2B making your eyes roll back in your head? I have to admit that the hype drives me a little nuts, too, and that chatting with high-tech hucksters about the virtues of B2B on a trade-show floor is not my favorite way to spend an afternoon, either.

Don't get me wrong: I'm not saying that B2B is a cure-all or even a done deal, but I'll hold firm in my conviction that, all hype notwithstanding, B2B is enormously promising. I'll even go so far as to predict that its impact on commerce will rival the Industrial Revolution in its reach. I won't say that it will happen tomorrow or even next year—these things often take more time than you think—but it will happen.

How dare I be so bold? Well, I think B2B will succeed because its concepts are built on a small framework of simple, universal, proven, and readily-available Internet technologies that are easy to understand and implement. Now because of this, everyone and his pot-bellied pig is putting together a prepackaged, off-the-shelf B2B system to sell you, and maybe that's the best way for you to go. But because I suffer from being cheap, curious, and confident, I ask, "Why let them have all the fun? I can do this myself."

I have not put together a full-blown, point-and-click B2B solution in this book. Far from it. But what I have provided is some instructions, some ideas, and a lot of examples on how you can put together your B2B package, without spending very much money. I believe that if you put the simple examples in this book into practice, you will have the pieces and resources you need to build your own basic B2B system, and you will have fun while you are at it.

> **NOTE**   I must mention that *B2B* also refers to the growing number of Web sites and resources dedicated to businesses doing business with each other in a common marketplace, from simple business-as-customer relationships to large-scale exchanges set up to do business online much as you would on the trading floor of a stock exchange. Although this is an exciting aspect of B2B, it is not the focus of this book.

## Rome, the Pony Express, Western Union, and Beyond

Message delivery systems have been around for a very long time. Ancient cultures from the Chinese to the Aztecs developed regular systems for carrying messages, usually by mercurial runners who galloped from one end of a kingdom to the other. Under Augustus Caesar (27 B.C. to 14 A.D.), the Romans established a mail system, complete with post offices or houses along the many roads that had been built to keep Rome's war machine rolling. Horsemen often carried these messages, mainly for military purposes, but some private mail was allowed in the empire's waning years (fourth and fifth centuries A.D.). Private mail flourished in the Middle Ages, such as ecclesiastical or guild-based systems, but these systems were inefficient and limited in scope. Modern mail, such as the system set up in colonial America, has grown from small beginnings to huge networks like the United States Post Office.

In April 1860, the Pony Express mail delivery service was established between Missouri and California. At that time, rail lines extending from the East coast of the United States reached west to St. Joseph, Missouri, but for a mere $5.00 per half-ounce, you could send a letter nearly 2,000 miles to Sacramento, California, usually in about 10 days. Mail was carried in a specially designed four-pocket saddle bag called a *mochila*. Riders had to meet strict qualifications. The newspaper ad read, "Wanted: Young, skinny, wiry fellows not over 18. Must be expert riders willing to risk death daily. Orphans preferred." Before saddling up, conscripts had to swear on a Bible that they would be honest in their dealings, not fight or cuss, nor abuse their mounts.

The following year, the Western Union Telegraph Company completed the transcontinental telegraph service on October 24, 1861. The Pony Express went out of business on October 26, 1861.

In 1878, Western Union tried to get into the telephone business but was legally forced to sell out to the Bell Telephone Company the following year. Nevertheless, Western Union stayed afloat by offering not only telegraph services but other communications services as well. In 1871, Western Union holds claim to the first electronic commerce transaction with a money order transfer. During the twentieth century, the company developed microwave radio and satellite messaging systems, and Western Union survives as a subsidiary of First Data Corporation. Today it offers such services as free email, loan and credit card services, and for less than $10, you can still have a telegram hand-delivered to just about anyone's doorstep—though you can now order it over the Internet.

In October 1969, the Internet was born when a brief message was transported across the fledgling ARPAnet, from a computer at UCLA's Network Measurement Center to a node at Stanford University. That message consisted of the letter *L*, as part of the word *login*. The message actually never got past the letter *G* before the system crashed, but at least the first two letters worked. A total of four nodes were on the network by the end of that year. Some 30 years later, the Internet connects millions of computers and people and carries billions of email messages everyday.

We certainly have changed the way we do things, but messages are still at the heart of the way we communicate, and messages are the key to B2B communication.

## What This Book Will and Will Not Do for You

I don't want to give you the wrong impression about this book. It doesn't cover everything there is to cover about B2B, but it covers a broad spectrum, so that even if you are new at this sort of thing, you will find the information you need to build your own system.

Even though you will find a lot of analysis and recommendations in this book, I cannot tell you how to get rich at light speed, nor can I tell you how to implement a solution or exactly how you should write your own B2B applications. Nonetheless, you should come away with enough information to decide what will and what will not work for you or your enterprise.

If you are a Web guru or a Java programmer with considerable experience, you might already know about some of the things I'll discuss in this book. These sections that might be familiar to you are well marked, so if you have already forgotten more about a certain subject than I know, you can just skip that section. But the way this book can help you, and your manager, is by putting the whole enchilada together on one plate, providing tips and ideas as well as directions on where to look for help and get definitive answers. But if it were me, I'd eat the whole meal—read the whole book—even though the recipe looks familiar.

You might even see a programming example and say to yourself, "There's a better way to do that." I hope that if you do, you will share your ideas with me and others. My dream it that this book will incite a riot of coding activity that will yield an open source B2B system project. I can't do it all by myself. I need your help.

The ultimate purpose behind this book is to provide you with a guided tour of how B2B communication works. You will learn about Extensible Markup Language, or XML, which largely forms the backbone of B2B communication. You will learn something of the standard Internet-related technologies that help XML do its job, such as Hypertext Transfer Protocol (HTTP), Multipurpose Internet Mail Extensions (MIME), and Java. You will get to know the consortia and companies that are developing XML vocabularies for B2B communication, such as Electronic Business XML (ebXML), XML Common Business Library (xCBL), Commerce XML (cXML), Simple Object Access Protocol (SOAP), and BizTalk.

## What's in It for You?

A recent report from Goldman Sachs conservatively estimates that gross revenues from B2B online commerce will reach $4.5 trillion by 2005, about 60 percent of all worldwide online commerce (B2B and B2C) combined. That's up from an estimate of only $135 billion in 1999. In 2005, the report also estimates that B2B commerce will amount to nearly 10 percent of the total value of world commerce.

The report also estimates that the B2B provider sector is undervalued by one-half. With the growth potential of B2B commerce, it seems likely that investors will flock to B2B issues, further strengthening overall movement to online business models. One of the strongest opportunities in this arena is for providers of B2B software with revenues in 2005 of an estimated $54 billion, with a trend toward purchased, off-the-shelf solutions rather than in-house software development.

Because the B2B opportunity is so large it is also likely to be pervasive, so pervasive that companies of all sizes that do not put some kind of B2B strategy in place are liable to be left far behind. It goes without saying (but I am going to say it anyway) that the business people, programmers, and Web developers who educate themselves about B2B technology and start down the B2B road as soon as possible will gain advantages over those slower to see the trend and recognize its importance.

## The Tools of Business Today

You are probably familiar, as I am, with how the tools of business work today. There is the ubiquitous PC on almost every desktop, many connected to the Internet. Next to that is a telephone with voice mail, and not far away, maybe along the next aisle of cubicles, are a fax machine and a networked printer.

Along with your regular ground mail, delivered to honeycombs of stacked cardboard mailboxes, you can drop a box off at the loading dock and have it shipped overnight by FedEx, UPS, or Airborne Express. Almost anywhere, sometimes in the most unlikely places, you can hear the bleating of a cellular phone or the chirping of a pager. And who isn't passionate about their new indispensable Palm Pilot or Handspring Visor?

What do all these devices have in common? They are all about people communicating, one person talking to another. In the last few days you probably have tapped out an email message on your computer at work. You probably in the same time frame have sent a letter or a fax or left a phone message, all for what? Most likely for you to communicate with another person. Communication is at the core of business, and humanity, for that matter, if I dare mention the two words in the same sentence.

Sure, those people you communicate with are at times anonymous, but they are still individuals with jobs, individuals who work for businesses or agencies or governments that need to communicate with other individuals. Companies don't talk to companies: Usually it's just one person who needs to talk to another, single person.

If business is largely made of communication, then B2B, likewise, is all about communication, often vital communication. It is also structured communication, which makes it more predictable and, we hope, more orderly than the chaos of communication to which we have grown so accustomed. Using a variety of Internet-related technologies, B2B makes sense of the morass of faxes, phone calls, orders, confirmation letters, invoices, error recovery, and so on that traditionally are all part of executing a single business transaction.

The overall goal of B2B-related software is to integrate business transactions, making them quicker and easier to track, quicker and easier to execute, and, ultimately, making it quicker and easier to ring the cash register.

## A Visit to My Insurance Agent

Not long ago, I sat across the desk from Jerry, my insurance agent. (Jerry isn't his real name, but to save him the embarrassment or unwanted notoriety, I'll just call him Jerry.) I'd come in to get a dental insurance policy.

I like my agent. Jerry is sharp, extremely well organized, hard working, and computer literate, even Web savvy. He does his homework, and I can rely on him to dig down and find a good value. I can't say the same about every insurance agent I have worked with, but Jerry is a standout.

When it came time to quote me the current premium, Jerry pulled a binder off the shelf, where, in an orderly way, he stores lists of his most recent premium quotes. He flipped to the dental section and in a matter of seconds found a list of quotes for the plan I picked out. But he hesitated when he discovered that it had been about a year since he had gotten an updated quote list in the mail.

He looked at his watch. It was about ten minutes to two o'clock Pacific time. That's not quite five o'clock on the East coast, so he figured he could hazard a phone call to Florida. He punched in a number on his telephone and in minutes had a live person on the other end. That person, whoever she was, verified that he did not have the latest prices but that she wouldn't mind faxing him a new list before going home for the day. We didn't have to wait long before Jerry's fax machine was chattering, and he had up-to-the-minute pricing in hand. A few minutes later, I signed the application.

## How B2B Could Help Jerry

What's wrong with Jerry's operation? Nothing at all, really. It's a pretty normal way of doing business these days. It's fairly effective, and I am a satisfied customer. What the system may lack in efficiency, Jerry makes up for in energy. But how could a B2B solution help?

Let's say that the insurance companies that Jerry represents stored all their premium data in XML files that are available on a Web site. These files would contain plain text data, identified by XML markup. This means that instead of being stored in a blind binary file format that requires a proprietary application to read them, the data could be stored in an open format that could be read by a Web browser or an assortment of other applications from a variety of vendors. In other words, XML provides a simple, open, easy-to-understand data or file format that is not locked into a single vendor's software but can be read by a number of applications.

Let's take this a little further. Suppose that a number of the insurance companies that Jerry represents formed a consortium to create or decide on an industry-wide standard XML format for all their insurance data. Given this consensus to use XML in a standard way, it is more likely that large amounts of data could be made available in a simple, agreed-upon format. It is also likely that this vast sea of data—not only premium quotes but all kinds of related data—could be made available easily and securely across the Internet, as well as updated daily. In addition, using different Internet technologies, this data could be accessed on demand, such as from a Web site—or Jerry could set up his computer system to accept nightly updates pushed across the Net.

It would not be much of a logical leap to set up insurance applications online, rather than mailing them in, so the insurance companies that have signed on with the consortium receive them in seconds rather than in days or weeks. And in the United States, since October 2000, an applicant's digital signature is just as legal as a handwritten one. When a company receives an application, it could automatically send a reply to Jerry so that he knows that it was received. In fact, data from the application form could be kept securely on Jerry's local hard drive (also as an encrypted XML document) and reused for other insurance applications. Jerry's life will be getting a whole lot easier.

It would also be easy for Jerry to send out many applications at once for me because he can send them over the Internet and populate the form with local data on disk. Because of this automation, the application process has gotten easier, faster, and highly accurate, making it easier for him to represent even more companies and to offer increasingly competitive rates. To keep up with this high-speed, competitive environment, actuaries would likely calculate a broader spectrum of premiums, and competition would get even stiffer, with reduced costs overall that benefit both the consumer and the vendor.

Similar data or document exchange models could be applied to just about any business. As you might guess, the potential savings and efficiency gains are staggering, if that is a strong enough word.

## OK, What's It Going to Cost?

If you are like me, one of the first questions that comes to mind when I am offered a panacea solution is "How much is it going to cost?" The answer to that question will vary widely depending on many factors, such as whether you buy a complete solution or write your own software, whether involvement in consortia or other coalitions can help reduce development costs, or how fast or how widely you implement a solution—in a department or across a worldwide operation.

If you are an enterprising software engineer, you could implement a worthy B2B system without spending much money at all. Nevertheless, you could devote hundreds of hours to such a project, which, if you are like me, requires you to affix a cost to your time.

On the other hand, if you go for a fully-blown, enterprise-wide, packaged solution, you probably are looking at a price tag somewhere between $250,000 and $500,000. A word to the wise: Learn all you can before you buy.

Regardless of your rollout strategy, a leading provider of B2B integration solutions estimates that the three-year return on investment (ROI) is about 10 times the cost of the investment, or, for a $100,000 investment you get $1,000,000 back. That's a lot better rate of return than my CD at the bank, but it's not FDIC-insured either. I'd take a hard look at data like this, especially if it were fed to me from a technical sales rep and I was shelling out hundreds of thousands of dollars, but they are interesting numbers at the very least.

## A Visit to My Insurance Agent, a Few Years Later

Imagine that a few years later, I visit Jerry's office again, only this time I find that a few things have changed. I'm in this time because I need a denture rider on my dental policy. I notice that Jerry's binders are gone and in their place are several solid bronze statues depicting scenes from the Old West.

After we have hashed over the details of my policy upgrade, Jerry swivels toward his flat-screened, small-form-factor PC, now just on the corner of his desk instead of being parked in a cabinet all its own. The sensitive microphone embedded in the lower-right corner of the screen picks up Jerry's voice.

"Michael Fitzgerald," he says.

After he authenticates himself with a password, my profile appears instantly on Jerry's screen. Vocally he details a few facts into a barely noticeable microphone and submits the denture rider change. In a few seconds, my policy makes a loop on the Internet and is updated with extended coverage and a new premium.

Jerry hesitates. "Before you sign this digitally, let's do a little shopping around." With a few more voice commands, he resubmits the same specs to 10 insurance companies and gets 10 competitive bids in return.

"I like the one with the AARP discount," I say. To confirm, I point a palm-sized handheld device at Jerry's infrared reader to transfer my digital signature, which secures a monthly, electronic draft from my checking account.

This scenario doesn't seem too far-fetched. The technology already exists, but it is not widely adopted. It could be, it should be, and it probably will be.

The fax machine was invented in 1842. It wasn't until the 1980s that it was cost-effective to have a fax machine in a small office. Twenty years later, the fax machine is nearly ubiquitous, though it eventually could be replaced by fax software and modems. Revolutions take time, but I will hazard a guess that it won't take 140 years to get B2B communication into the small office.

# CHAPTER 2

# The XML Foundation

You've probably already asked yourself the obvious question: What's so great about XML? It's good for you to wonder if it is really what folks say it is, or just another "Excellent Marketing Language." Why does every company in the Fortune 1000 seem to be catching the XML fire, and why are XML conferences selling out?

XML seems to be worth a little of your attention; otherwise, why are you wasting time reading this book? I don't think you are wasting your time, unless you are already an expert in XML. If you are, don't feel guilty if you skip this chapter. If you are not an XML expert, it will give you a good overview of what XML is, what it can do, and why it's vital for folks doing B2B.

## A Short History of Markup Languages

I relate computer markup languages to time-tested proofreaders' marks. Proofreaders' marks have been around for centuries, about as long as there have been manuscripts. These marks are a shorthand system that has developed into a somewhat standard way for editors to communicate changes to manuscripts that are being prepared for publication. Still in

**Table 2.1**   Proofreaders' Marks

| MARK | MEANING |
| --- | --- |
| *bf* | Change type to bold face |
| *ital* | Change type to italic |
| *cap* | Set in CAPITALS |
| *stet* | Let it stand; scratch the suggested change |
| ¶ | Insert new paragraph |
| ‖ | Line up or straighten type |

wide use, lists of proofreaders' marks usually appear in a dictionary or a writer's handbook. You'll find a few samples in Table 2.1.

These handwritten marks or notes on printed copies or galley proofs of a manuscript suggest changes to authors or help typesetters know how to format a printed page. They provide information about information or, in other words, meta information, which is an underlying concept behind markup languages.

## Generalized Markup Language

Mainframe computers came into common use in large businesses in the 1960s, and computerized typesetting systems were also developed around this time. The Graphic Communications Association (GCA) created a standard for embedding formatting and typesetting information in text files. The standard was called GenCode. A little later, IBM created something similar called Generalized Markup Language, or GML.

In 1969, the year the original Internet came into being, IBM was putting together a system for publishing legal information. The problem was that the various computer systems in the company could not talk to each other because of differing command languages and file formats. Sound like a familiar problem?

Three researchers at IBM, Charles Goldfarb, Ed Mosher, and Ray Lorie, solved this problem with GML, a markup system that allowed output coming from different sources to be marked up and processed uniformly.

Other markup systems have emerged since that time, such as troff and Rich Text Format (RTF). Troff is a Unix system designed for typesetting plain text files with markup composed of directives that are preceded with a period (.) and start at the leftmost column of a page. The following fragment issues three requests: The `.ft` request sets the font to Times, `.ps` sets the font point size to 11 points, and `.sp` inserts a single vertical line.

```
.ft Times
.ps 11
.sp
Troff is a Unix system designed for typesetting plain text files…
```

RTF is a kind of markup language that produces a file format allowing word processors like Microsoft Word or Corel WordPerfect to store typographical information, such as **bold** and *italics*. Because they are stored as text files rather than as proprietary binary files, you can easily see in the example here a few RTF symbols or tags that mark up the type. The \par tag sets off a paragraph, while  \b and \i, along with the braces that enclose them, indicate bold and italic fonts.

```
\par RTF is a kind of markup language resulting in a file format that
allows word processors like Microsoft Word or Corel WordPerfect to store
typographical information, such as }{\b bold}{ and }{\i italics}{.
```

Other schemes include Adobe PostScript, a page description language that issues precise instructions to output devices like printers, and Portable Document Format (PDF), also from Adobe, which describes documents compactly, putting a premium on economy to ensure fast transport of files across networks.

## Standard Generalized Markup Language

The American National Standards Institute (ANSI) liked the idea of a standard document file format, so in the late 1970s it invited Charles Goldfarb and others to form a group that studied the issue. That group produced the 1980 draft of Standard Generalized Markup Language, or SGML. By 1986, SGML grew into an international standard (ISO 8879:1986).

But there is one little problem: SGML is a behemoth. Although it is powerful and comprehensive, it is also complex, if not unwieldy. It caught on in some circles, especially those that had gargantuan document management tasks, such as the government and military, but it has never enjoyed broad popularity, except by those who took the time to learn it and understand it. It has ardent defenders, but it does not have a huge fan club because so few understand what it can really do. I am not doing SGML justice here because I think it is an unparalleled standard deserving more credit than it has ever gotten, but it is so complex that the uninitiated are put off; understandably, people did not flock to it in droves.

## Tim Berners-Lee and HTML

In March 1989, Tim Berners-Lee was working for CERN, the European Particle Physics Laboratory. That month, he circulated a paper he had written entitled "Information Management: A Proposal." This document explored a method for scientists to share papers using hypertext and the Internet. With that little paper, the seeds of the World Wide Web were planted.

Berners-Lee wanted to figure out how to present information so that it would be easily transported across the Internet and readable when it got to where it was going. In the early 1990s, he and his associates created an SGML application or document type called HyperText Markup Language, that is, HTML. HTML put an application of SGML into the hands of common folk, providing a set of comparatively simple tags for marking up text for presentation and display in early browsers.

You are likely familiar with what an HTML document looks like. Here is a simple example:

```
<html>
<head>
<title>HTML</title>
</head>
<body>

<p>You are likely familiar with what an HTML document looks like. Here
is a simple example.</p>

</body>
</html>
```

The paragraph element is marked up with a p start-tag and end-tag (in practice the end-tag is often omitted). The body element contains the body of the page, while title contains the page's title. The first or root element of the document is html.

## The Web and HTML Grow Up

As the Web flourished in the 1990s, the profession of Web designer emerged, and HTML was soon stretched and pulled beyond reason. Berners-Lee founded the World Wide Web Consortium (W3C) in 1994 to keep tabs on Web-related de facto standards, such as HTML, and to develop other recommendations.

**NOTE** We often think of the W3C as a standards body, but the consortium really is not, not in the same way that ANSI and ISO are standards bodies. W3C enjoys popular confidence, and it promotes would-be standards to what's known as recommendation status, but that's as far as it goes.

After HTML version 2.0 was released, a struggle ensued over what tags and attributes to include in the next release of HTML, largely between Microsoft and Netscape factions, which are both W3C members. It was during the protracted conflict over what HTML 3.0 should look like that XML was born, born it seems of a need to get beyond the limitations of HTML, to tap into the might of SGML, and to address the future needs of the Web.

## Where Did XML Come From?

Activity on XML began in the summer of 1996. Originally it was called the "Web SGML" activity at W3C. Jon Bosak of Sun Microsystems—the father of XML—Jean Paoli of Microsoft, Tim Bray, and James Clark, who coined the term *XML*, were among the committee that eventually invented a language that was like its predecessors SGML and HTML, but different in some important respects.

Three consequential differences are these:

- XML does not lock its users into predetermined elements or tags. If you want to create a new element, you do not have to wait around for a committee to approve it: You can just create the tags yourself.

- XML left behind a great deal of SGML's complexity, making it easier to create document types.

- Perhaps not by design, XML allows you to easily use tags to describe not just documents but data, making it easier to parse and exchange data between different applications on a variety of platforms.

In February 1998, a mere 20 months after activity started, XML became a W3C recommendation. XML was not released with a big splash, however, but those who understood what was going on saw big waves rolling toward shore. Word about XML seemed to get out slowly at first, but the online world is now beginning to take it more seriously.

XML is here to stay, and here are some good reasons why:

**XML is free.** You don't have to pay anything for XML. No license fees. No break-the-seal contracts. You owe nothing except to congratulate yourself for being so frugal and stingy. When a standard like XML is widely accepted in industry, and free on top of that, it is hard to come up with reasons for not adopting it. Why is it free? W3C is a not-for-profit consortium, and XML is one of its gifts to the world.

**XML is structured.** Structure is inherent in XML as elements in XML have parent-child relationships. This allows you to structure text-based data in a clear, logical way. You cannot get away from it, and that is a good thing because this structure helps software—and humans—to organize, find, read, and interpret documents and data quickly and accurately.

**XML is the basis for a file format.** I like to think of XML as the basis for universal file formats. Because XML's structure is orderly and pre-dictable and because its data content can be clearly and easily labeled, XML documents can potentially be shared between entirely different computer and software systems. This is one reason why I think, in the next few years, XML will become the backbone of electronic com-merce worldwide.

**XML is open.** The W3C, which manages the XML recommendation, allows anyone to comment on XML. Granted, you have to be a W3C member to participate in private XML committee work, but W3C pub-lishes working drafts of all its XML-related work, and it does not keep all its work locked away as a private company would.

**XML is nonproprietary.** It's not owned by Microsoft, IBM, AOL Time Warner, or Sun Microsystems, nor is it strictly tied to any proprietary software or hardware. It does work within proprietary software, such as the Microsoft Internet Explorer or Netscape Navigator browsers, but not to the exclusion of other software or platforms.

**XML is platform independent.** It's not tied to a PC, Macintosh, Unix, or any other operating system or platform. You can develop XML on any platform that can handle a plain text file, which covers all of them. Some of the applications you can use to create XML may not be platform independent, but XML itself is. Don't let anyone tell you otherwise.

> **NOTE** The XML recommendation, now in its second edition, is available online at www.w3.org/tr/rec-xml.

## A Markup Language for Creating Markup Languages

XML really is not a markup language in and of itself, but it provides a framework—the rules and the tools—for creating your own markup language. You can use these rules and conventions to design, name, and organize XML elements, attributes, and entities.

HTML, on the other hand, is limited to a set of predefined elements. Here are a few of them:

- body for the body of a Web page
- p for a paragraph
- hr for a horizontal rule or line

XML does not offer ready-made, predefined elements. You must define them yourself or use someone else's vocabulary or collection of XML elements. Some examples of XML vocabularies for B2B are the following:

- Electronic Business XML (ebXML) is jointly sponsored by OASIS and UN/CEFACT (see www.ebxml.org).
- RosettaNet makes possible the exchange of business documents and other business-to-business exchanges (see www.rosettanet.org).
- Commerce XML (cXML) is an XML vocabulary developed by Ariba for online catalog transactions, among other things (see www.cxml .org/home/index.htm).

You'll learn more about these XML vocabularies in later chapters of this book.

## What's Going to Happen to HTML?

XML is not really a replacement for HTML, and there is no reason to believe that HTML will disappear soon just because of XML. The predefined elements and attributes that HTML offers are easy to learn, well established, well known, and sufficient for many purposes, especially when combined with other related technologies such as Cascading Style Sheets (CSS).

XML is similar to HTML, but it did not grow out of it. HTML is an SGML application. XML, likewise, is not really an application of SGML but is a restricted subset of it. This means that XML looks a lot like SGML but is not as complex.

With the advent of XHTML (see *XHTML: The Marriage of HTML and XML* later in this chapter) and statements by the W3C Working Group, it appears that HTML work will focus on its reformulation as XML, rather than following on a separate track.

# Anatomy of an XML Document

You've had a look at a simple HTML document. Now it is time to plunge ahead and look at a simple XML document. You will notice some similarities instantly, and this should help make XML easier to grasp. The following is an example of an XML document designed for use with a B2B application:

```
<?xml version="1.0" encoding="iso-8859-1" ?>

<Order partner="06-853-2535">
 <Date>2001-03-05</Date>
 <Item type="ISBN">0471404012</Item>
 <Quantity>22</Quantity>
 <Comments>None.</Comments>
 <ShippingMethod class="4th">USPS</ShippingMethod>
</Order>
```

> **NOTE** This document, order.xml, is not based on a standard B2B vocabulary but is meant for demonstration purposes in this book.

## The XML Declaration

The first line of the XML document is called the *XML declaration*. It looks like this:

```
<?xml version="1.0" encoding="iso-8859-1" ?>
```

This declaration tells the processing software that this is an XML document. The version attribute says that the document that follows conforms to the version 1.0 recommendation of XML. The XML declaration is not mandatory, but the version attribute is mandatory if such a declaration is present.

The optional encoding attribute indicates the character set or encoding used in the document. This document uses the ISO-8859-1 or Latin-1 character set, which is based on characters used in Western Europe and is composed of 256 characters. (The US-ASCII character set has 128 characters.) XML 1.0 supports character sets registered by the Internet Assigned Numbers Authority (IANA), but XML processors are not required to support all the character sets registered by IANA. Some of the most common are UTF-8, UTF-16, and ISO-8859-1 through ISO-8859-9. Character set values used with encoding are not case sensitive.

The `standalone` attribute, which is also optional and not shown, provides a way to state explicitly the presence or absence of external declarations, such as those in a document type definition (DTD). The `standalone` attribute, it seems, is not often used because an XML processor detects external declarations without it

The XML declaration is an example of a *processing instruction*. Processing instructions pass instructions to the program that processes the XML document; they begin with `<?` and end with `?>`. The XML recommendation does not stipulate that you must include an XML declaration in every XML document, but it does say that you *should* include one. Actually, it is always a good idea to include an XML declaration because it is a precise indicator, both to the human eye and to the software reading the file, that the document is supposed to be XML.

## The Root Element in XML

Like the HTML document, an XML document must have a root element. HTML's root is always `html`. In XML, though, the root element can be whatever you want. In the case of this example, the root is the `Order` element.

The root element must always be the first element in an XML document. The root is like a container that holds all the other elements in the document and is the first element in the hierarchy of elements. The root element is also called the *document element*.

The `Order` element also happens to have an attribute, `partner`. The value of the attribute is a Data Universal Numbering System, or DUNS number. Dun & Bradstreet's nine-digit DUNS numbers are a de facto standard for identifying and finding data for more than 57 million businesses worldwide.

### Child Elements

The root element `Order` is also a parent element. It has five child elements in this example, namely `Date`, `Item`, `Quantity`, `Comment`, and `ShippingMethod`. Each of these child elements is a sibling of the others. Without a DTD or other schema, the order of the elements is not strictly enforced. DTDs and XML Schemas are used to validate or constrain XML documents so that elements may be presented, for example, in a certain order. This goes for attributes, content datatypes, and other things as well. The `order.xml` example is considered well formed, though it is not yet tested for validity.

## Well-Formed XML

XML must be well formed. This means that it follows certain rules enforced by a complying XML processor. HTML processors are pretty forgiving, and this accounts for lots of sloppy HTML coding. You can't get away with slipshod coding in XML.

Four important rules of well-formedness are as follows:

**Each element must have a start-tag and an end-tag.** Notice that the document begins with the Order start-tag and ends with the proper end-tag. In HTML, end-tags, such as for the p element, can often be omitted. Such flakiness is not allowed in XML.

**Empty elements must terminate properly.** For example, the HTML element hr is an empty element, that is, it can have attributes but has no content such as text or other elements. In XML, an empty element is represented as <horizontalrule/>, that is, with a slash (/) and right angle bracket (>) at the end.

**XML is case sensitive, so start-tags and end-tags must match.** The tags <Date> and </Date> match, but the tags <date> and </DATE> do not. HTML tags are not case sensitive.

**In XML, attribute values must always be enclosed in either single (') or double (") quotes.** For example, version="1.0" is legal, but version=1.0 is not. Leaving quotes off is permissible in HTML.

## Valid XML

You can validate your XML documents against a special document that defines the elements, attributes, and so forth contained in an XML document. This special document can be a DTD or some other schema. In order for a document to be valid, it must conform to an associated DTD and also be well formed. Validating an XML document against a schema requires a validating XML parser. An XML parser is likely to be part of an XML processor, the software that processes XML documents, such as Microsoft's MSXML.

### The Document Type Declaration

In the following example, a document type declaration, highlighted in bold, is added to order.xml. If present, this declaration must appear before any elements in an XML document. The XML and document type declarations make up what is called the *prolog*.

```
<?xml version="1.0" encoding="iso-8859-1" ?>
<!DOCTYPE Order SYSTEM "Order.dtd">

<Order partner="06-853-2535">
 <Date>2001-03-05</Date>
 <Item type="ISBN">0471404012</Item>
 <Quantity>22</Quantity>
 <Comments>None.</Comments>
 <ShippingMethod class="4th">USPS</ShippingMethod>
</Order>
```

The DOCTYPE keyword must always be uppercase and preceded by a right angle bracket and an exclamation point (<!), with no intervening space. Next is the name of the document type, Order, which must also match the root element of the XML document. The SYSTEM keyword clues the XML processor in that a path to a file will follow, the local file in this case being Order.dtd. A URL, such as http://testb2b.org/order/Order.dtd, could also used. Always end the document type declaration with a right angle bracket (>).

## The Document Type Definition

As you know, a DTD contains definitions or declarations for XML elements, attributes, and entities, among other things. These definitions are called *markup declarations*. An external DTD (or external subset) for order.xml would look like this:

```
<!ELEMENT Order (Date,Item+,Quantity,Comments*,ShippingMethod)>
<!ATTLIST Order partner CDATA #REQUIRED>
<!ELEMENT Date (#PCDATA)>
<!ELEMENT Item (#PCDATA)>
<!ATTLIST Item type (ISBN | title) "title">
<!ELEMENT Quantity (#PCDATA)>
<!ELEMENT Comments (#PCDATA)>
<!ELEMENT ShippingMethod (#PCDATA)>
<!ATTLIST ShippingMethod class (Express|1st|Parcel|4th) "1st">
```

With an internal subset, a DTD is included in an XML document. Here is an instance of order.xml with an internal subset DTD:

```
<?xml version="1.0" encoding="iso-8859-1" ?>
<!DOCTYPE Order [
<!ELEMENT Order (Date,Item+,Quantity,Comments*,ShippingMethod)>
<!ATTLIST Order partner CDATA #REQUIRED>
<!ELEMENT Date (#PCDATA)>
<!ELEMENT Item (#PCDATA)>
```

```
<!ATTLIST Item type (ISBN | title) "title">
<!ELEMENT Quantity (#PCDATA)>
<!ELEMENT Comments (#PCDATA)>
<!ELEMENT ShippingMethod (#PCDATA)>
<!ATTLIST ShippingMethod class (Express|1st|Parcel|4th) "1st">
]>

<Order partner="06-853-2535">
 <Date>2001-03-05</Date>
 <Item type="ISBN">0471404012</Item>
 <Quantity>22</Quantity>
 <Comments>None.</Comments>
 <ShippingMethod class="4th">USPS</ShippingMethod>
</Order>
```

An element markup declaration begins with the ELEMENT keyword. It must always be uppercase and preceded by <! with no space. Element declarations, like all declarations, always end with a close angle bracket (>).

The first declaration in the DTD, for the Order element, is defined to contain other elements, that is, Date, Item, Quantity, Comments, and ShippingMethod. These elements are enclosed in parentheses to form what is called a *content model*.

### Content Models

The content model determines the sequence and number of occurrences of these elements. Generally speaking, when an element is constrained in a DTD, it can contain three things: (1) parsed character data (#PCDATA), (2) other ordered elements, or (3) mixed content. Mixed content consists of parsed character data and other elements in no particular order. These, unfortunately, are the only content types you can specify for elements in a DTD based on XML 1.0.

In its own syntax, the model states the element content of Order:

**There will be one and only one occurrence of the Date element.** Date can contain parsed character data (#PCDATA). This means it can't contain any characters that might be interpreted by a parser to be markup, such as angle brackets (< or >) or ampersands (&). (For a workaround, see the section titled *Built-in Entities* later in this chapter.) The Date element is expected to contain a date based on the ISO 8601 format, but this cannot be enforced by the #PCDATA type alone. (You might more accurately define a date in a DTD by breaking down its components and storing them in attributes and using an empty element, such as <Date year="2000" month="03" day="05" />, but XML Schema helps overcome the limitations of DTDs by adding datatypes, as you will see in the section titled *XML Schema* later in this chapter.)

**Following the `Order` declaration is an attribute declaration.** The `ATTLIST` keyword is preceded by `<!`, as are other declarations. It then names the element it is providing an attribute for, namely, `Order`. Then it names the attribute `partner`, followed by the `CDATA` keyword, which indicates that the attribute content can be unparsed character data. Unlike `#PCDATA`, the content of this attribute is not parsed, so you have broader options as to what characters you can use (that is, any legal XML character, including those used in markup, such as &). The expected value is a nine-digit DUNS number, identifying the business entity that is making the order, but the DTD cannot strictly enforce this. The `#REQUIRED` keyword means that the `partner` attribute is required, but it does not have a default value. Attribute values can occur once in a start-tag or an empty element tag, but never in an end-tag.

**The `Date` element will be followed immediately by one or more occurrences of `Item`.** The + operator, called an *occurrence operator*, indicates that an element can appear one or more times. Other occurrence operators are * for zero or more times and ? for zero or one occurrence. The absence of an operator in a content model means that the element can occur exactly once. The `Item` element contains `#PCDATA` and is expected to contain either a book title or an International Standard Book Number (ISBN), as indicated by the attribute `type`, but alas, a DTD cannot strictly constrain this intended content.

**Following this is a declaration for an attribute called `type`.** The attribute `type` has an enumerated list of two possible values. The default value, `title`, is indicated in quote marks. If a default attribute is omitted in an XML document, the XML processor must act as if the attribute were present, along with its default value.

**Next come declarations for two more elements, `Quantity` and `Comments`, both containing `#PCDATA`.** `Quantity` should be a positive integer indicating the number of `Items` ordered. `Comments` contain, well, comments. This element can appear zero or more times (*). Normally, you can include comments in an XML document with the `<!--comment -->` construct. Both XML and HTML inherited this construct from SGML. The `Comments` element must contain `#PCDATA`, but regular comments can contain any character data, except --. You also can't end a comment with --->. It's got to be -->.

**ShippingMethod contains #PCDATA as well.** It also carries an enumerated attribute called class with a default value of 1st. The content of the element is expected to be the name of a shipping carrier (again, this constraint is unenforceable by the DTD).

## Entities

Another markup declaration, not shown in the example DTD, defines entities. In general, an entity in XML is like an abbreviation. With an entity name contained in an ampersand (&) and semicolon (;), it can represent a general entity, a built-in entity, or a character reference, which I will show you presently. DTDs can also contain parameter entities that allow you to reuse text in a DTD. Parameter entities work only in DTDs.

The following declaration in a DTD would define a general entity:

```
<!ENTITY nt "Note: An entity is like an abbreviation.">
```

With this declaration in a DTD, the XML processor will expand &nt; to the phrase *Note: An entity is like an abbreviation*.

## Built-in Entities

XML 1.0 comes with several built-in entities that represent special, markup-related characters so that they can be present in parsed character data without a parser chewing them up and spitting them out. For example, an XML processor won't like ampersands (&) in parsed character data, but on examination of the built-in entity &amp;, it will render & in its output stream. The built-in entities are listed in Table 2.2.

**Table 2.2**    XML 1.0 Built-in Entities

| ENTITY | DESCRIPTION |
| --- | --- |
| &lt; | Less than or left angle bracket (<) |
| &gt; | Greater than or right angle bracket (>) |
| &amp; | Ampersand (&) |
| &apos; | Apostrophe or single quote (') |
| &quot; | Double quote (") |

### Character References

XML 1.0 supports ISO/IEC 10646 or the implementation of 10646 called Unicode. If you have a Unicode-compliant browser, you can display these Unicode characters in XML documents with character references. Character references are composed of the four-digit hexadecimal code representing the character, bounded by &#x and ; (the x must be lowercase).

For example, the Latin capital letter A is represented with &#x0041;, the registered trademark sign is &#x00AE; (®), and the Greek small letter alpha is &#x03B1; (α).

> **NOTE**  Even though XML may support a particular Unicode character, that doesn't mean that your browser will be able to render it. Unicode has thousands of characters, and the number is growing. It may take a little patience before we get to see them all in our browser of choice.

### The XML Namespace

It is possible that two developers creating separate XML documents and collections might give the same name to an element or an attribute. If a software application happens to bring those two vocabularies together in one document, those names would clash and an XML processor could overheat.

XML namespaces provide the answer. The namespace specification provided by W3C shows how to identify element and attribute names uniquely, thus avoiding a fender-bender when elements or attributes of the same name collide. This is done with a namespace declaration.

In general terms, a namespace is identified with a Uniform Resource Identifier or URI. This URI does not, according to the current W3C model, have to point to a resource such as a schema defining the elements and attributes contained in the namespace. Instead, it usually just acts as a naming scheme, a means to identify elements and attributes uniquely. It may be confusing to use a URL as a namespace identifier, as we are accustomed to using URLs to dereference or get a resource on the Web. They may point to a resource, such as a schema that defines the resource, or they may not. If they don't point to a resource, just consider the URL as a unique ID.

You can also associate a namespace with a prefix. Think of this prefix as a sort of shorthand for the URI that identifies the namespace. You declare a namespace with a prefix, if desired, in an element start-tag using the xmlns declaration, as shown in bold type in the following example:

```
<?xml version="1.0" encoding="iso-8859-1" ?>
<!DOCTYPE Order SYSTEM "Order.dtd">

<order:Order partner="06-853-2535"
        xmlns:order="http://testb2b.org/order">
  <order:Date>2001-03-05</order:Date>
  <order:Item order:type="ISBN">0471404012</order:Item>
  <order:Quantity>22</order:Quantity>
  <order:Comments>None.</order:Comments>
  <order:ShippingMethod
        order:class="4th">USPS</order:ShippingMethod>
</order:Order>
```

The value of the xmlns declaration is http://testb2b.org/order, and the prefix associated with this namespace is order. The prefix may be used to label all the elements and attributes that belong to the given namespace. If you drop the prefix in the declaration, as in xmlns=http://testb2b.org/order, then that element and its children are included in a default namespace where no prefix is applied.

The namespace in this example just happened to be declared in the root element, but you can associate a namespace with any element. Attributes, on the other hand, cannot be in a default namespace. They require a namespace prefix in order to be in a namespace. Nevertheless, attributes without prefixes do not normally pose naming conflicts because they are associated with the scope of a single instance of an element.

## XML Schema

The XML DTD syntax trickled down from SGML and was part of the original XML 1.0 recommendation. XML Schema, another W3C-sponsored initiative, picks up where the DTD left off as means to define and describe valid XML documents and data. XML Schema uses XML syntax whereas DTDs have their own syntax.

One of XML Schema's strengths is that it offers much stronger datatyping than the DTD offers. XML 1.0 has somewhat limited datatypes. For example, attributes defined in XML 1.0 DTDs can have types such as CDATA (character data, unparsed) or ID (a unique identifier), but elements can be defined only as #PCDATA, contain other elements, or have mixed content (unordered #PCDATA and elements). XML Schema allows you to apply datatypes to both element and attribute content. You can even define your own new datatypes.

Following is a brief example of an XML Schema document that may be used to validate the XML document sample (order.xml) presented earlier.

```
<schema xmlns="http://www.w3.org/2000/08/XMLSchema"
        xmlns:order="http://testb2b.org/order"
        targetNamespace="http://testb2b.org/order">

<complexType name="Order">
 <sequence>
  <element name="Date" type="date"/>
  <element name="Item" maxOccurs="unbounded">
  <complexType>
   <attribute name="type" type="itemType" />
  </complexType>
  </element>
  <element name="Quantity" type="positiveInteger"/>
  <element name="Comments" minOccurs="0"
           maxOccurs="unbounded" type="string"/>
  <element name="ShippingMethod">
   <complexType>
    <attribute name="class" type="mailClass" />
   </complexType>
  </element>
 </sequence>
 <attribute name="partner" type="DUNS" />
</complexType>

<simpleType name="DUNS">
 <restriction base="string">
  <pattern value="\d{2}-\d{3}-\d{4}"/>
 </restriction>
</simpleType>

<simpleType name="itemType">
 <restriction base="string">
  <enumeration value="ISBN" />
  <enumeration value="title" />
 </restriction>
</simpleType>

<simpleType name="mailClass">
 <restriction base="string">
  <enumeration value="Express" />
  <enumeration value="1st" />
  <enumeration value="Parcel" />
  <enumeration value="4th" />
 </restriction>
</simpleType>

</schema>
```

**NOTE** At this writing, XML Schema is in the final phases of becoming a W3C recommendation. This XML Schema document may be slightly different from what is stated in the final recommendation.

Let's take a closer look at what is happening in this schema document, `Order.xsd`.

## The XML Schema Root Element

An XML Schema begins with its root element `schema`. Inside the start-tag for this element is a declaration for the schema language namespace (`http://www.w3.org/2000/08/XMLSchema`), plus declarations for the target namespace (`http://testb2b.org/order`) and its prefix (`order`). A target is any instance of an XML document based on the schema. Once you have namespaces squared away, it's time to start defining elements or types.

Conventionally, the XML Schema specification uses the `xsd` prefix for its namespace, but the example declares it as the default namespace, so no prefix is used. If you want to use `xsd` or another prefix, it's your choice—it doesn't have to be `xsd`.

## Complex and Simple Types

A complex type in XML Schema contains elements and attributes. A simple type, on the other hand, contains only character data. In this schema, the name of the first complex type is the element `Order`. It contains five elements that must appear in the instance document in the same sequence given in the schema, namely, in the order `Date`, `Item`, `Quantity`, `Comments`, and `ShippingMethod`. The `sequence` element indicates that the elements must, in an instance document, follow the order given in the schema. More about complex types and attributes in a few paragraphs.

## The Date Datatype

The `Date` element has a simple type of `date`. An element of this type must have content that conforms to the ISO 8601 standard for date formats—for example, 2001-01-01 (CCYY-MM-DD). This datatype, along with many others, comes along with XML Schema. In a DTD, you can't constrain element data other than with #PCDATA or with an element or mixed content model, but XML Schema allows you to constrain element content based on a variety of datatypes. It even allows you to define your own datatypes.

Attributes defined in DTDs can have one of a few types, such as ID and NMTOKEN, but elements are left behind. XML Schema provides a rich set of simple datatypes that can constrain not only attributes but elements as well. Table 2.3 shows a sampling of datatypes that come standard with XML Schema.

**Table 2.3**  A Sample of XML Schema Datatypes

| DATATYPE | DESCRIPTION | EXAMPLES |
|---|---|---|
| `int` | Integer in the range –214748647 to 214748648 | `-13, 7, 144, 32655` |
| `float` | 32-bit floating-point number | `2e64, 12.63, INF, NaN` |
| `date` | Time instant with a duration of one day, in the form CCYY-MM-DD (C = century, Y = year, M = month, D = day) | `2001-08-19, 2024-01-01` |
| `boolean` | Boolean value | `true, false` |
| `uriReference` | Absolute or relative URI reference | `http://www.wiley.com/index.html`(absolute) or `index.html` (relative) |

## The Item and ShippingMethod Elements

Both the `Item` and `ShippingMethod` element definitions carry the `max-Occurs` attribute with a value of `unbounded`. The `minOccurs` and `max-Occurs` attributes in XML Schema dictate how often elements appear. By default (or if omitted), `minOccurs` is assumed to equal `1` and `maxOccurs` is likewise assumed to equal `1`, so an element so constrained appears exactly once.

I'll compare the DTD and XML Schema syntax to make this a little clearer. For simplicity, assume that the `Order` element contains only one element, `Item`, that occurs one or more times. In a DTD, the declaration would look like this:

```
<!ELEMENT Order (Item+)>
```

In other words, the element `Order` may have one or more (+) `Item` child elements. In XML Schema, you would achieve the same result by declaring `Order` in this way:

```
<complexType name="Order">
 <sequence>
  <element name="Item" minOccurs="1" maxOccurs="unbounded">
 </sequence>
</complexType>
```

A DTD content model formed in this way in XML Schema is called a *model group*. It takes more keystrokes in XML Schema than in a DTD, but the tags and attributes give you clearer indications than the DTD about what is going on.

Taking the example further, let's say you wanted exactly one occurrence of Item in Order. The DTD would look like this:

```
<!ELEMENT Order (Item)>
```

The XML Schema, though, would look this way:

```
<complexType name="Order">
 <sequence>
  <element name="Item" minOccurs="1" maxOccurs="1">
 </sequence>
</complexType>
```

Or like this, if the attributes minOccurs and maxOccurs are omitted, so that the default value (1) is assumed for each:

```
<complexType name="Order">
 <sequence>
  <element name="Item">
 </sequence>
</complexType>
```

For zero or more (*) occurrences of Item, the declaration in a DTD would be:

```
<!ELEMENT Order (Item*)>
```

In XML Schema, the same declaration would be:

```
<complexType name="Order">
 <sequnce>
  <element name="Item" minOccurs="0" maxOccurs="unbounded">
 </sequence>
</complexType>
```

Finally, to declare zero or exactly one (?) occurrence of Item in a DTD, declare Order this way:

```
<!ELEMENT Order (Item?)>
```

Converting this to XML Schema would make the declaration look like this:

```
<complexType name="Order">
 <sequence>
  <element name="Item" minOccurs="0" maxOccurs="1">
 </sequence>
</complexType>
```

## Attributes in XML Schema

Now back to `Order.xsd`. After the `sequence` element end-tag, but before the `complexType` end-tag, you see an attribute declaration. The `partner` attribute is associated with the complex type `Order`. It has a type of `DUNS`, which is a new, user-defined simple type.

`DUNS` is a type that restricts the `string` type to a special pattern. The `value` attribute of the `pattern` element uses a regular expression to form a nine-digit number. Regular expressions refer to a syntax for textual pattern matching. Given `\d{2}-\d{3}-\d{4}`, a value of type `DUNS` will match a text pattern of two digits followed by a hyphen (-) and three digits followed by a hyphen and then four digits, looking something like `06-853-2535`. (Sometimes you see DUNS numbers without the hyphens. That's OK, but the `partner` attribute in this schema will not accept them.)

### Attributes and Anonymous Types

Here's one last trick. Simple types in XML Schema cannot contain attributes, but you can associate an attribute with a simple type by using an anonymous complex type. Following the start-tags for `Item` and `ShippingMethod` you see the `complexType` element without a `name` attribute. This occurs because it is anonymous or, in essence, nameless. Following the anonymous declarations come the `attribute` element, declaring either `type` or `class`.

Like the `partner` attribute, these attributes have user-defined simple types. Each has a value that is a restricted form of the `string` type. The `enumeration` element (a facet) lists the precise legal values for the attributes, that is, `ISBN` and `title` for `type` (of type `itemType`), and `Express`, `1st`, `Parcel`, and `4th` for `class` (of type `mailClass`). If you specify any value other than these, a validating XML Schema processor should kick back an error.

## The Quantity and Comments Elements

The `Quantity` element has a simple type of `positiveInteger`. This is another type that is built into XML Schema. The possible range for this type is `1` through infinity (if you can count that high). You can prepend a value with a plus sign if you want. The Comments element is a string that can occur zero or more times. A string in XML Schema, by the way, is a sequence of valid XML characters.

## Validating against XML Schema

Finally, a few lines inserted in your root element start-tag will let the schema processor know where your schema document is located. You can do so with the schemaLocation attribute that belongs to the XMLSchema-instance namespace. This namespace provides a few attributes for use in instances of XML documents, not in schema documents. The xsi prefix is a convention that comes from the schema recommendation; you can use a different prefix if you wish. A prefix is necessary because attributes do not fall into a default namespace and must be qualified if and when a namespace is required.

```
<?xml version="1.0" encoding="iso-8859-1" ?>

<order:Order partner="06-853-2535"
  xmlns:order="http://testb2b.org/order"
  xmlns:xsi="http://www.w3.org/2000/08/XMLSchema-instance"
  xsi:schemaLocation="http://testb2b.org/order
  http://testb2b.org/order/Order.xsd">

  <order:Date>2001-03-05</order:Date>
  <order:Item order:type="ISBN">0471404012</order:Item>
  <order:Quantity>22</order:Quantity>
  <order:Comments>None.</order:Comments>
  <order:ShippingMethod
       order:class="4th">USPS</order:ShippingMethod>
</order:Order>
```

The example now has a declaration for the XMLSchema-instance namespace with a conventional xsi prefix. The prefix prepends the schemaLocation attribute, designating that it is part of the XMLSchema-instance namespace. The value of schemaLocation is first the namespace identifier associated with the target schema and then, after a space, the URI for the location of the resource, that is, the actual file containing the schema against which the XML document is to be validated. In order for this to work, your XML processor must accept this construct.

## Adding Style

In the beginning days of the Web, HTML content and presentation were tied together closely. Then along came Cascading Style Sheets (CSS), now at level 2 but inching closer to level 3. CSS allows you to apply styles to HTML and XML documents either from within the document or with a separate stylesheet; in other words, it separates the concept of content and presentation. This allows you to reuse and refit content to meet more than one need. For example, with the original content file, you could apply different stylesheets to produce both Web and print versions of the same content.

Here is a simple example of how to apply a separate CSS stylesheet. The following applies a block display property and a font size of 12 points to the p element (72 points equals an inch):

```
/* CSS stylesheet */

p {display: block; font-size: 12pt}
```

The first line is a C or Java style comment. The p is the selector: It selects the element to which you want to apply a style. Display and font-size are the properties; block and 12pt are the values for those properties. A block style or characteristic blocks a chunk of text, usually with a bit of whitespace above and below it, like a paragraph in a book.

## A CSS Stylesheet for order.xml

Now let's create a CSS stylesheet for order.xml and apply the stylesheet for display in a browser. Here's an example of what such a stylesheet might look like:

```
/* CSS stylesheet for order.xml */

Order {font-family: Arial,Helvetica,sans-serif;font-size: 12pt}
Date {display: block}
Item {display: block; font-weight: bold}
Quantity {display: block}
Comments {display: block}
ShippingMethod {display: block}
```

In this little stylesheet (order.css), all child elements of Order are given the display property of block. This property value simply means that, without other alterations, the element will be rendered by itself in a block, having, by comparison, the same effect as a carriage return/line feed on a line of text. Another value for this property is inline, which directs that an element shall be rendered *inline,* that is, on a line without a break. For example, the b (bold) element in HTML is an inline element.

The properties associated with the Order element affect Order and all of its children. The font-family property has a prioritized value of

Arial, Helvetica, sans-serif. This means that the software that renders an XML document (such as a browser) will render textual content in Order and its children first in the Arial font, then, if Arial is not available, in the Helvetica font. Finally, if neither the Arial nor Helvetica font is available, it will render the text in some sans-serif font. This is a fail-safe mechanism that recovers when all platforms do not have the same fonts.

The presentation of Order is also modified by the font-size property, which has a value of 12 points (12 pt). The Item element is also given a font-weight of bold.

## Applying a Stylesheet to an XML Document

The following simplified version of order.xml applies the CSS stylesheet order.css by using the XML stylesheet processing instruction, shown in bold:

```
<?xml version="1.0" encoding="iso-8859-1" ?>
<?xml-stylesheet href="order.css" type="text/css" ?>

<Order partner="06-853-2535" xmlns="http://testb2b.org/order">
 <Date>2001-03-05</Date>
 <Item type="ISBN">0471404012</Item>
 <Quantity>22</Quantity>
 <Comments>None.</Comments>
 <ShippingMethod class="4th">USPS</ShippingMethod>
</Order>
```

The value of href assumes that the stylesheet order.css is in the same directory as the XML document order.xml, and type indicates that the content or media type for order.css is text/css. I changed the namespace http://testb2b.org/order to the default namespace and removed the prefix order from all the elements and attributes because CSS cannot yet select a prefixed element. It is proposed in CSS level 3 that the basic syntax for selecting a prefixed element will, for example, be order|Date, where order is the prefix for the namespace, followed by a vertical bar (|) and then by the Date element that is associated with the prefix. The proposed declaration in CSS will be the rule @namespace order url(http://testb2b.org);.

Figure 2.1 shows how the document would look in a browser when this CSS stylesheet is applied.

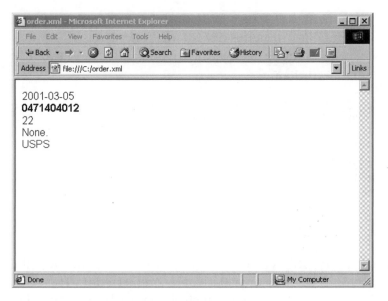

**Figure 2.1**    order.xml with order.css applied.

## Extensible Stylesheet Language

XML by itself focuses on content alone and was not designed with presentation in mind. You can use CSS with XML to apply style to an XML document, or you can use a powerful new language called Extensible Stylesheet Language (XSL). XSL is divided into two parts: (1) Extensible Stylesheet Language Transformations (XSLT) and (2) Extensible Stylesheet Language formatting objects (XSLFO in the vernacular).

### XSLT

XSLT was approved as a W3C recommendation late in 1999. It can transform XML documents, taking a source document or tree and transforming it into a new result tree. For example, with XSLT, you can transform an XML document into an HTML document, kick out plain text, or recreate the XML document in a new form, with new elements and attributes. An XSLT stylesheet uses a pattern-matching template to select and transform parts of an XML document. XSLT uses XML Path Language (XPath) as a way to address different parts or nodes of XML documents.

I'd like to show you an example of how XSLT works. First, have a look at a simplified version of order.xml.

```
<?xml version="1.0" encoding="iso-8859-1" ?>
<?xml-stylesheet href="order.xsl" type="text/xsl" ?>

<Order partner="06-853-2535">
 <Date>2001-03-05</Date>
 <Item type="ISBN">0471404012</Item>
 <Quantity>22</Quantity>
 <Comments>None.</Comments>
 <ShippingMethod class="4th">USPS</ShippingMethod>
</Order>
```

For the sake of clarity, this version of order.xml does not use the http://testb2b.org/order namespace or its prefix order. The value of href in the XML stylesheet processing instruction has been changed to order.xsl, and type has been changed to text/xsl.

The following XSLT example transforms order.xml, which essentially is just a data file, into a text file that is a bit more readable. This is a simple if inelegant example, but it demonstrates pretty clearly what XSLT can do:

```
<transform version="1.0" xmlns="http://www.w3.org/1999/XSL/Transform">
<output method="text" />

<template match="Order">
Purchase Order
Date: <apply-templates select="Date"/>
Partner: <apply-templates select="@partner"/>
Item: <apply-templates select="Item"/> Type: <apply-templates
select="Item/@type"/>
Quantity: <apply-templates select="Quantity"/>
Comments: <apply-templates select="Comments"/>
Shipping Method: <apply-templates select="ShippingMethod"/> Class:
<apply-templates select="ShippingMethod/@class"/>
</template>

</transform>
```

There are several XSL processors available, including Michael Kay's Saxon (from http://users.iclway.co.uk/mhkay/saxon/) and Apache's Xalan (from http://xml.apache.org). (See the end notes for this chapter for references to other XSLT processors.) If you are on the Windows platform, you can quickly download Instant Saxon, a command-line executable (saxon.exe) that consists of the full Saxon product, minus source code, full documentation, and a few other things. It comes in a ZIP file containing just a few files—it's a fast download even if you have a slow Internet connection. After you extract the ZIP file and place saxon.exe in your path so that Windows can execute it, type a command line like this:

```
saxon -a order.xml
```

The −a option tells the processor that the XSL stylesheet is specified in a processing instruction in the XML document. If it were not, your command line would look like this, where the XML document is the first argument and the stylesheet is the second:

```
saxon order.xml order.xsl
```

The Xalan XSLT processor was originally developed at IBM's alpha-Works, where it was known as Lotus, and later donated to Apache. After you download and install Xalan (Java version), a Windows command line for transforming an XML document with a separate XSL stylesheet will look something like this:

```
java -classpath xerces.jar;xalan.jar org.apache.xalan.xslt.Process -IN
order.xml -XSL order.xsl -OUT order.txt
```

In Unix, replace the semicolon (;) between the JAR (Java Archive) files with a colon (:). The files xerces.jar and xalan.jar must be stated in the given order in the classpath. I won't go into all the particulars of the classpath here, but I will mention that putting the JARs in the −classpath (or −cp) option on the command line is the preferred method because it won't affect other Java applications running on your system that require different classpath values. If you want the particulars of setting the classpath environment variable, I suggest that you read Sun's Java classpath documentation.

I have placed the JAR files in my current directory for convenience; they will be under the bin directory in Xalan, provided Xalan is installed or extracted in a standard way. For example, the bin directory might be C:\xalan-j_2_0_D01\bin on Windows or /home/mike/xalan-j_2_0_D01/bin on Unix. By the way, the file xerces.jar that comes with Xalan is smaller than the one that comes with the separate Xerces software from Apache.

The full package name org.apache.xalan.xslt.Process is followed by the option for the XML input document (-IN order.xml) and the XSLT file you want to use to transform the XML file (-XSL order.xsl). Optionally, you can direct the output of the transformation to a file (-OUT order.txt). You can direct the output to standard output (such as your screen) by leaving the –OUT option and value off the command line.

You can place this command in a batch file in the Windows environment. The batch file xalan.bat command can contain the following:

```
java -classpath xerces.jar;xalan.jar org.apache.xalan.xslt.Process -IN
%1 -XSL %2 %3 %4
```

With the replacement parameters %1 and %2, you can provide the names of the XML document input file and the XSLT file at the command line:

```
xalan order.xml order.xsl
```

If you want to redirect the output to a file, try:

```
xalan order.xml order.xsl -OUT order.txt
```

When processed with either Saxon or Xalan, you will get the following text as output:

```
Purchase Order
Date: 2001-03-05
Partner: 06-853-2535
Item: 0471404012 Type: ISBN
Quantity: 22
Comments: None.
Shipping Method: USPS Class: 4th
```

Perhaps you have worked with XSLT before, perhaps not. If not, you'll probably want to read the rest of this section to understand what is going on here.

I like to think of an XSLT stylesheet as a sort of filter. When you run an XML file through it, so to speak, you get a filtered version on the other end. If you're an XSLT aficionado, I'll admit that was a crude, imprecise description of what's going on, but that's the general idea.

In order.xml, you see a processing instruction associating the stylesheet order.xsl with the document. This stylesheet has a content type of text/xsl.

The first element in the stylesheet is the root element transform. You can also use the stylesheet element, which is a synonym for transform. This root element must have a version attribute that reflects the appropriate XSLT version (currently 1.0). It also must declare a namespace for XSLT, namely `http://www.w3.org/1999/XSL/Transform`. The conventional prefix for the XSLT namespace is `xsl`, but this prefix is not mandatory, as you have seen in other cases. I set aside the prefix in this example to make it a bit easier to read.

Immediately following the root element is the optional `output` element. Among other things, it tells the XSLT processor what kind of output to spit out—just plain `text` in this instance. The values `html` and `xml` are also valid. By default, the first apparent thing the XSLT processor outputs is an XML declaration. Because the output is plain text, the processor will omit this declaration. If you were outputting an XML document, you'd want to leave it in.

The real core of XSLT is the template. The template searches for a pattern and then tells the processor what to do once it finds the pattern. The `template` element specifies a pattern to match, such as an element node and its children, while the `apply-templates` element applies the transformation to the node or to a more specific node, as indicated by the value of the optional `select` attribute. The values in either `match` or `select` are examples of abbreviated XPath constructs.

The plain text, such as `Purchase Order`, `Date:`, and so forth, is output as it is in the result tree. The result tree is the result or output of a transformation on a source tree such as an XML document. Both the source and result can be files, but according to the XSLT recommendation, they don't have to be files. They could be arbitrary I/O streams, chunks of memory, whatever, but usually they are files.

After the text `Date:` in the example, `apply-templates` is invoked, selecting specifically an element with the abbreviated XPath value `Date`. This will print in the result tree the content of `Date` (that is, `2001-01-02`). Following that you see the text `Partner:`, with `apply-templates` selecting the `partner` attribute (`@partner`, another XPath value) from the `Order` element. As you can guess, XSLT allows you to manipulate the result output so that it is in a different order than the source. Remember, the operative term here is *transformation*.

Next the example grabs the content of `Item` and its attribute `type`. You can see that the syntax is a little different, though, as in `Item/@type`. You have to specify the element and attribute in `select`. Earlier, you just specified `@partner` because it is a child node of `Order` specified in the `template` element attribute `match`. You have to get more specific so that the processor knows what node you are talking about. The remaining element and attribute nodes, `Quantity`, `Comments`, `ShippingMethod`, and `class`, are all similarly transformed.

When using an XSLT processor such as Xalan or Saxon, you can also redirect the output to a file, so you can store your transformed B2B document in a file. With Saxon, for example, the command line would look like this:

```
saxon -a -o order-2001-03-05-0001.xml order.xml
```

The –o option is followed by the name of an output file for the result tree. The filename appends a date and numeral to order to make it unique.

## XSL Formatting Objects (XSLFO)

At the time of this writing, XSLFO is still not a W3C recommendation, but it likely will become one in 2001, so this section is not the last word on XSLFO (though it won't be far off from the final recommendation). Like CSS, XSLFO applies formatting objects and properties to XML documents. These objects and properties control the appearance of the document.

In the next example, an XSL stylesheet applies styles beyond the earlier CSS example. It adds the http://www.w3.org/1999/XSL/Format namespace with the conventional fo prefixes. It also adds the xsl prefix to the Transform namespace. The block characteristic is applied by the fo:block element. This is called a *formatting object*. Within the start-tag of this element you see attributes such as font-family, font-size, and font-weight. These attributes represent a sampling of *formatting properties*. Here is the stylesheet:

```
<xsl:stylesheet version="1.0"
  xmlns:xsl="http://www.w3.org/1999/XSL/Transform"
  xmlns:fo="http://www.w3.org/1999/XSL/Format">

<xsl:template match="/">
 <fo:root>
  <fo:layout-master-set>
   <fo:simple-page-master master-name="PO" height="11in"
       width="8.5in" margin-top="1in" margin-bottom=".5in"
       margin-left="1in" margin-right="1in">
    <fo:region-body margin-top=".5in"/>
   </fo:simple-page-master>
  </fo:layout-master-set>
  <fo:page-sequence master-name="PO" initial-page-number="1">
   <fo:flow flow-name="PO-body">

    <xsl:apply-templates select="Order"/>

   </fo:flow>
```

```
        </fo:page-sequence>
      </fo:root>
</xsl:template>

<xsl:template match="Order">
  <fo:block font-weight="bold" font-size="24pt"
       text-align="center" space-after.optimum="20pt">
    Purchase Order
  </fo:block>

  <fo:block font-weight="bold">
   Date: <fo:inline font-weight="normal"><xsl:apply-templates
              select="Date"/></fo:inline>
  </fo:block>

  <fo:block font-weight="bold">
   Partner: <fo:inline font-weight="normal"><xsl:apply-templates
                select="@partner"/></fo:inline>
  </fo:block>

  <fo:block font-weight="bold">
   Item: <fo:inline font-weight="normal">
          <xsl:apply-templates select="Item"/>
          </fo:inline>
          <fo:inline font-weight="bold">
              Type: <fo:inline font-weight="normal">
                     <xsl:apply-templates select="Item/@type"/>
                     </fo:inline>
          </fo:inline>
  </fo:block>

  <fo:block font-weight="bold">
   Quantity: <fo:inline font-weight="normal">
               <xsl:apply-templates select="Quantity"/>
             </fo:inline>
  </fo:block>

  <fo:block font-weight="bold">
   Comments: <fo:inline font-weight="normal">
               <xsl:apply-templates select="Comments"/>
             </fo:inline>
  </fo:block>

  <fo:block font-weight="bold">
   Shipping Method: <fo:inline font-weight="normal">
                  <xsl:apply-templates select="ShippingMethod"/>
                  </fo:inline>
    <fo:inline font-weight="bold">
     Class: <fo:inline font-weight="normal">
            <xsl:apply-templates select="ShippingMethod/@class"/>
```

```
          </fo:inline>
      </fo:inline>

   </fo:block>
  </xsl:template>
  </xsl:stylesheet>
```

To apply this stylesheet to order.xml with Xalan, you would type this line in Windows:

```
java -cp xerces.jar;xalan.jar org.apache.xalan.xslt.Process -IN
order.xml -XSL order-fo.xsl -OUT order.fo
```

Or, you could apply it with Saxon like this:

```
saxon -o order.fo order.xml order-fo.xsl
```

After performing the transformation, you get a result tree that is saved as the file order.fo, which looks like this:

```
<?xml version="1.0" encoding="UTF-8"?>

<fo:root xmlns:fo="http://www.w3.org/1999/XSL/Format">
 <fo:layout-master-set>
  <fo:simple-page-master
      margin-right="1in" margin-left="1in"
      margin-bottom=".5in" margin-top="1in"
      width="8.5in" height="11in"
      master-name="PO">
   <fo:region-body margin-top=".5in"/>
  </fo:simple-page-master>
 </fo:layout-master-set>

<fo:page-sequence initial-page-number="1" master-name="PO">
<fo:flow flow-name="PO-body">
<fo:block space-after.optimum="20pt" text-align="center"
    font-size="24pt" font-weight="bold">
     Purchase Order
</fo:block>

<fo:block font-weight="bold">
  Date: <fo:inline font-weight="normal">2001-03-05</fo:inline>
</fo:block>

<fo:block font-weight="bold">
  Partner: <fo:inline font-weight="normal">06-853-2535</fo:inline>
</fo:block>

<fo:block font-weight="bold">
  Item: <fo:inline font-weight="normal">0471404012</fo:inline>
```

```
    <fo:inline font-weight="bold">
      Type: <fo:inline font-weight="normal">ISBN</fo:inline>
    </fo:inline>
  </fo:block>

  <fo:block font-weight="bold">
    Quantity: <fo:inline font-weight="normal">22</fo:inline>
  </fo:block>

  <fo:block font-weight="bold">
    Comments: <fo:inline font-weight="normal">None.</fo:inline>
  </fo:block>

  <fo:block font-weight="bold">
    Shipping Method:
    <fo:inline font-weight="normal">USPS</fo:inline>
    <fo:inline font-weight="bold">
      Class: <fo:inline font-weight="normal">4th</fo:inline>
    </fo:inline>
  </fo:block>
  </fo:flow>
</fo:page-sequence>
</fo:root>
```

FOP is a Java-based program from Apache that lets you render a result tree like this as a PDF file. Once you have downloaded and installed FOP (from http://xml.apache.org), if you want to render a transformed file, one option is a Windows command line like this:

```
java -classpath fop.jar;xerces.jar;xalan.jar;w3c.jar
org.apache.fop.apps.CommandLine order.fo order.pdf
```

You'll find other command-line alternatives in the FOP documentation—you can experiment with the others, but I'll stick with one to simplify the illustration. In addition, this command line worked at writing time, but new developments in FOP may make it inoperable. This is often the case when you are using emerging software and tools, so you are probably used to it.

The screen output resulting from this command—provided that the command is successful—will look similar to this:

```
FOP 1.0 [dev]
using SAX parser org.apache.xerces.parsers.SAXParser
using renderer org.apache.fop.render.pdf.PDFRenderer
using element mapping org.apache.fop.fo.StandardElementMapping
using element mapping org.apache.fop.svg.SVGElementMapping
using property list mapping
org.apache.fop.fo.StandardPropertyListMapping
```

```
using property list mapping org.apache.fop.svg.SVGPropertyListMapping
building formatting object tree
setting up fonts
formatting FOs into areas
 [1]
rendering areas to PDF
writing out PDF
```

As before, the JAR files are in the current directory in this example, but they could be elsewhere. The example also renames the most recent FOP JAR file to `fop.jar`.

The package name from `fop.jar`, `org.apache.fop.apps.Command-Line`, is followed by the name of the transformed or formatting object file (`order.fo`) followed by the output file to receive the Portable Document Format (PDF) formatting (`order.pdf`).

In the Windows environment, you could place this command line in a batch file. For example, in the batch file `fop.bat` is the following command:

```
java -classpath fop.jar;xerces.jar;xalan.jar;w3c.jar
org.apache.fop.apps.CommandLine %1 %2
```

The replacement parameters `%1` and `%2` allow me to provide the filenames at the command line:

```
fop order.fo order.pdf
```

After executing this command successfully, you can display `order.pdf` with Adobe Acrobat Reader, as represented in Figure 2.2.

# Other XML Initiatives

The W3C is sponsoring a large number of recommendations and initiatives related to XML. I will talk about each of these briefly in the descriptions that follow.

## XHTML: The Marriage of HTML and XML

HTML and XML tied the knot early in 2000 with the specification XHTML 1.0: the Extensible HyperText Markup Language. This means that as long as your existing HTML files follow certain rules, you can reuse them as XHTML, allowing you to add XML to them. You can also add the familiar HTML elements to XML documents. This mingling of XML and HTML may well be the *lingua franca* of the Web in the foreseeable future.

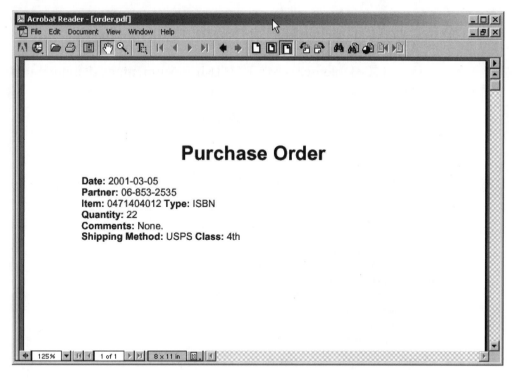

**Figure 2.2**   order.pdf in Adobe Acrobat Reader.

You remember the simple HTML example earlier. Here it is again, converted to XHTML (changes in bold):

```
<!DOCTYPE html PUBLIC "-//W3C//DTD XHTML 1.0 Strict//EN" "xhtml1-
strict.dtd">
<html xmlns="http://www.w3.org/1999/xhtml">
<head>
<title>XHTML</title>
</head>
<body>

<p>You are likely familiar with what an XHTML document looks like. Here
    is a simple example.</p>

</body>
</html>
```

Added is the document type declaration for the strict XHTML DTD, which has a standard PUBLIC identifier (-//W3C//DTD XHTML 1.0 Strict//EN). Other DTDs are also available, namely, the transitional and frameset DTDS. The XHTML namespace (http://www.w3.org/1999/

xhtml) has also been added, and it is declared as the default (no prefix). XHTML tags must be lowercase. Like XML, XHTML must be well-formed, but I won't go into all the rules now.

You can add XML elements to an XHTML document, as demonstrated in the next example:

```
<html xmlns="http://www.w3.org/1999/xhtml">
<head>
<title>XHTML</title>
</head>
<body>

<p>You are likely familiar with what an XHTML document looks like. Here
is a simple example.</p>

<order:Order order:partner="06-853-2535"
xmlns:order="http://testb2b.org/order">
 <order:Date>2001-03-05</order:Date>
 <order:Item order:type="ISBN">0471404012</order:Item>
 <order:Quantity>22</order:Quantity>
 <order:Comments>None.</order:Comments>
 <order:ShippingMethod order:class="4th">
  USPS
 </order:ShippingMethod>
</order:Order>

</body>
</html>
```

With XHTML, you are free to drop in XML as long as you associate it with a namespace so that the processor can sort out XHTML, its set of elements, and so forth, from well-formed XML.

XHTML is advancing a series of recommendations beyond its original specification, for example, XHTML Basic. These recommendations describe the modularization of XHTML, which simply means that XHTML can be defined by DTDs and XML Schema that are broken down into smaller modules. This will allow for a more compact definition of XHTML that will enable it to be used efficiently on small devices.

## XLink and XPointer

XML Linking Language (XLink) should become a W3C recommendation in 2001. It defines a way to link documents, going way beyond the capabilities of the a element in HTML. XLink will allow you to have two-way links and collect groups of links called *extended links*. XPointer defines ways to address documents and will allow documents to link to parts of remote documents without having to edit or add an anchor to the remote document. Work on XPointer will also be complete soon, perhaps by the time you read this.

The following fragment shows a simple XLink link:

```
<xlink:link xmlns:xlink="http://www.w3.org/1999/xlink"
xlink:type="simple" xlink:show="replace"
xlink:href="http://www.testb2b.org">This is a simple link.
</xlink:link>
```

First of all, you'll notice the xlink namespace. A simple type link works just like the traditional, one-way a tag in HTML. XLink, however, allows you to get beyond the simple link with extended links. Generally, extended links permit a single link to point to more than one resource. Much more could be said about extended links, but I'll leave it at that for now.

The show attribute specifies that the linked resource will replace the current resource in the browser or other agent. Other values for show include embed, which should embed the requested resource in the current resource without replacing it, and new, which should load the resource in a new window or in some other suitable framework. The attribute href is analogous to href in the a element in HTML. There aren't a lot of XLink implementations yet, but Netscape Navigator 6 does support simple XLink links.

## Document Object Model (DOM) and Simple API for XML (SAX)

DOM level 2 is a W3C recommendation that defines objects that describe either an HTML or XML document. Championed by David Megginson, SAX was developed outside of W3C by the XML-DEV mail list community, but with the broad support from the XML developers.

Both DOM and SAX have their strengths, but one is not normally used to the exclusion of the other. It depends on what you want to do to an XML document. While DOM can store an entire document in memory, and thereby access and change it, SAX traverses an XML document in one pass and is essentially event-based, handling each distinctive part of a document as a unit.

While DOM and/or SAX are likely candidates for processing XML applications, I'll only touch on them lightly in this chapter—in this book, for that matter. The Apache Xerces project (available at http://xml.apache.org) offers a validating XML parser plus example programs that use both DOM and SAX. The project includes source code, too. I'll show you how to run a couple of the sample programs to get you going.

First of all, let's start with `SAXCount.java`. This program invokes the Xerces parser for a given XML document. At a Windows command line, type:

```
java -cp xerces.jar;xercesSamples.jar sax.SAXCount order.xml
```

The output will look like this:

```
order.xml: 80 ms (6 elems, 3 attrs, 0 spaces, 47 chars)
```

As the name of the program suggests, it does some counting while SAX traverses the document (tree). It reports the amount of time it took to complete the traversal in milliseconds. Then it outputs the count of elements (`6 elems`), attributes (`3 attrs`), ignorable whitespace characters (`0 spaces`), and text characters (`47 chars`) in the document. By default, the program is nonvalidating. You can turn on validation by adding the –v option at the end of the command line:

```
java -cp xerces.jar;xercesSamples.jar sax.SAXCount order.xml -v
```

The program `DOMFilter.java` uses the DOM to search a tree for elements and attributes. It searches for all elements and attributes by default using this command line:

```
java -cp xerces.jar;xercesSamples.jar dom.DOMFilter order.xml
```

It outputs the start-tag for all elements, including any attributes, if present. You can search for a particular element with the –e option or an attribute with –a. For example, if you wanted to search for any instance of the `Item` element, you would add the –e option and the element name to the command:

```
java -cp xerces.jar;xercesSamples.jar dom.DOMFilter -e Item order.xml
```

Likewise, if you are hunting for an attribute, add the –a attribute with the attribute name:

```
java -cp xerces.jar;xercesSamples.jar dom.DOMFilter -a type order.xml
```

Use the –h option (help) for more information about what the program can do.

One last sample program I'll mention is `TreeViewer.java`. It uses the Java Swing library, so it has a graphical interface (see Figure 2.3). This program uses DOM to traverse an XML file. It displays the source file (right pane) as well a tree view (left pane). The File menu lets you open an XML file or quit the program, while the Shortcuts menu lets you expand and collapse the tree as well as reload the XML document. The lower pane displays values for whatever node is highlighted in the tree view. You invoke this program with the command:

```
java -cp xerces.jar;xercesSamples.jar ui.TreeViewer order.xml
```

In closing, Table 2.4 lists a few other W3C XML initiatives worth noting. Of those listed, only Resource Description Framework (RDF) is a recommendation, but the others are maturing rapidly and will have an impact on the wider XML scene in due time.

**Figure 2.3** TreeViewer from Apache's Xerces project.

**Table 2.4**    Other XML Initiatives

| NAME | DESCRIPTION |
|---|---|
| RDF | Resource Description Framework (RDF) provides a uniform way to add metadata to an XML document and is an aid to organizing, categorizing, and cataloging online information. It is an approved recommendation of the W3C, and it is beginning to catch on. It will likely be an important building block for the Semantic Web, which is only in the early stages of development. |
| XML Query | XML Query will deliver a means to query and extract reports from documents. It is not yet a W3C recommendation. |
| XForms | HTML forms, while essential to ecommerce, have become outdated. The XForms initiative will update Web form technology so that, among other improvements, data from forms will be delivered as XML. |
| XBase | In HTML, the base element lets you specify the document's base URI so that it can automatically resolve relative URIs. In XML, this will be done through the xml:base attribute. The value of xml:base must be a URI. W3C is not ready to release XBase yet. |
| XInclude | XML Inclusions or XInclude is an inclusion mechanism for merging XML documents. For example, you could include a separate XML document in another XML document. Work on XInclude is not yet complete. |
| XML Signature | This initiative will permit the creation of digital signatures—a method for secure, online identification—using XML. It is not yet fully approved, but it soon will be. (XML Signature is discussed further in Chapter 4, "Security.") |
| XML Infoset | The XML Information Set (Infoset) provides a level of abstraction for an XML document using a set of information items that make it easier for XML-related standards and applications to interoperate. It is not a recommendation yet. |
| Canonical XML | Canonical XML provides a strict, streamlined way to represent XML documents. XML documents, while physically different, may be logically identical as long as they conform to the Canonical XML specification. This also is not a recommendation yet. |

# Beyond XML

Now you should have a pretty good grasp of what XML is and how to use it, but transport and security mechanisms are also essential parts of a working B2B system. In the next chapters, I explore other important technologies that will help you move or transport XML documents (Chapter 3) and how to keep XML documents secure (Chapter 4).

# Transport

This book is for people who want a clear picture of how B2B works. If you read the last chapter, you probably have a good idea of how XML works. Now we are going to start from a lower transport level.

I need to talk about transport-related technologies because they are used regularly in B2B implementations or are integral parts of them. For example, Multipurpose Internet Message Extensions (MIME) is an essential protocol for B2B systems. Also, every B2B implementation discussed in this book uses Hypertext Transfer Protocol (HTTP), which uses headers that are similar to MIME and its predecessor, a mail format sometimes called Internet Mail, based on the Internet Engineering Task Force Request for Comment 822 (IETF RFCC 822, also known as Standard 11). Simple Mail Transfer Protocol (SMTP) and File Transfer Protocol (FTP) are other means for transporting files across the Internet.

I will cover transport protocols in this chapter, the programs that move data from one place to another or are used to encapsulate or describe data that is being moved. These protocols are TCP/IP, HTTP, FTP, RFC 822, SMTP, POP3, IMAP4, and MIME. In the next chapter, I'll discuss security measures, such as encryption and digital signatures.

# Transmission Control Protocol and Internet Protocol

The underbelly of the Internet lies in a pair of layered programs: *Transmission Control Protocol* (TCP) and *Internet Protocol* (IP), called TCP/IP for short. TCP/IP has been around for about 20 years, and together these programs transport billions of packets of data all over the Internet every single day.

TCP/IP is not the only kind of network protocol used on the Internet—User Datagram Protocol (UDP) is another example—but by and large, TCP/IP is the dominant networking protocol used. It was created to connect a vast array of computers over great distances, many of which had incompatible network protocols, and it works well.

TCP and IP work together, but each has a different purpose. TCP is the higher-level, top layer, and IP is the low-level, bottom layer. These layers together are called a TCP/IP stack. To put it simply, IP moves the data and TCP referees. Above TCP are higher-level layers or interfaces, such as the capabilities that are built into a Web browser. TCP talks to user-level applications in the layers above it and talks to IP in the layer below it.

I'll start from the bottom and work my way back up.

## How IP Works

IP—that's *Internet Protocol*, not *intellectual property*—is the real workhorse of the Internet. It transmits huge amounts of data all over the world at any given second on any given day. The trick is in this: IP doesn't send everything out in one big chunk, but it breaks data into fragments, or packets, and then sends them out toward a destination identified by an addressing scheme. After the packets arrive, IP—with the help of TCP—reassembles them in the correct order at the destination.

Sounds a little messy, but given that it was originally part of U.S. military research, it's not surprising that's the way IP was designed. In the event of a nuclear strike, IP could route its packets around the damaged areas of the network until it found their destination. By design, robustness and recovery outweighed efficiency and speed.

IP also does not keep a connection open until it finishes sending all the data, making it possible for data packets to travel different routes on their way to a destination and then have a little reunion once they get there.

Packets of data sent by IP are said to be unreliable because IP cannot guarantee whether the packets will be delivered, the time it will take for them to get where they are going, or in what order the packets may arrive. I like to think of TCP as IP's parole officer. IP may go a little nuts, but TCP keeps it accountable.

If data is undeliverable over a certain period of time, it just self-destructs. If such is the case, packets are retransmitted until they get to where they are supposed to go and until its preset time-to-live runs out. This means that if a packet fails along a route, it can be rerouted to the same destination using a different course and retransmitted until it succeeds. If part of the Web infrastructure, such as phone and fiber-optic lines, is down or out of commission, IP can find alternative paths to get the data to where it needs to go, unless the down-and-out infrastructure is a severed fiber-optic cable dangling from the shovel of a backhoe in your front yard.

When IP gives the data it sends a header. The header provides information about the data, such as the IP version number, the length of the packet, and source and destination addresses. These addresses are known as *IP addresses*.

### The IP Address

No doubt you have heard about and seen an IP address, sometimes called a *dotted decimal*. It is part of the IP header. An IP address is a unique identifier that is composed of four bytes or octets (32 bits). For human consumption, each octet is converted into a decimal number in the range 0–255 and separated by a dot or period (.). For example, the IP address for `http://testb2b.org` is 205.204.47.30, which is a lot easier for you and I to grasp than its binary equivalent.

> **NOTE**    IP version 4 (IPv4) specifies 32-bit addresses. This address is based on RFC 820, "Assigned Numbers." IPv4 is still the most common version of IP. The draft Internet standard for IP version 6 (IPv6) accomodates128-bit addresses, among many other enhancements. Vendors are just beginning to deploy IPv6, though it has been a draft standard since 1998. Eventually it will be universal.

In a browser, you could type in a Web address as either `http://testb2b.com` or `http://205.204.47.30` and get the same result. An IP address identifies the location or home address of a resource such as a Web server. The domain name *testb2b.org* is actually an alias for its IP address. This alias is usually resolved by the Domain Name System (DNS). DNS servers provide huge lookup tables that match IP addresses with domain names, so we can use mnemonics to save us from remembering and typing all those numbers.

IP also communicates with Ethernet in a local area network (LAN) environment. It relies on Address Resolution Protocol (ARP) to match up Ethernet addresses with IP addresses. Like DNS, your local, neighborhood ARP updates its database regularly and uses simple tables to associate these addresses with each other.

## How TCP Works

TCP, as mentioned earlier, works on the layer just above IP. When TCP opens a connection across the Internet, unlike IP, it keeps that connection open until it has completed its work. As TCP fires packets of data through the IP layer and then across a network connection, the receiving TCP process sends an acknowledgment for each chunk of data, reassuring the sender that all went well. Packets are each given a header, and they may vary in size. IP, the layer below TCP, can explode packets into 64-bit fragments, reassembling them at the terminal end. TCP similarly reassembles the larger packets.

Each packet is assigned a sequence number so that these blocks of data can be reassembled in their proper sequence at the receiving end. A checksum is also added, so that TCP can check to see if the data it receives is sound and correct. TCP also monitors the flow of packets, opening and closing the data spigot as needed to make sure data flows smoothly and efficiently.

Because it was necessary for local applications on a computer to use the TCP layer simultaneously, TCP was designed to provide a range of addressable points, allowing what is known as *multiplexing*. These points are called *ports*. Each port is numbered, and you can have up to 65,535 ports on a machine. A *socket* is a port that connects applications or operating systems to TCP/IP and allows them to talk to each other. TCP connections are made between sockets at each end. TCP keeps the connection alive until, with the help of IP, it finishes its job.

## Hypertext Transfer Protocol

Tim Berners-Lee did not invent the Internet, but he did invent the systematic use of the Internet that we call the *World Wide Web*, or the Web for short. The Web was built on the foundation of HTML and Hypertext Transfer Protocol (HTTP). Instead of just transporting binary data or files across the Internet, Web browsers help us skip cumbersome steps—such as moving documents separately with one program and then using a local application to read them—in retrieving data in the form of documents.

The Internet, in its earliest form, has been with us since the early 1970s. One of the initial programs or clients available to use on the Internet was File Transfer Protocol, or FTP. FTP allows you to transfer files, individually or in groups, between remote computers.

Back before the Web, say in the mid- to late 1980s, if you wanted to share a file with me, you could use FTP to log in to my local host computer and push a file onto it. If it was a document in the form of a US-ASCII or plain-text file, I could then use some sort of local program to read that file, such as `cat`, a Unix command, or the `vi` editor, a Unix screen editor. You could also send binary files to me, provided that I could dig up a program to read or execute your binary.

This is where the Web enters the scene. With HTML, you can define a document that could be readable across the Internet, and with HTTP, you can transport an HTML document to a local client such as a Web browser, thus avoiding a couple of steps or obstacles:

- You no longer needed to download or upload the file; you could just view a temporary copy of it in a user agent such as a browser.

- You no longer needed to open the file with another local program. You could read the file with the browser you used to retrieve it.

- HTML provides a means to share not only text but also binary graphics.

Though the Web was originally intended to help engineers collaborate across distances, people dreamed up all kinds of ways to exploit it for their own purposes. If an engineer could share a single scientific document this way, couldn't I just as well host a bunch of documents? We call this kind of repository a Web site. Why not create more than just scientific documents: How about a document that just describes the agency I work for?

Then, why not documents describing the businesses that use our scientific data to build super-colliders? While I'm at it, I'll use this thing called a link to connect that scientific page to the business page. In fact, I can use the company's logo, convert it into CompuServe's Graphical Image Format (GIF), and then display it on my page. Now I'm advertising for you! How about a little cash to compensate me for my trouble? If I can advertise, why don't I also sell directly to my customers? Once in the hands of marketers, the evolution of the Internet from a scientific-centric to a business-oriented network did not take long.

This is how, back in the early 1990s, one thing led to another. B2B continues the trend and often relies on the main engine of the Web, HTTP, to do its work. Here's how.

## How HTTP Works

HTTP has been around since 1990, right around when the Web began. Tim Berners-Lee documented his work on HTTP, but various implementations of it arose, and HTTP got a little wild for a while. Finally, in 1996, Berners-Lee and others described HTTP version 1.0 in an Internet Engineering Task Force (IETF) document called Request for Comment (RFC) 1945. Any version prior to 1.0 was generally referred to as version 0.9. HTTP version 1.1 appeared three years later (RFC 2616).

If you surf the Web about everyday like me, you are using HTTP without really noticing it. HTTP is yet another application, like FTP, that operates in the layer that sits atop TCP/IP and whose simple commands retrieve resources (documents and other kinds of files or entities) over the Internet. HTTP requires that a computer that stores Web documents must be connected to the Internet and have a Web server installed on it to handle the HTTP requests.

A Web server listens to port 80, the default HTTP port, waiting patiently for requests from a client for documents and other resources. From another computer, perhaps a remote one, a client such as a Web browser sends a request to a server with a given IP address. The server then retrieves the requested resource and sends it to the requester. Once it arrives, the client usually renders or otherwise processes the resource. You can also push resources with HTTP, but by and large it makes requests for documents and other resources.

**NOTE**   While HTTP version 1.1 is the most recent protocol version, servers may not support all its capabilities as specified in RFC 2616.

Following is an example of a manual HTTP GET request, which you use when you bring up a page on the Web, but which you usually don't see because the browser hides it from you. This time you are going to get a chance to use GET by hand.

The first step is to make sure that you have an Internet connection. Once you are connected, type the following line, at either a Windows or Unix command prompt:

```
telnet testb2b.org 80
```

This line opens up port 80, the dedicated HTTP port, on the server testb2b.org. Now enter the following line:

```
GET /B2B/order.xml HTTP/1.0
```

The server on `testb2b.org` supports HTTP 1.1, but because HTTP is backward-compatible, it will support a version 1.0 request. Be sure to preserve case when typing, as a request that is even slightly different may fail. Also, at a Windows command prompt, your typing may not be echoed, but on Unix it should.

Then press Enter twice. The server will send the requested document, plus several headers, back to you. After the transaction, your connection to the host is lost. It may not look so great on the screen, but we are dealing with the raw Internet here, so let's not get fussy.

HTTP 1.0 assumes the domain `testb2b.org` because it is already connected to that host via `telnet`. If you change the version to HTTP 1.1, the server will return a "400 Bad Request" error. Here is the correct command in version 1.1. Press Enter after the first line, twice after the second line:

```
GET /B2B/order.xml HTTP/1.1
Host: www.testb2b.org
```

Here is an explanation of each part of this method call:

- The GET method or command at the beginning of the line is the request method for a Web page. Method names in HTTP must be uppercase.

- Next is the relative Uniform Resource Identifier (URI) that names the resource, that is, the B2B document `/B2B/order.xml`, that you want to retrieve from the host.

- At the end of the line is the protocol name HTTP and its version number, 1.0 in the first instance, 1.1 in the second. The slash (/) between the protocol and version number is mandatory.

- In the case of version 1.1, you add the domain name following the `Host:` field identifier. This works in 1.0 as well, but 1.1 requires this form.

A response from the server lets you know whether the transaction was successful. This is an example of a response from the HTTP server on `testb2b.org`:

```
HTTP/1.1 200 OK
Date: Mon, 05 mar 2001 13:10:24 GMT
Server: Apache/1.3.4 (Unix) FrontPage/4.0.4.3 PHP/3.0.14
Last-Modified: Mon, 05 mar 2001 12:45:05 GMT
ETag: "10b0b4-13c-39f7e116"
Accept-Ranges: bytes
Content-Length: 421
```

```
Connection: close
Content-Type: text/plain

<?xml version="1.0" encoding="iso-8859-1" ?>
<!DOCTYPE Order SYSTEM "Order.dtd">

<order:Order order:partner="06-853-2535"
xmlns:order="http://testb2b.org/order">
 <order:Date>2001-03-05</order:Date>
 <order:Item order:type="ISBN">0471404012</order:Item>
 <order:Quantity>22</order:Quantity>
 <order:Comments>None.<order:Comments>
 <order:ShippingMethod order:class="4th">USPS</ShippingMethod>
</order:Order>
```

An explanation of each line of the HTTP response follows.

The first part of the response is a series of headers; the second part is the actual XML document that the GET method requested. The header and the document are separated by a single blank line.

The first line of the header gives the HTTP protocol name and version number. Again, the slash is required. The server on testb2b.org supports HTTP 1.1, so HTTP/1.1 is appropriate. Following the protocol and version information is the status code "200 OK," which means the request succeeded. HTTP issues status codes to let the recipient know about the success or failure of the request. The 200 series HTTP status codes indicate success, while the 400 series means there was a client error. For example, one such error is the familiar "404 Not Found," which means that the server couldn't find anything to match the requested URI. Later in this chapter, Table 3.2 lists the HTTP 1.1 status codes.

After the first line come several header fields. The order and content of these fields may vary, but these are representative examples. Date, the first header field, indicates the date and time that the response message originated from the server. Following that is the server type with its version number identifying the server that responded to the request. It also lists its Microsoft FrontPage and PHP support. The Last-Modified field indicates the date and time that the resource—an XML document, order.xml, in this case—was last modified.

The Etag or entity tag is a cache validator. This value helps a cache determine if it has a stale entry or not. A browser, for example, can keep pages (entities, generally) in cache so that it won't have to go through the work of retrieving a page if the page hasn't been modified. Normally, cache is evaluated against the Date field, so a page modified in the same second would not appear different. The Etag validator makes more precise comparisons than the Date field can because the Date field entry has a granularity of one second—a long time when you are dealing with the Internet.

The Accept-Ranges field value is bytes, but in version 1.1, the only acceptable values are either bytes or none, anyway. In fact, it is an optional header field that the server may or may not send. The interesting thing about it is that you can set byte offsets and ranges, allowing you to retrieve only certain, selected bytes from a resource.

The next header field is Content-Length. This specifies how many characters or octets are in the requested document.

After the requested document is sent, the connection to the server will be closed. That is what the header field Connection: close means. HTTP 1.1 has the ability to open a connection between a client and server and keep it open for a time. Earlier versions of HTTP did not support this. Persistent connections make it possible to conduct a number of request-response transactions quickly and efficiently, rather than the stateless, one-at-a-time approach of HTTP 1.0 and earlier.

The Content-Type field points to the Internet media or MIME type text/plain. The first term is the type, and the second term, following the slash, is a subtype. The media type text/plain means that the content of the requested document will be plain-text format. A more suitable media type would be text/xml, but apparently the HTTP server does not support it yet.

Following the header is a blank line (carriage return/line feed, or CRLF) and the actual XML document, all 421 octets of it.

## Java and XML

Java and XML are a pretty good match. While XML is a neutral language that describes data that can be handled by a variety of applications, Java applications complement XML's portability as well. The Java/XML combination has not achieved perfection, but it is about the best thing going for business and partners that operate networks that connect different platforms using different operating systems. Any other combination either has a proprietary bent, which is aimed at getting more of your money, or requires recompiling code for each platform.

The Java and XML combination is not your only option, but at this time it is about the best overall bet for B2B applications. With any resource constraints, you have to make choices and take your best shot. That's why I chose Java for the sample programs in this book.

## *Compiling and Running Java*

If you are an experienced Java programmer, you'll be awfully bored for the next few paragraphs, so you can skip ahead to the next section. If not, hang with me for a few minutes to get some Java mechanics out of the way. You don't have to know everything about Java to do something with it. Even if you have never programmed in Java before, if you will follow a few simple steps, you can begin today.

First of all, you have to get Java on your computer. You may already have a Java Runtime Environment (JRE) on your computer. A JRE includes a Java Virtual Machine (JVM), which is the engine that actually executes Java programs. A JVM can be installed on just about any platform, be it Windows, Unix, Linux, Mac OS, or whatever, so that a compiled Java program will run on any platform.

You might have a JRE on your system without knowing it because many times a JRE gets installed as part of another program. For example, if you have installed Netscape 6 on your system, you have the option of installing a JRE with it, so that you can run Java applets in your browser. A simple test to see if you have Java on your system is to go to a command line and type:

```
java -version
```

If you have Java on your system, you will get a message back stating the version number. If Java is not on your system or in the proper path, you will get a hiccup saying that the command was not recognized. If it isn't there, you can put it there, for free. Let's get it done.

If you want to compile Java programs in addition to running them, you can install the Java Development Kit (JDK), which you can download for free from Sun's Java Web site. The JDK offers you Sun's Java compiler (javac), as well as a debugger and other development tools. As of this writing, the current version is the Java 2 Platform, Standard Edition, Version 1.3. This version of the JDK is adequate for compiling and running the programs in this book—you don't need the Enterprise Edition of the JDK or an Integrated Development Environment (IDE), such as Webgain's Visual Café, until you expand your use of Java, but that's out of scope for this book.

To download the JDK, go to http://java.sun.com/j2se/ and select the current release for the platform you are using, either Sun's Solaris, Linux, or Microsoft Windows. On Solaris, you have to log in to the Java Developer's Connection (JDC) in order to get to the file, but the steps are simple and self-explanatory. Then elect the download size, whether in one big package or smaller chunks, and accept the license agreement (or that's as far as you will go). Next you'll have to select the site from which you want to download the package. You can pick from a variety of sites, so you have a chance to circumvent high Web traffic. On Windows, you will download a self-extracting file. On Linux, you get the option of either a RedHat RPM package or a GNUZIP script. On Solaris, you can get either a `bin` or `tar.Z` file for either the SPARC or Intel platforms.

After you finish downloading the archive file, install it on your system. On Windows, for example, you will be asked to open or install the file after the download completes. Other platforms will require you to be familiar with the `tar` or `rpm` utilities in order to extract the files. The installation process is guided by easy-to-follow instructions, so I won't cover those closely.

## Compiling and Running a Java Program

Assuming that the JDK installed successfully, you can now compile and run Java programs from the command line. Before you do that, however, you must set that `path` and the `classpath` variables on your system so that you can run the Java executables. I'll cover the `path` first.

### The Path Variable

On Windows, it is likely that you installed the JDK at `c:\jdk1.3`. Under that directory will be the `bin` directory, which holds executables such as `javac.exe` and `java.exe`. Your command interpreter must be able to "see" where these executables are in order to run them. It does so through the `path` variable. You can set the path in a variety of ways.

On Windows 2000 Server, for example, one way to do this is to bring up the Environment Variables dialog box. First select Settings from the Start menu. Then choose Control Panel. Select System and click the Advanced tab and then the Environment Variables button. Select Path in the System Variables pane at the bottom of the dialog box. In the Edit System Variable box (shown in Figure 3.1), add `;c:\jdk1.3\bin` to the Variable Value, then click OK until all the dialog boxes are dismissed. Now the path variable is reset, without rebooting your system, though you have to close and reopen your command window. You can also set the path in the `autoexec.bat` file on Windows or even at the command line, but if you don't know how to do that, I'll leave that to you for a research project—one method is enough for now. (Refer to the end notes for a reference to information on how to set the path on a Linux platform.)

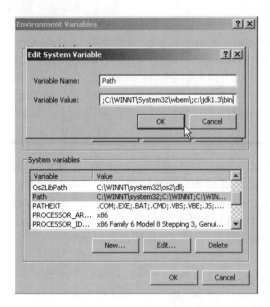

**Figure 3.1**   System Variable and Edit System Variable dialog boxes from Windows 2000 Server.

## The Classpath Variable

The classpath variable informs the system where to find class (Java executable) and Java Archive (JAR) files. A class file essentially is a byte-code file or the result of compiling a Java program. The JVM interprets these bytecodes when you run a Java program. A JAR file is a collection of class files bundled into a ZIP file.

The default classpath is the current directory, represented by a single period (.). Sometimes the classpath gets messed up in one way or another so that you get the error Exception in thread "main" java.lang.NoClassDefFoundError: ProgramName when you try to run a program. To add or establish a classpath, for example, on Windows 2000 Server, follow the same instructions for adding to the path variable, but instead of clicking the Edit button, click New instead. When the Edit System Variable dialog box appears, enter a variable name of classpath and a variable value of a single period (.). Dismiss the dialog boxes by clicking OK, and you are ready to roll in a new command window. (Again, see the end notes for more references to instructions on setting classpaths on Windows and other platforms.)

### Compiling a Java Program

With the JDK installed and your `path` and `classpath` variables properly set, you can now compile a Java program. In an archive file on the companion Web site for this book (www.wiley.com/compbooks/fitzgerald/testb2b.zip), you will find, among others, a program called `Get.java`. After you download this archive file to a local system and extract `Get.java`, you can compile this program by typing the following on a command line:

```
javac Get.java
```

This will produce the file `Get.class`, a bytecode file that is interpretable by a JVM. If you get an error, I am ready to predict it is one of four things: (1) the JDK is not installed properly or installed at all; (2) the `path` variable is not set correctly; (3) the `classpath` variable is not set correctly; or (4) any combination of the first three. Because I can't be there to see what you're doing, my advice is to go back and follow the earlier instructions as closely as you can, especially those covering the `path` and `classpath` variables. Another good choice is to join Java Developer's Connection (JDC), where you can get a lot of free help.

To run the program, type:

```
java Get /B2B/order.xml
```

The JVM will now execute the program. You don't have to type the `.class` file extension, just the name of the class file. Now if you are trying to execute a Java program from a directory other than the one in which it is located, you can include the value of `classpath` on the command line. For example, say you were currently in the root directory `c:\`, but the program you wanted to execute was in the directory `c:\java`, you could include the `-cp` or `-classpath` option at the command line, like this:

```
java -cp c:\java Get /B2B/order.xml
```

When the `classpath` is in good order, the program will execute. Sometimes you include JAR files in the `classpath` because a particular program needs to access a whole mess of `class` files, all neatly archived in a JAR. For example, in the last chapter, you saw a command like this:

```
java -classpath fop.jar;xerces.jar;xalan.jar;w3c.jar
org.apache.fop.apps.CommandLine order.fo order.pdf
```

In this command, four JARs, all in the current directory, are in the classpath. The program CommandLine is found in fop.jar. Order can be important, as a Java program may expect to find some class files earlier than others.

### Retrieving order.xml with Get.java

The Java program Get.java requests a document with HTTP. This program assumes that you have an Internet connection at execution time. Provided that the path and classpath variables are in good shape, extract Get.class from the program archive to your current working directory and just type in the following at a command line:

```
java Get /B2B/order.xml
```

The output of this program, displayed on your screen, will look something like this:

```
HTTP/1.1 200 OK
Date: Mon, 05 Mar 2001 20:46:17 GMT
Server: Apache/1.3.4 (Unix) FrontPage/4.0.4.3 PHP/3.0.14
Last-Modified: Mon, 05 Mar 2001 17:54:52 GMT
ETag: "10b029-1a5-3a09936c"
Accept-Ranges: bytes
Content-Length: 421
Connection: close
Content-Type: text/plain

<?xml version="1.0" encoding="iso-8859-1" ?>
<!DOCTYPE Order SYSTEM "Order.dtd">

<order:Order order:partner="06-853-2535"
  xmlns:order="http://testb2b.org/order">
  <order:Date>2001-03-05</order:Date>
  <order:Item order:type="ISBN">0471404012</order:Item>
  <order:Quantity>22</order:Quantity>
  <order:Comments>None.</order:Comments>
  <order:ShippingMethod
    order:class="4th">USPS</order:ShippingMethod>
</order:Order>
```

Here is a listing of the Java source file.

```
/*
//
// Get.java
//
// Using HTTP, requests a document from testb2b.org.
//
*/

import java.net.*;
import java.io.*;

public class Get {

 public static void main(String args[]) {

   try {

     // Make sure there is one argument; if not, fail

     if (args.length != 1)
       throw new IllegalArgumentException("Need file or /");

     // Create socket object

     Socket testb2b = new Socket("testb2b.org", 80);

     // Set up input/output to/from host

     InputStream fromhost = testb2b.getInputStream();
     PrintWriter tohost = new PrintWriter(new
       OutputStreamWriter(testb2b.getOutputStream()));

     // Make HTTP Get request

     tohost.println("GET " + args[0] + " HTTP/1.0\n");
     tohost.flush();

     // Buffer for download

     byte[] buffer = new byte[1024];
     int readbytes;
     while((readbytes = fromhost.read(buffer)) != -1)
       System.out.write(buffer, 0, readbytes);

     // Close socket

     testb2b.close();

   }
```

```
    // Handle exceptions

    catch (Exception err) {
     System.err.println(err);
     System.err.println("Usage: java Get <file [or /]>");
     }
    }
   }
```

## What's Going on in Get.java?

For readers who aren't familiar with Java, this section walks through
Get.java so you have an idea of what it's doing. Experienced programmers need not apply. I won't cover all the gritty details of Java here—that's
not the purpose of this book—but I will give you a general rundown of
what the program does.

After a few comments at the beginning (// comments out a single line,
/* */ can comment out multiple lines), the program imports two packages. These packages are composed of groups of classes and/or interfaces
(types). Classes from these packages will be used later in the program.
Classes contain definitions for variables and methods (functions or routines), among other things. The Socket class is part of the java.net.*
package, while the InputStream class is part of java.util.*. An aster-
isk (*) is a convenience that lets you import all the classes that are part of a
given package.

The user-defined public (accessible) class Get encapsulates the entire
Java program, and this class name must be the same name as the program
file. The main method is where the program begins its execution. The try
block defines a chunk of code that may generate errors (exceptions). The
catch block that follows try will handle the output of any exceptions that
get generated.

The if statement tests to see if Get has an argument, throwing an exception if it does not. The Socket class creates a new socket, connecting it to
a port (80) at a specified host address (testb2b.org). InputStream creates a means to get input from the socket and PrintWriter, a means for
output to the socket. Using println, the program submits the HTTP GET
method to the socket, then pushes the request out the hatch (flush()).

The input from the socket is read into a buffer 1024 bytes at a time, then
written to the output stream (standard output or the screen) until there
is nothing left to read (-1). The socket is closed for good measure, and
the main block ends, without, we hope, catch having to throw any
exceptions.

### *Retrieving order.xml with GetOrder.java*

The following simple Java program, `GetOrder.java`, requests the document `order.xml` via the Java URL class and then saves the document in the same local directory where the program was invoked. Like the last program, this one assumes that you have a live connection with the Internet at execution time. Extract `GetOrder.class` from the archive to your current working directory and just type in the following at a command line:

```
java GetOrder
```

The program will execute. In your current local directory, you should find a file with a unique filename that looks something like this:

```
2001-02-28-8558-order.xml
```

Here is a listing of the Java source file.

```
/*
//
// GetOrder.java
//
// Gets a known URL for order.xml, opens a file output stream,
// and saves the file locally with a unique name.
//
*/

import java.net.*;
import java.io.*;
import java.util.*;
import java.text.*;

public class GetOrder {

 public static void main(String args[]) {

 // Start off with a clean slate

 InputStream input = null;
 OutputStream output = null;

 // Random number for unique filename

 Random rn = new Random();

 // Formatted date for unique filename
 // Date format conforms to ISO 8601 and XML Schema date

 DateFormat today = new SimpleDateFormat("yyyy-MM-dd");

 // Form unique filename
```

```
String ufn = new String(today.format(new
  Date()) + "-" + rn.nextInt(10000) + "-order.xml");

try {

  // Open URL, input stream, file output stream

  URL url = new URL("http://testb2b.org/B2B/order.xml");
  input = url.openStream();
  output = new FileOutputStream(ufn);

  // Buffer for download

  byte[] buffer = new byte[1024];
  int readbytes;
  while((readbytes = input.read(buffer)) != -1)
    output.write(buffer, 0, readbytes);

  // Close input

  input.close();

}

// Handle exceptions

catch (Exception err) {
  System.err.println(err);
}

  }
}
```

### What's Happening in GetOrder.java?

New `input` and `output` streams are assigned `null` values. A new random number object is created (`rn`) as well as a date format (`today`) that conforms to ISO 8601, a standard for the representation of dates and times (`yyyy-MM-dd`). This format is used for the `date` simple type in XML Schema as well. The random number and formatted date are then used to give a file a unique name (`ufn`).

A new object of type `URL` is created with the address of `http://testb2b.org/B2B/order.xml`. The input stream the program created earlier (`input`) is hooked up with the stream from the URL, which amounts to the contents of the file `order.xml`. The output stream is assigned a file output stream for the unique file `ufn`. The date is followed by a random number and then ends with the original filename, `order.xml`.

## Retrieving Any Document with GetAny.java

You don't have to stay locked in to one file. Perhaps you would like to retrieve other documents besides order.xml. With a few alterations to the program, you can specify a URL for a document on the command line at runtime. The new program GetAny.java allows you to do just that (available from the program archive). At the command line, type:

```
java GetAny http://testb2b.org/B2B/summ.xml
```

This program makes a few changes to GetOrder.java.

```java
/*
//
// GetAny.java
//
// Gets a URL, given as an argument on the command line,
// opens a file output stream, and saves the file locally
// with a unique name.
//
*/

import java.net.*;
import java.io.*;
import java.util.*;
import java.text.*;

public class GetAny {

 public static void main(String args[]) {

  // Start off with clean slate

  InputStream input = null;
  OutputStream output = null;

  // Random number for unique filename

  Random rn = new Random();

  // Formatted date for unique filename
  // Date format conforms to ISO 8601 and XML Schema date

  DateFormat today = new SimpleDateFormat("yyyy-MM-dd");

   try {

    // Test argument
```

```
    if (args.length != 1)
     throw new IllegalArgumentException("Needs URL!");

    // Open URL, input stream

    URL url = new URL(args[0]);
    input = url.openStream();

    // Extract filename

    String name = url.getFile();
    File filename = new File(name);
    String fn = filename.getName();
    if (fn.equals(""))
     fn = "any.txt";

    // Output file

    String ufn = new String(today.format(new Date()) + "-" +
     rn.nextInt(10000) + "-" + fn);
    output = new FileOutputStream(ufn);

    // Buffer for download

    byte[] buffer = new byte[1024];
    int readbytes;
    while((readbytes = input.read(buffer)) != -1)
     output.write(buffer, 0, readbytes);
    System.out.println("\nWrote file: " + ufn);

    // Close input

    input.close();

   }

   // Handle exceptions

   catch (Exception err) {
    System.err.println(err);
    System.err.println("Usage: java GetAny <url>");
   }
  }
 }
```

## What's Happening in GetAny.java?

Unlike GetOrder.java, GetAny.java accepts a URL as a command-line argument (args[0]). It extracts the filename from the URL, breaking it down to a filename part (such as order) plus the extension part (such as .xml) and placing the name in a String variable (fn). If it can't get a filename from, for example, a URL like http://testb2b.org/, it uses a default filename (any.txt). From this filename (fn), it creates a unique filename (ufn), and like GetOrder.java, writes the file to the current local directory.

### Putting a Document on a Server with Put.java

The following Java program is similar to the Get.java program you saw earlier, but rather than using the GET method it uses PUT. In order for it to work, the PUT method must be enabled on the server, presenting potential security risks, which can be dealt with in different ways, depending on your server.

From the program archive, extract Put.class and ack.xml and place them in your local working directory. Then at a command line, type:

```
java Put 2001-02-28-8558-ack.xml
```

The prefixed date and random number is merely an example; you can change it if you wish. This program will put the file 2001-02-28-ack.xml on http://localhost. I use http://localhost because, as you might guess, it would not be wise for me to open up testb2b.org for you to put any file on it! The example assumes that you open up the directory B2B in your local Web root for writing. Following is the source code for the program.

```
/*
//
// Put.java
//
// Puts a local file on localhost
//
*/

import java.io.*;
import java.net.*;

public class Put {

  public static void main(String[] args) {

    try {
```

```java
// Test argument

String fn = "new.xml";

if (args.length == 0) {
 System.out.println("Using default filename " + fn + "...\n");
 System.out.flush();
}
else {
 fn = args[0];
 System.out.println("Using filename " + fn + "...\n");
 System.out.flush();
}

// Set up connection

URL url = new URL("http://localhost/B2B/" + fn);
HttpURLConnection c = (HttpURLConnection)url.openConnection();
c.setDoInput(true);
c.setDoOutput(true);
c.setRequestMethod("PUT");

// Read local file order.xml

FileInputStream fs = new FileInputStream("order.xml");
BufferedInputStream bf = new BufferedInputStream(fs);

// Output file to destination

OutputStream out = c.getOutputStream();
byte[] buf = new byte[512];
int len;
while (bf.available() != 0) {
 len = bf.read(buf);
 out.write(buf, 0, len);
 }
bf.close();

// Print response information plus

int rc = c.getResponseCode();
String r = c.getResponseMessage();
System.out.println(rc + " " + r);

String hf = c.getHeaderField("Date");
System.out.println("Date: " + hf);

String m = c.getRequestMethod();
System.out.println("Method: " + m);

// Disconnect from host
```

```
    c.disconnect();

  }

   catch (Exception x) {
    System.err.println("Usage: java Put [filename]");
    System.err.println("Without filename, defaults to new.xml");
    System.err.println(x);
   }
  }

 }
```

**NOTE** For obvious reasons, this program will not work on www.testb2b.org because of the danger of opening up the server to someone writing a harmful file to it. You can change the program to work with some other remote server, as long as you have control over whether the server will accept the PUT method. For example, you can control the PUT method with the mod_put module on an Apache server. On Windows Server 2000, you can change permissions to the directory under the Web root (`http://localhost/B2B` in this example) to accept PUTs.

### What's Happening in Put.java

The `Put.java` program uses the HTTP method PUT to place a copy of the local file `order.xml` on `http://localhost/B2B`. It first tests to see if you have included an argument on the command line to use as the remote filename. If not, it uses a default filename (`new.xml`) for the file you will put on the host. Then it sets up a URL connection for the new file and sets the method to PUT. The local file `order.xml` is read and this file is buffered. Some HTTP header information is then printed on standard output (your screen), demonstrating that the operation was successful.

### W3C's Winie

In addition to this program, W3C's Winie product (downloadable from http://jigsaw.w3.org/Winie/) offers several programs that use the PUT HTTP methods, either from a command line or with a nice user interface. For example, the JWPut program is invoked like this.

```
java -cp client.jar;winie.jar;sax.jar;xp.jar org.w3c.jwput.JWput
order.xml http://localhost/B2B/order.xml
```

The JAR files, which come with the Winie download, are placed explicitly in the `classpath` for illustration. (Use colons instead of semi-colons in the Unix environment.) The first argument, `order.xml`, is the local file that you want to PUT, and the second argument, the URL `http://localhost/B2B/order.xml`, indicates where you want to put the named resource. With a successful PUT, you should see the following output to the screen, or something comparable to it:

```
Winie - HTTP/1.1 PUT tool
Version: 1.0.7
Uploading order.xml...
Uploading order.xml: 100% of 419 bytes at 41900 bytes/sec

File order.xml uploaded at

http://localhost/B2B/order.xml
```

## WebDAV

Web-based Distributed Authoring and Versioning (WebDAV) deserves a mention here. It is a collection of extensions to HTTP that allows you to edit and manage resources, such as XML files, on remote Web servers. Some of the features of WebDAV include the ability to lock files so others can't overwrite them, the use of properties to identify authors, dates, and so forth, and the ability to collect documents and manipulate them as groups. Popular tools, such as Macromedia Dreamweaver and Adobe Go Live, have recently added WebDAV support. WebDAV features may prove to be useful tools in B2B solutions.

## HTTP Methods

Object-oriented programming languages also used the term *method* to refer to what are called routines or procedures in traditional programming. HTTP has a number of methods other than GET or PUT, and HTTP version 1.1 offers a few more than HTTP 1.0. These methods are listed in Table 3.1.

As defined in RFC 1945, HTTP 1.0 had only three methods, GET, HEAD, and POST, though several others appeared in an appendix. Earlier versions, referred to generally as version 0.9, had proposed additional methods, such as CHECKIN and CHECKOUT, to lock outstanding files, but they apparently did not pass muster.

PUT and DELETE were proposed as early as 1992, made it to the appendix of version 1.0, and have fully resurfaced in version 1.1. LINK and UNLINK were also proposed in 1992, were relegated to a 1.0 appendix, and seemed to have evaporated in 1.1.

**Table 3.1**    HTTP Methods

| METHOD | VERSION | DESCRIPTION |
| --- | --- | --- |
| GET | 1.0, 1.1 | Requests a resource, such as a document |
| HEAD | 1.0, 1.1 | Requests only that a header be returned |
| POST | 1.0, 1.1 | Submits data to a server, such as from an HTML form |
| PUT | 1.0, 1.1 | Places a resource on the server rather than retrieves it |
| DELETE | 1.0, 1.1 | Deletes a named resource |
| LINK | 1.0 | Establishes links between resources |
| UNLINK | 1.0 | Removes links between resources |
| OPTIONS | 1.1 | Tests a server for capability but does not request a resource |
| TRACE | 1.1 | Traces what is being received at the destination |
| CONNECT | 1.1 | Is reserved for TCP-based or SSL tunneling |

## HTTP 1.1 Features

HTTP 1.1 includes a number of improvements over earlier incarnations of HTTP, though not all of them are fully supported yet. Not only does version 1.1 include performance enhancements and help reduce Web traffic, but it also has greater versatility.

Take ranges, for example. This feature, as mentioned earlier, allows you to select ranges of bytes to retrieve, so rather than refreshing an entire document, you could potentially refresh only part of it, perhaps only the part that has changed.

In HTTP 1.1, you have much more control over caching. A server can restrict what can or cannot be cached. Further, the expiration model has been improved so that a server can assign a heuristic expiration time and calculate the age of items in the cache in a more sophisticated way.

Persistent connections in HTTP 1.1 make it possible to run through several transactions more efficiently. The version 1.0 model makes it necessary to close a network connection after each and every transaction. Persistent connections will hold those connections open long enough to conduct a number of transactions in one session, reducing network overhead.

## HTTP Status Codes

HTTP 1.1 has added a number of status codes to the protocol. A brief description is provided for each code in Table 3.2.

**Table 3.2**   HTTP Status Codes

| CODE | VERSION | DESCRIPTION |
|------|---------|-------------|
| **100 SERIES: INFORMATIONAL** | | |
| 100 | 1.1 | Continue |
| 101 | 1.1 | Switching protocols |
| **200 SERIES: SUCCESS** | | |
| 200 | 1.0, 1.1 | OK |
| 201 | 1.0, 1.1 | Created |
| 202 | 1.0, 1.1 | Accepted |
| 203 | 1.1 | Nonauthoritative Information |
| 204 | 1.0, 1.1 | No Content |
| 205 | 1.1 | Reset Content |
| 206 | 1.1 | Partial Content |
| **300 SERIES: REDIRECTION** | | |
| 300 | 1.0, 1.1 | Multiple Choices |
| 301 | 1.0, 1.1 | Moved Permanently |
| 302 | 1.0, 1.1 | Moved Temporarily (1.0) or Found (1.1) |
| 303 | 1.1 | See Other |
| 304 | 1.0, 1.1 | Not Modified |
| 305 | 1.1 | Use Proxy |
| 306 | 1.1 | Unused |
| 307 | 1.1 | Temporary Redirect |
| **400 SERIES: CLIENT ERRORS** | | |
| 400 | 1.0, 1.1 | Bad Request |
| 401 | 1.0, 1.1 | Unauthorized |
| 402 | 1.1 | Payment Required |
| 403 | 1.0, 1.1 | Forbidden |
| 404 | 1.0, 1.1 | Not Found |
| 405 | 1.1 | Method Not Allowed |
| 406 | 1.1 | Not Acceptable |
| 407 | 1.1 | Proxy Authentication Required |
| 408 | 1.1 | Request Timeout |

**Table 3.2** (Continued)

| CODE | VERSION | DESCRIPTION |
|------|---------|-------------|
| **400 SERIES: CLIENT ERRORS** | | |
| 409 | 1.1 | Conflict |
| 410 | 1.1 | Gone |
| 411 | 1.1 | Length Required |
| 412 | 1.1 | Precondition Failed |
| 413 | 1.1 | Request Entity Too Large |
| 414 | 1.1 | Request-URI Too Long |
| 415 | 1.1 | Unsupported Media Type |
| 416 | 1.1 | Requestable Range Not Satisfiable |
| 417 | 1.1 | Expectation Failed |
| **500 SERIES: SERVER ERRORS** | | |
| 500 | 1.0, 1.1 | Internal Server Error |
| 501 | 1.0, 1.1 | Not Implemented |
| 502 | 1.0, 1.1 | Bad Gateway |
| 503 | 1.0, 1.1 | Service Unavailable |
| 504 | 1.1 | Gateway Timeout |
| 505 | 1.1 | HTTP Version Not Supported |

# File Transfer Protocol

File Transfer Protocol, or FTP, is a standard Internet program for moving files over the Net. It has been around since 1971 and is freely available on Unix and Windows platforms. It's easy to use, and you can create scripts to move the files automatically or at a certain given time, such as with Scheduled Tasks on Windows, or `at` on Unix.

First of all, I take it for granted that you have an active Internet connection, such as one through a LAN or a dial-up connection. Without such a connection, you won't be able to do anything useful or fun with FTP. If you already comfortable with FTP, you can skip ahead to the next section in this chapter, *FTP Scripts*.

Let's get started by simply connecting to a host using the *anonymous FTP* convention. Normally an Internet host is set up with a special, protected directory where you can upload and download files, even though you do not have an account on that particular machine. To get started, type the following line at a command prompt:

```
ftp testb2b.org
```

The answers you get back from FTP might be a little different depending on what operating system is installed on the host, but it shouldn't be that much different. (By the way, in this example, I am connecting to a Linux system from a Windows Server 2000 system.) Here's what you might get:

```
Connected to testb2b.org.
220-
220-Welcome to testb2b.org!
220-
220 testb2b.org FTP server (Version wu-2.6.0(2) Fri Aug 25 20:09:50 CDT
2000) ready.
User (testb2b.org:(none)): anonymous
331 Guest login ok, send your complete e-mail address as password.
Password: testb2b@testb2b.org
230 Guest login ok, access restrictions apply.
ftp>
```

The bold text is what you type in. If you did as the example shows, you just logged in using anonymous FTP with an email address as the password. I could also have used guest as the password. Though the password is shown here, it will be hidden from you on the screen as you type it in.

The FTP server software sends back reply codes, each preceded with a three-digit number—such as 331 Guest login ok...—to let you know if things are going well or if you are going astray. (You can turn off these reply codes with the -v switch on the command line.)

To log in anonymously without having to enter a username or password, use the -A switch (from Windows only). Type the following:

```
ftp -A testb2b.org
```

The username anonymous and your email address are then entered automatically after the FTP service connects with the host testb2b.org.

You can't tell at the moment, but if you connect this way, you wind up in the /ftp/testb2b directory where you don't have write privileges, or in other words, where you can't upload a file. One way I can tell that I can't write files to this directory is by performing a dir command:

```
ftp> dir
200 PORT command successful.
150 Opening ASCII mode data connection for /bin/ls.
total 9
```

```
drwxr-xr-x    8 594      1638         1024 Aug 31 16:47 .
drwxr-xr-x    8 594      1638         1024 Aug 31 16:47 ..
-rw-r—r—      1 594      1638           25 Aug 31 16:47 .banner
d—x—x—x       2 root     root         1024 Apr  5  1997 bin
drwxr-xr-x    2 root     root         1024 Apr  5  1997 dev
d—x—x—x       2 root     root         1024 Apr  5  1997 etc
drwxrwsrwt    2 594      1638         1024 Oct 25 16:42 incoming
drwxr-xr-x    2 root     root         1024 Aug 31 16:47 lib
drwxrwxr-x    2 594      1638         1024 Apr  5  1997 pub
226 Transfer complete.
ftp: 555 bytes received in 1.89Seconds 0.29Kbytes/sec.
ftp>
```

The directory identified with a single period (.), the first of the nine items returned by dir, is the current directory where I can't do much of anything. The field drwxr-xr-x at the beginning of the line means that the item is a directory (d); the following triplet means that the owner of the file can read, write, or execute or access it (rwx); and the second triplet (for user group) and the third triplet (others or anyone else) indicate that the group and others have only read and execute or access rights (r-x) to the directory. As an anonymous user, you are classified as an "other or anyone else," so you can only read the directory or access it. All this illustrates why you can't write a file to this particular directory.

I want to upload a file, so I am going to change directories to the incoming directory, another common convention where an anonymous user, like me, is given write privileges, as long as I behave myself.

```
ftp> cd incoming
250 CWD command successful.
ftp> dir
200 PORT command successful.
150 Opening ASCII mode data connection for /bin/ls.
total 2
drwxrwsrwt    2 testb2b  testb2bg     1024 Oct 25 13:14 .
drwxr-xr-x    8 testb2b  testb2bg     1024 Aug 31 11:47 ..
226 Transfer complete.
ftp: 126 bytes received in 0.01Seconds 12.60Kbytes/sec.
ftp>
```

The current directory (incoming or .) is almost wide open. "Others" are given rwt privileges. This means that anonymous folks like you can read and write files (rw), but you can't remove files that you don't own (t).

On my home system, I've got an XML file that is part of my own B2B process and based on my own schema. It's called orders.xml. I'm using simplistic files like this to show how transport and other processes work, though you probably will not use files based on this ordinary schema for your actual B2B interchange. Let's put the file up on the site:

```
ftp> lcd B2B
Local directory now C:\B2B.
ftp> ascii
200 Type set to A.
ftp> put order.xml
200 PORT command successful.
150 Opening ASCII mode data connection for order.xml.
226 Transfer complete.
ftp: 379 bytes sent in 0.00Seconds 379000.00Kbytes/sec.
ftp>
```

First, I changed to the directory B2B on my local system with lcd (local change directory). Then, because I am sending an XML text file, I set the type to ascii, just to make sure FTP was in ASCII mode. This is usually the default, but not always. You can also set the mode to binary when you send binary files. You can also set the file type with the commands type ascii or type binary.

The put command sends a single file, order.xml in this example, from my local system to the remote system, that is, from C:\B2B on my computer to /ftp/testb2b/incoming on the host testb2b.org, and it doesn't take very long, either. The send command is a synonym for put.

Now let's reverse the process. The get command (synonym recv) grabs a single file off a remote system and downloads it to the current directory on the local computer. This is how you do it:

```
ftp> get order.xml
200 PORT command successful.
550 order.xml: Permission denied.
ftp> dir
200 PORT command successful.
150 Opening ASCII mode data connection for /bin/ls.
total 3
drwxrwsrwt   2 594       1638        1024 Oct 25 20:45 .
drwxr-xr-x   8 594       1638        1024 Aug 31 16:47 ..
----rw----   1 ftp       1638         370 Oct 25 20:45 order.xml
226 Transfer complete.
ftp: 192 bytes received in 0.80Seconds 0.24Kbytes/sec.
ftp>
```

Well, ouch. You can't get a copy of the file back. The owner of the file is now ftp, but only members of the group 1638 (a code name for testb2bg) can read or write the file. The owner or others cannot read, write, or execute it (---), and that includes you. Let's end this session and try another method.

```
ftp> bye
221-You have transferred 370 bytes in 1 files.
221-Total traffic for this session was 1404 bytes in 2 transfers.
221-Thank you for using the FTP service on testb2b.org.
221 Goodbye.
```

You can also use the quit or close command to end an FTP session. Let's try to download a file from a private FTP directory with the following username and password (for security reasons, this won't actually work on testb2b.org—sorry):

```
ftp -i testb2b.org
Connected to testb2b.org.
220-
220-Welcome to testb2b.org!
220-
220 testb2b.org FTP server (Version wu-2.6.0(2) Fri Aug 25 20:09:50 CDT
2000) ready.
User (testb2b.org:(none)): b2buser
331 Password required for b2buser.
Password: b2buser
230 User b2buser logged in.
ftp> ls
200 PORT command successful.
150 Opening ASCII mode data connection for file list.
order-2000-10-25.xml
order-2000-11-19.xml
order-2001-01-02.xml
order-2001-01-09.xml
order.xml
226 Transfer complete.
ftp: 99 bytes received in 0.01Seconds 9.90Kbytes/sec.
ftp>
```

The -i switch in the command line tells FTP to turn off interactive prompting, the effect of which you will see in a moment or two. Again, when you type the password, you won't see it.

After issuing the ls command, the file order.xml, among others, is listed on the screen. This time, I think you'll have better luck downloading it:

```
ftp> get order.xml
200 PORT command successful.
150 Opening ASCII mode data connection for order.xml (370 bytes).
226 Transfer complete.
ftp: 379 bytes received in 0.01Seconds 37.90Kbytes/sec.
ftp>
```

If you wanted to get all the files at once, use the mget command, instead of get, which downloads a single file only. This is how you do it:

```
ftp> mget *.xml
200 Type set to A.
200 PORT command successful.
150 Opening ASCII mode data connection for order-2000-10-25.xml (365
    bytes).
226 Transfer complete.
ftp: 374 bytes received in 0.01Seconds 37.40Kbytes/sec.
200 PORT command successful.
150 Opening ASCII mode data connection for order-2000-11-19.xml (395
    bytes).
226 Transfer complete.
ftp: 404 bytes received in 0.00Seconds 404000.00Kbytes/sec.
200 PORT command successful.
150 Opening ASCII mode data connection for order-2001-01-02.xml (388
    bytes).
226 Transfer complete.
ftp: 397 bytes received in 0.01Seconds 39.70Kbytes/sec.
200 PORT command successful.
150 Opening ASCII mode data connection for order-2001-01-09.xml (372
    bytes).
226 Transfer complete.
ftp: 381 bytes received in 0.01Seconds 38.10Kbytes/sec.
200 PORT command successful.
150 Opening ASCII mode data connection for order.xml (316 bytes).
226 Transfer complete.
ftp: 325 bytes received in 0.00Seconds 325000.00Kbytes/sec.
ftp> quit
```

The mget command downloads all the files with the .xml extension to the current directory of your local computer. The -i switch, which you invoked at the command line, turns off interactive prompting. Otherwise, FTP would ask you to confirm whether to transfer each file with y (yes) or n (no) or to confirm all files with a (all). With interactive prompting off, you can grab the whole bunch of files in one move, which works well when you are running FTP from batch files or scripts, as you will see in the next section. You can also issue the prompt command during the FTP session to enable/disable prompting.

## FTP Scripts

You can place FTP commands in a batch file in Windows. The first catch is that you have to store the FTP commands in a separate file. The example that follows is for Windows only.

On the Windows platform, in an editor that can save a plain-text file, such as Notepad, type the following:

```
user b2buser
b2buser
ascii
lcd c:\b2b
mget *.xml
bye
```

After typing this, save the file as `cmds.txt`. You should already be familiar with the FTP commands in this file. Now in the same directory, open another file, and enter the following lines:

```
# FTP script

start "B2B: Get Files" ftp -n -s:cmds.txt testb2b.org
```

Save this file as `getfiles.bat`. The pound sign (#) indicates a comment. The `start` command starts the FTP program in a separate window, with the quoted text appearing in the title of the window. The `-n` switch after `ftp` suppresses auto-login so that you can log in with the `user` command and password in `cmds.txt`. The `-s` switch, followed by a filename (`-s:cmds.txt`), specifies the file containing the FTP commands. Of course, `testb2b.org` is the host to which you want to connect.

With these two files in place, type on the command line:

```
getfiles
```

The batch file launches a separate window, executes all the FTP commands in `cmds.txt`, and exits the session (for security reasons, this won't work).

Let's say that you want to execute this batch file every morning at 2:00 A.M. On the Windows platform, you can create a Scheduled Task to do it for you. From the Start menu, select Programs, Accessories, System Tools, Scheduled Tasks. Then select File, New, Scheduled Task. Name the task whatever you want—I'm calling mine `FTPDaily`. Right-click on the task and select Properties. Now you can set up what and how often this task will run.

First, you'll see the Task tab of the dialog box. Find the file you want to run (`getfiles.bat`), and put it in the Run field. You can also set what user will be set as the user when this task runs. This allows you some password protection. Click the Schedule tab, and put in the time and frequency you want the task to run, daily at 2:00 A.M., for example. You can set it even more frequently with the Advanced button. Under the Security tab, you can limit who has access to this task. Another option is the `at` command, which is available both on Unix and Windows platforms. The following command is from Windows 2000 Server:

```
at 02:00:00 /every:M,T,W,Th,F,S,Su "getfiles.bat"
```

# Multipurpose Internet Mail Extensions

Another protocol found in B2B implementations is Multipurpose Internet Mail Extensions, or MIME. Building on a standard for Internet text messages published in 1982, MIME in 1993 extended the earlier message format to allow for the inclusion of encoded binary entities inside an email message. MIME built on the header layout of its predecessor and lionized a standard encoding mechanism called base64 for converting binary code into a text form that is suitable for fast, simple transport across the Internet, with encoding and decoding happening on each end.

## Internet Text Messages and Standard Mail Transfer Protocol

When the Internet came into being about 30 years ago, one of its exciting developments was the ability to send text files or messages back and forth between far-flung hosts on the network. About 10 years later, in 1982, recommendations emerged from the Internet community to help systemize and standardize the content of text messages or what came to be called electronic mail, or email. These standards, still important today, are Simple Mail Transfer Protocol (SMTP), a protocol for sending email messages, and the "Standard for ARPA Internet Text Messages," or RFC 822, which laid down the pattern for email headers and content. I'll call it 822 for short.

RFC 822 was based on RFC 733, which came out in 1977. RFC 733 attempted to consolidate previous efforts to define text messages, but it also encouraged several features that were not widely implemented. The Internet community, comparatively small back then, regrouped with 822.

### How 822 Works

The 822 standard defines the way email headers and content should look. This, of course, makes it easier for programs such as mail clients to read or parse incoming mail and then figure out what to do with it. Every piece of email you get has a header, though it's probably hidden from your view by your mail client.

Today these headers are usually called MIME headers. We will first look at an example of 822 message headers. They are different from MIME fields, but they will help show you the differences between MIME and 822. Here's an 822 header and message right now, a fictitious message I never sent:

```
Date:   Fri, 13 Aug 82 1204 MDT
From:   Mike Fitzgerald <mike@hiawatha>
To:     Dave Crocker <DCrocker@udel-relay>
CC:     Jon Postel <Postel(RFC Editor)@ISIC>
Subject:   Congratulations!
X-Derelict:   no
Message-ID:   <1001.101.aaa-mike@tecumseh>

Dave,

Let me say thanks for your excellent work on RFC 822 that was just
submitted today. You can see from my message that I am eager to comply
with the new standard. I hope to get you to sign my copy of the RFC next
time we cross paths.

Thanks again,

Mike
.
```

Do the fields in the mail header look familiar? These are not all the fields that you might see in 822 mail headers, but they are common. The arrangement of the fields is not set in concrete, so the order can vary. The only stipulation is that the header fields must precede the message body. The general structure of a header field is:

```
Field-name: Field-body CRLF
```

A header field consists of a field-name and field-body that must be separated by a colon (:). A field is one line long, with a length of up to about 72 characters, but the standard does not impose an exact line length. The line is terminated by a carriage return/line feed or CRLF combination (in decimal, the US-ASCII characters are 13 and 10, respectively).

Let's walk through the header and message format.

First is the Date field. The form of this date is similar to the form used in HTTP or MIME, with an important difference. A two-digit year was acceptable when 822 was released, but it is no longer suitable because of the year 2000 issue. This was corrected in MIME. You can also see that the hours and minutes are not separated by a colon or some other delimiter. This was permissible, though colon separators are specified in the 822 syntax.

The From field is next. It identifies the person sending the mail. A message must have this field or a Sender field. A Sender field can identify not just a person but also an agent, including a machine, system, or process that sends a message. From and Sender are in a class called *originator fields*.

First in the `From` field comes the human-readable name of the sender, which may be quoted, followed by an address enclosed in angle brackets (< and >). The angle brackets indicate a machine-readable reference or address.

An address is a mailbox that contains a local part such as a username, followed by an at sign (@), followed by a domain name. The @ sign was standardized in 822, whereas RFC 733 permitted the word *at* with a single space on either side of it. The local part, according to 822, must be case-sensitive, but this does not seem to be the practice now in mail clients. Domain names have always been case-insensitive.

## *Domain Names*

The rightmost part of a domain name is known as the top-level domain. Today you commonly see such top-level domain names as `.com`, `.org`, or `.edu`. Though not yet in use, the Internet Corporation for Assigned Numbers and Names (ICANN) approved a new set of top-level domains late in 2000. They are `.aero`, `.biz`, `.coop`, `.info`, `.museum`, `.name`, and `.pro`.

Each part of a domain name, divided by periods (.) and moving from right to left, is known as a subdomain name with the first subdomain commonly called the second-level domain. This scheme is illustrated in Figure 3.2.

At the time 822 was published, it was not uncommon to use only a single domain name, such as in `mike@hiawatha`. One reason was that the Internet was much smaller than it is now. About five years later, yet another Internet standard appeared to help resolve domain names with their IP addresses. It's called the Domain Name System (DNS), and it is still in very broad use today.

### Domain Name System

As I mentioned earlier in this chapter, DNS contains a huge database of domain names—literally millions of them—that are matched in a table against IP addresses. DNS is not a central authority through which all network traffic must pass, but it is duplicated on servers at various locations on the Internet. Your company, for example, may have its own DNS server, or you may access it via your Internet Service Providers' (ISP) infrastructure. DNS is really a network of interconnected DNS servers, so if a particular server can't do its job, it will contact another server along the way until it can find the correct match. The DNS database is updated constantly, with changes being propagated from registries such as Network Solutions, Inc., among others, to servers all over the world.

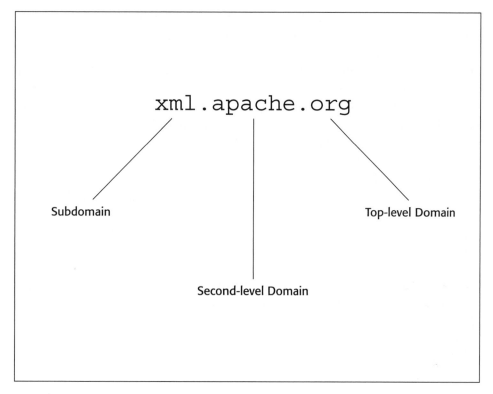

**Figure 3.2**   The domain name.

For example, an email message may be addressed to `testb2b@` `testb2b.org`. If you were to send a message to this address, as with all messages, a DNS server would be one of the message's first stops along its journey to the mail server `mail.testb2b.org`. DNS would resolve the domain name with its IP address (205.244.47.30), then shove it along to its intended destination.

The Internet doesn't really rely on domain names to do its work. Domain names are there for humans to read, while underlying software will resolve those names to IP addresses. In the early days, when there was less traffic on the Internet, shorter lists of addresses could be stored and looked up locally. Those days are over. From now on, we will need DNS or any of its successors to do this work for us.

## Back to Header Fields

The `To` field is the primary recipient of the message, with the address written in the same form as the `From` field. This field, as well as the `CC` and `Bcc` fields, are called *receiver fields*. The CC or *carbon-copy* field is next, containing the name of a secondary or informational recipient.

The content of a Bcc or *blind carbon copy* field (not shown) will not appear in the mail delivered to recipients listed in the To and CC fields. The parenthetical statement *(RFC Editor)* is a comment, and as specified in 822, it will be gobbled up and discarded by local mail software. Though rare, parentheses are legal in the local part of an email address, but the comment mechanism is now largely ignored.

The Subject field provides a summary or key language relating to the message. The field is common but not mandatory.

X-Derelict is an optional, user-defined field. The 822 standard allowed for both extension fields, to be developed uniformly some time in the future, and user-defined fields, which must be preceded with an *X-*. User-defined fields allow mail software to accept proprietary information in a field without going through a standards process; however, there is no way to keep someone else from using your field in a different way than you intended.

The Message-ID identifies a message with a unique, individual, arbitrary string in the local part of the address. The sender's address is always part of this ID. The example string *1001.101.aaa-mike* can be anything that makes sense for your implementation, but often it is a sequential number and always is unique.

Just preceding the message body is a null or blank line—that is, two successive CRLFs. This signals to a processing client that the header fields are finished and that which follows is the actual message. The message text or body is an unstructured string of US-ASCII text. You can type characters and whitespace any which way. The only combination you are forbidden to use is a period alone on a line because it has a special meaning.

As shown in the preceding example, the final period at the end of the message body is there for a purpose. A period alone on a line, followed by a CRLF, signals that the message is complete and will be sent to the addressees. The mail client then passes the message on to be sent by Simple Mail Transfer Protocol, or SMTP.

## How SMTP Works

Now that you have a good understanding of the 822 format, I'll show you how SMTP (RFC 821) sends that message along. A mail client depends on SMTP to send a mail message to a mail server so that it can be delivered to your mailbox.

Behind the scenes, a mail client spins off a mail message for SMTP to process. You can then open a two-way channel, on port 25 by default, with an SMTP mail server, using the Internet as a means for interprocess communication. You can actually use SMTP on the command line, as long as you have a live Internet connection. Here's how.

You can connect to port 25 via a telnet session with a mail server. I'll show you how to connect to your own, where `yourhost` is your domain name:

```
telnet mail.yourhost.com 25
```

If everything goes well, you will get a message that looks something like this:

```
220 mail.yourhost.com ESMTP Sendmail 8.8.5/8.8.5; Mon, 01 Jan 2001
00:00:01 -0800
```

This is an example message from an extended SMTP `sendmail` software on a Linux mail server. The message you receive will vary, depending on what sort of software is installed on your mail server. Once the connection is made, you can communicate with the SMTP process directly. According to 821, the actual commands should be in uppercase, but this is not always a strict requirement because mail servers, like browsers, are often more liberal than the standards. If you would like to try SMTP out for yourself, type the following lines that appear in bold. Your mail server should respond with the messages that follow, shown in regular face.

```
HELO mail.yourhost.com
250 mail.yourhost.com Hello otherhost.com [XXX.XXX.XXX.XXX], pleased to
meet you
MAIL FROM:<user@otherhost.com>
250 <user@otherhost.com>... Sender ok
RCPT TO:<user@yourhost.com>
250 <otheruser@yourhost.com>... Recipient ok
DATA
354 Enter mail, end with "." on a line by itself
From: user@otherhost.com
To: user@yourhost.com
Subject: B2B

Please send me more information about B2B and XML!
.
250 DAA04905 Message accepted for delivery
QUIT
221 mail.yourhost.com closing connection
```

The first command is `HELO` (one *L*, that's right). This call rings up the server, so to speak, establishing a connection with it. A more recent alternative is `EHLO`, which not only greets the server but also requests extended

SMTP mode, but we not going to get into ESMTP here. The server politely responds and repeats the name of the server to which you just connected. The response message may remind you of the 200-series responses from HTTP. SMTP predates HTTP by about seven years, and HTTP status messages are reminiscent of SMTP messages.

The next command, MAIL FROM, specifies, with a machine-readable address, who the mail is from. A congenial "...Sender ok" lets you know that the address was formed properly and is acceptable. In accordance with 821, SMTP expects only one MAIL FROM.

Following that command is RCPT TO for identifying the recipients of the message. If all is well with the command, a reply repeats the address and acknowledges it as "...Recipient ok." Multiple RCPT TO commands are acceptable, but additional addresses on one line are ignored.

The DATA command signals that what follows is the actual message, starting with headers. SMTP does not rely on MAIL FROM or RCPT TO to supply field bodies for the From and To fields. Those come from the header lines in the DATA section. The 354 message tells you to enter the message. It reminds you, too, that a single period on a line signals the end of the message.

The first part of the message should be the header fields, such as From: user@otherhost.com, and Subject: B2B. The header section is followed by a blank line (two CRLFs) and then the message body. After typing the period on a blank line, your message is queued. You can send another message or close the connection with the QUIT command.

Now that the email is on the server, how do you retrieve it?

### POP3 and IMAP4

SMTP carts messages around on the Internet from server to server, but you can't use it to download messages from a server to your mail client. This is where Post Office Protocol version 3 (POP3) and Internet Message Access Protocol version 4 (IMAP4) come in. It isn't always necessary or economical to keep a computer attached to the Internet all the time, so rather than hosting a full-fledged mail server, it makes sense to be able to just grab mail when you need to and then shut down. This is what POP3 and IMAP4 allow you to do.

Figure 3.3 shows the relationship between SMTP, POP3, and IMAP4. Mail messages are transported across the Internet from SMTP server to SMTP server. Local nodes can connect to the server temporarily, also via the Internet, download mail with POP3 or IMAP4, and then disconnect

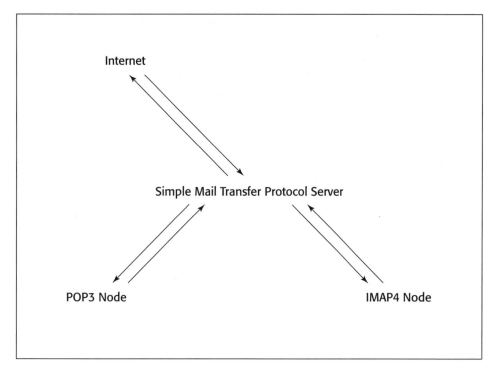

**Figure 3.3** SMTP, POP3, and IMAP4.

from the mail server and, if necessary, from the Internet, too. The local nodes are relieved of the burden and cost of a full-time connection to the server and Internet. Basically, this is the reason to be for either IMAP4 or POP3.

### POP3

POP3 can retrieve mail from a server, and once it is retrieved to a local system, the mail can be deleted from the server. The protocol is not unlike HTTP or SMTP in that you can connect to it directly with `telnet`. This is probably the best way to demonstrate how POP3 works.

The first step is to open a connection with POP3 with `telnet` via port 110:

```
telnet mail.yourhost.com 110
```

You then get a response that looks something like this:

```
+OK POP3 yourhost.com v4.47 server ready
```

Generally, a +OK prefix for a message sent back from the server indicates a successful command, and an -ERR prefix indicates an error.

Once you make a connection with a POP3 server, you have to prove who you are before you can go any further; that is, to gain entrance, you must submit a name and password. The following listing shows this authentication procedure as well as other commands for collecting email:

```
USER user
+OK Username accepted, password please
PASS
+OK Mailbox open, 1 messages
LIST
+OK Mailbox scan listing follows
1 507
.
RETR 1
+OK 507 octets
Return-Path: <user@otherhost.com>
Received: …
Date: Mon, 01 Jan 2001 00:00:02 -0500
From: <user@otherhost.com>
Message-Id: <200010260829.DAA04905@mail.yourhost.com>
Status:
From: user@otherhost.com
To: user@yourhost.com
Subject: B2B

Please send me more information about B2B and XML!
.
STAT
+OK 1 507
QUIT
+OK Sayonara
```

After establishing a connection with the POP server, your session is in an authorization state. You then have to submit a login or username with USER and a password with PASS. You can also submit an APOP command, which includes a login name and an MD5 digest. An MD5 (Message Digest version 5) digest is a string produced by applying an algorithm to a text message and thereby forming a digest. You will learn more about digests and digital signatures in Chapter 4, "Security."

After the server authenticates you, you are then authorized to retrieve mail from it. The example first issues a LIST command that lists the email currently on the server in your mailbox (also called a *maildrop*). It gives the number of messages and the length in octets of those messages. It also gives the unique ID number for each message and how long each message is in octets. There was only one message on the server at the time of this session. The single period on a line by itself shows the end of the list or the end of some other response from the server.

The next step is to retrieve a message with RETR. The command RETR 1 grabs the message with the ID 1 and displays it on your screen. A mail client would read and save such input, but in the absence of software to do otherwise, the message simply is dumped out on the screen. A single period marks the end of the server's response.

The STAT command lists the total number of messages in the mailbox and the total size in octets of all the messages. As you have undoubtedly guessed, the QUIT command closes your POP3 connection and returns you to the command prompt or shell.

### IMAP4

IMAP4 is similar to POP3. It doesn't post mail like SMTP but helps a mail program access messages on a mail server. Like POP3, IMAP4 can check a server for new messages or remove them permanently. It can also create, delete, and rename the mailboxes that hold messages.

One of the key differences between IMAP4 and POP3 is that it can work with remote mailboxes just as it would local ones. It can also synchronize with a server after being offline, which is an advantage if you don't have a full-time connection to the Internet and if you are a traveler and access email from different locations. It essentially, at your option, leaves messages on the server so that you can access them from all over, rather than always downloading them to a single local host, such as your desktop computer.

A few other things that IMAP4 can do is search for and retrieve messages based on attributes or fragments of text. Messages are identified by sequenced numbers or by other unique but noncontiguous values. IMAP4 can handle both 822 and MIME messages.

## How MIME Works

Multipurpose Internet Mail Extensions, or MIME, extends, as the title suggests, the earlier RFC 822 mail paragon. Emerging about a decade after 822 appeared, MIME retained much of the flavor of 822, while offering an important difference: You are no longer limited to plain US-ASCII text. You can now include or attach binary files containing graphics, video, or audio. This is usually done through base64 processing.

More about this later, but in a nutshell, a base64 algorithm encodes or converts sequences of digits into sequences of alphanumeric characters and then decodes them at the destination. When you attach a large binary file to an email, it takes a while to send or receive because a module in your mail client must encode or decode the attached file in base64.

## The MIME Header

You have already seen an example of a MIME header in the preceding POP3 example. You can view a MIME mail header for any email with a mail client such as Microsoft Outlook 2000. In Outlook, select the message in the message pane, click the right mouse button, and select Options. The Message Options dialog box appears. At the bottom of the dialog box you will see the Internet Headers field. This field will contain the MIME header for the selected email message, as shown in Figure 3.4.

A more thorough explanation is in order, so the header is repeated here for your convenience.

```
Received: from wyeast [63.229.130.140] by mail.wyeast.net
(SMTPD32-6.00) id AAEE390500F4; Tue, 08 Aug 2000 19:42:38 -0400
```

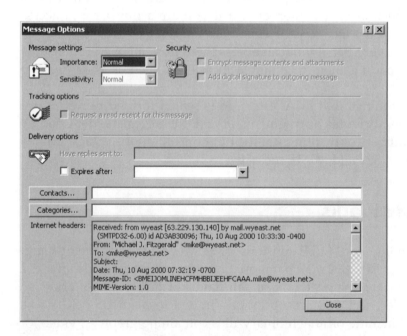

**Figure 3.4**  Outlook 2000 Message Options dialog box.

```
From: "Michael J. Fitzgerald" <mike@wyeast.net>
To: <rango@wyeast.net>
Subject:
Date: Tue, 8 Aug 2000 16:41:27 -0700
Message-ID: <BMEIJOMLINEHCFMHBBIJCEGJCAAA.mike@wyeast.net>
MIME-Version: 1.0
Content-Type: text/plain;
        charset="iso-8859-1"
Content-Transfer-Encoding: 7bit
X-Priority: 3 (Normal)
X-MSMail-Priority: Normal
X-Mailer: Microsoft Outlook IMO, Build 9.0.2416 (9.0.2910.0)
Importance: Normal
X-MimeOLE: Produced By Microsoft MimeOLE V5.50.4133.2400
X-RCPT-TO: <mike@wyeast.net>
X-UIDL: 261799451
Status: U
```

The `Received` field comes to us from 822. It provides a little journal of the activity of the transport service that has got the mail to you. The message was both sent by and received from `mail.wyeast.net`. It also gives you information about the SMTP server that pushed the mail along, plus an `id` associated with the message queue on the mail server. Finally, you get the day, date, and time of receipt of the message. Figure 3.5 shows a break down of the timestamp.

The days of the week and months are abbreviated to three letters, just as in 822. The year must be four digits long, whereas two digits sufficed in 822. (Given the Y2K fiasco, though, I suppose it's never too early to start preparing for the Year 10,000 bug.) Hours, minutes, and seconds are readily recognizable. The offset from Coordinated Universal Time (UTC)—we used to call it Greenwich Mean Time (GMT)—is minus four hours (-400) in the server's time zone.

Because the message may have made a number of hops between mail servers, there may be a number of instances of the `Received` header at the top of your mail message.

The `From`, `To`, `Subject`, `Date`, and `Message-ID` header fields are the same in MIME and 822. Addresses can be prepended with human-readable names, in quotes or not, and machine-readable addresses are enclosed in angle brackets. The `Message-ID`, a unique value, is associated with the sender's address.

The `MIME-Version` field helps the client to know by what rules it has to abide in order to process the message correctly. The MIME version has been 1.0 since 1993. That's a pretty stable standard.

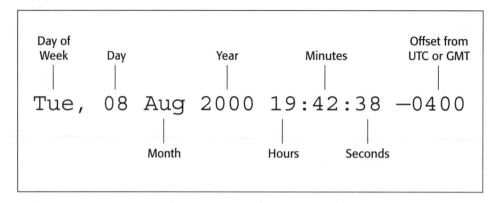

**Figure 3.5**    MIME timestamp.

The Content-Type field associates a MIME type such as text/plain with the message. More about this in the section titled *MIME Types*, later in this chapter. The Content-Transfer-Encoding header indicates the encoding for the overall message and helps the mail client determine if the entire message—not just an inserted attachment—needs to be encoded to make it suitable for SMTP. See the section called *Transfer Encoding* later in this chapter.

The fields that begin with X-, such as X-Priority, are user-defined fields, proprietary to Microsoft, I suppose, but we can make a few guesses at what they are about. RCPT TO, suggested in the field name X-RCPT-TO, is an SMTP command; the field body <mike@wyeast.net> would be correct for the RCPT TO command as well. UIDL (unique ID listing) is a POP3 command. The Importance header indicates the importance, such as Normal (default), High, or Low, that the sender gave the message before sending it. Status headers are added to the mail in the mailbox, indicating such status as U (unread), R (read), N (new), and O (old).

## MIME Types

A content type or Internet media type is often called a MIME type. In 1988, the Content-Type header field was proposed in RFC 1049 as a uniform way to indicate to a mail client that the content of the mail message body was something other than plain, unstructured US-ASCII text, such as troff commands, SGML, or PostScript. Five years later, MIME embraced the Content-Type header as a suitable way to describe the data that is contained in the message. The header is formed like this:

```
Content-type: type/subtype
```

The first term, also called a top-level media type, describes the general type of the content while the second term, after the slash, pinpoints a subtype. Table 3.3 lists a few prominent examples of content types.

The most common type of data in MIME-conforming messages is `text/plain`. This content type means that the text in the message is just plain vanilla text, with no bold, italics, or what have you. There is no graphics, audio, video, or other binary data, just traditional 7-bit ASCII text as you would have under 822.

A content type of `text/plain` can have a `charset` parameter that gives the character set of the text included in the message. The parameter is specified as follows (quotation marks are optional):

```
Content-Type: text/plain; charset="US-ASCII"
```

You are not limited to the US-ASCII character set; you can also use the extended ISO standard character sets that are related to SGML. The Latin-1 set, known as ISO-8859-1, has 256 characters as opposed to US-ASCII's 128. The other characters sets in the series, IS0-8859-2 through ISO-8859-9, are also supported.

## Transfer Encoding

Data sent by way of the original SMTP was limited to 7-bit US-ASCII. This is a conflict with the 8-bit ISO character sets (ISO-8879-1, for example). More modern mail servers can handle 8-bit encoding, but not all mail

**Table 3.3** Content Types

| TYPE/SUBTYPE | DESCRIPTION |
|---|---|
| text/plain | Plain, ordinary, unformatted text |
| text/html | Text in HyperText Markup Language (HTML) format |
| text/xml | Text in Extensible Markup Language (XML) format |
| image/jpeg | Graphical image in Joint Picture Experts Group (JPEG) format |
| audio/basic | Single channel audio, 8-bit mu-law at 8000 Hz |
| video/mpeg | MPEG video |
| application/octet-stream | Arbitrary binary data |
| multipart/mixed | MIME message body contains different content parts |

servers can be expected to do so. MIME overcomes this with transfer encoding; that is, the client can encode everything it sends into the 7-bit format that is acceptable to SMTP or decode it from 7-bit to 8-bit or binary. MIME's default header field for this is:

```
Content-Transfer-Encoding: 7bit
```

If this header field is absent, MIME acts as if it were present anyway. Other possible values are: 8bit, binary, quoted-printable, and base64. The 7bit value is appropriate if your message is US-ASCII—that is, if no conversion or encoding is necessary—while 8bit is suitable for ISO-8879-1 through ISO-8879-9. If the field body is binary, any octet sequence is permitted. The values quoted-printable and base64 signify transforms that are discussed in some detail in the following sections.

### Quoted-Printable Encoding

Quoted-printable encoding is fairly simple and is intended to be somewhat readable by humans when encoded. It represents printable US-ASCII, SMTP-conforming characters as themselves while allowing other characters outside this range to be quoted as a hexadecimal value preceded by an equal (=) sign. Printable characters are equivalent to US-ASCII decimals 33 through 60 (! through <) and 62 through 126 (> through ~).

Characters 0 through 32 (NUL or null through SP or space) and 127 (DEL or delete) are not printable, so they don't pass the test, but exceptions are made for 9 and 32 as intercharacter whitespace, but not at the end of an encoded line. The value 61 (=) is dropped from the printable list because it has special meaning in the encoding scheme.

To represent an actual equal sign, for example, in a quoted-printable stream, = is converted to =3D. The hexadecimal value 3D is equivalent to decimal value 61, both of which represent the equal sign. The hex value is preceded immediately by an equal sign for encoding purposes. Your encoding algorithm can take the same approach with any nonprintable character, that is, representing it with an equal sign followed hard by the character's hexadecimal equivalent. Lines must not exceed 76 characters in length; longer lines are broken with equal signs as placeholders. End-of-line characters, such as CRLF, representing the actual end of a line, are not encoded, but they can be encoded in a message body. In general, quoted-printable is used far less than its sibling, base64 encoding.

### Base64 Encoding

Base64 encoding converts arbitrary binary octets into characters from a 64-character subset of US-ASCII. Once a binary stream is encoded, it can be presented as a set of legal characters to an old-fashioned SMTP server. On the other end, the base64 characters can be decoded back into their original binary selves. This is why you can attach a Microsoft Word file or a digital photo in JPEG format to an email: These binary files are converted to base64 at the sending end and reconverted to their binary representation on the other end. Data grows only about one-third larger when converted to base64.

The encoding values are shown in Table 3.4. A 65th character (Value 64), the equal sign (=), is used for padding rather than being encoded into another character.

**Table 3.4**   Base64 Encoding Values

| VALUE | CODE | VALUE | CODE | VALUE | CODE | VALUE | CODE |
|-------|------|-------|------|-------|------|-------|------|
| 0 | A | 17 | R | 34 | I | 51 | z |
| 1 | B | 18 | S | 35 | j | 52 | 0 |
| 2 | C | 19 | T | 36 | k | 53 | 1 |
| 3 | D | 20 | U | 37 | l | 54 | 2 |
| 4 | E | 21 | V | 38 | m | 55 | 3 |
| 5 | F | 22 | W | 39 | n | 56 | 4 |
| 6 | G | 23 | X | 40 | o | 57 | 5 |
| 7 | H | 24 | Y | 41 | p | 58 | 6 |
| 8 | I | 25 | Z | 42 | q | 59 | 7 |
| 9 | J | 26 | a | 43 | r | 60 | 8 |
| 10 | K | 27 | b | 44 | s | 61 | 9 |
| 11 | L | 28 | c | 45 | t | 62 | + |
| 12 | M | 29 | d | 46 | u | 63 | / |
| 13 | N | 30 | e | 47 | v | Padding | = |
| 14 | O | 31 | f | 48 | w | | |
| 15 | P | 32 | g | 49 | x | | |
| 16 | Q | 33 | h | 50 | y | | |

### A Base64 Algorithm

This is how a base64 algorithm encodes arbitrary binary data into the base64 character set. First of all, it assumes that the binary input stream is read from left to right, with the leftmost bits as the most-significant, that is, the high-order bits. It processes the stream in 24-bit chunks or three 8-bit octets and then treats the 24-bit group as four 6-bit groups. Each 6-bit group acts as an index into the array of 64 printable characters that make up the base64 character set shown in the preceding table. To decode, generally, you must walk backward through the steps.

Using this formula, Table 3.5 shows how to convert the 24 bits making up the word *You* from US-ASCII to its decimal equivalent to binary. The next table, Table 3.6, shows the resulting 24-bit group carved into four 6-bit groups, using the resulting decimal value as an index into the base64 array.

You can download a free Windows program from Azalea Software (www.azalea.com) that converts text strings and files into base64 on the fly, or vice versa. Azalea Base 64 is shown in Figure 3.6.

## The multipart/mixed Content Type

A MIME message with a content type of multipart/mixed can have several parts, each with a different content type. The parts of the message are

**Table 3.5** Converting to a 24-Bit Group

| US-ASCII | DECIMAL | BINARY | COMBINED 24-BIT GROUP |
|----------|---------|----------|------------------------|
| Y | 89 | 01011001 | |
| o | 111 | 01101111 | 010110010110111101110101 |
| u | 117 | 01110101 | |

**Table 3.6** Converting a 24-Bit Group to Base64

| COMBINED 24-BIT GROUP | 6-BIT GROUPS | DECIMAL INDEX | BASE64 |
|------------------------|--------------|---------------|--------|
| | 010110 | 22 | W |
| 010110010110111101110101 | 010110 | 22 | W |
| | 111101 | 61 | 9 |
| | 110101 | 53 | 1 |

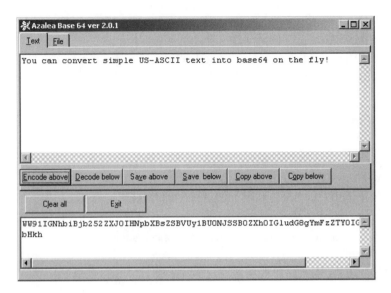

**Figure 3.6**   Azalea Base 64.

separated by a unique boundary marker. This kind of mixed message is called a *compound message*.

For example, if you attached a Microsoft Word binary file, after the regular text message, a boundary would appear, followed by the attached file encoded as base64. In the example message that follows, you can see (in bold) that the content type is multipart/mixed. This is followed by a boundary parameter whose value is the unique, precise text that will delineate the boundary. The boundary makes it easier for a mail client or other software to process a queue of messages concatenated together—it can keep track of what boundary belongs to what discrete message.

Boundaries always begin with two hyphens (--), with no intervening space, and they are preceded by a blank line. A Microsoft algorithm creates a unique boundary value, using optionally four hyphens instead of two, at least in this instance. The last boundary, after all content, must use two hyphens at the end of the boundary name. The hyphen helps the client to search for where the boundaries are, which helps it figure out where to process base64 or other data. The value for the boundary parameter is

----=_NextPart_000_0033_01C003C2.6671D9D0, not particularly an attractive boundary, but one that will surely be unique.

Only a portion of the base64 version of the Word file is shown in the following example:

```
Received: from wyeast [63.229.130.140] by mail.wyeast.net
    (SMTPD32-6.00) id A942430132; Fri, 11 Aug 2000 21:32:50 -0400
From: "Michael J. Fitzgerald" <mike@wyeast.net>
To: <rango@wyeast.net>
Subject: Document attached
Date: Fri, 11 Aug 2000 18:31:42 -0700
Message-ID: <BMEIJOMLINEHCFMHBBIJMEIFCAAA.mike@wyeast.net>
MIME-Version: 1.0
Content-Type: multipart/mixed;
     boundary="----=_NextPart_000_0033_01C003C2.6671D9D0"
X-Priority: 3 (Normal)
X-MSMail-Priority: Normal
X-Mailer: Microsoft Outlook IMO, Build 9.0.2416 (9.0.2910.0)
Importance: Normal
X-MimeOLE: Produced By Microsoft MimeOLE V5.50.4133.2400
X-RCPT-TO: <rango@wyeast.net>
X-UIDL: 261799495
Status: U


Rango,

For your reading pleasure, a Microsoft Word file is attached to this
message.

Mike
==========
Michael Fitzgerald
mailto:mike@wyeast.net
http://www.wyeast.net


------=_NextPart_000_0033_01C003C2.6671D9D0
Content-Type: application/msword;
     name="mime-attachment.doc"
Content-Transfer-Encoding: base64
Content-Disposition: attachment;
     filename="mime-attachment.doc"


0M8R4KGxGuEAAAAAAAAAAAAAAAAAAAAAPgADAP7/CQAGAAAAAAAAAAAAAAAABAAAAIQAAAAA
AAAAEAAAIwAAAAEAAAD+////AAAACAAAAD////////////////////////////////////////
////////////////////////////////////////////////////////////////////////
////////////////////////////////////////////////////////////////////////
////////////////////////////////////////////////////////////////////////
////////////////////////////////////////////////////////////////////////
/////////////////////////////////////////////////////////...


------=_NextPart_000_0033_01C003C2.6671D9D0--
```

You can see in the preceding example where the boundary marking the beginning of the attached file is. Two hyphens are added to the beginning of the boundary value for a total of six. Immediately following the first boundary marker are three field names:

- `Content-Type` with a field body of `application/msword`. It's not hard to guess to what that value is pointing. This header field adds a `name` parameter, which names the attached file that is encoded.

- `Content-Transfer-Encoding` indicates the type of transfer encoding used, which is base64, as you already know.

- The final field name, `Content-Disposition`, describes where the base64 content came from, that is, an `attachment`, and the `file-name` as it was attached and the name by which it can be saved, for that matter.

At the end of the truncated base64 code is the second and last boundary marker, which has two hyphens added to the end of it.

The `multipart/mixed` type is common in email applications. Another multipart type is `multipart/related`. This type is considered more generic than `multipart/mixed` and is used in the SOAP and ebXML message envelopes. One of its advantages is the `start` parameter. With `start`, you can designate a part other than the first part as the root of a compound message. With this flexibility and other features, `multipart/related` is commonly used in B2B systems. You will see several demonstrations of the `multipart/related` type in later chapters of this book.

## A Simple Transport Example

Now we will walk through a simple example that shows you how to push and pull by hand a small, well-formed B2B XML document across the Internet. The document is a copy of `order.xml`, which you have seen before.

First of all, you will send the small XML document by SMTP, then grab the document with POP3. You enter the commands in boldface.

```
telnet mail.yourhost.com 25
220 mail.yourhost.com ESMTP Sendmail 8.8.5/8.8.5; Mon, 01 Jan 2001
00:00:03 -0800
MAIL FROM:<user@otherhost.com>
250 <user@otherhost.com>... Sender ok
RCPT TO:<user@yourhost.com>
250 <user@yourhost.com>... Recipient ok
```

```
DATA
354 Enter mail, end with "." on a line by itself
From: user@otherhost.com
To: user@yourhost.com
Subject: b2b

<?xml version="1.0" encoding="iso-8859-1" ?>
<!DOCTYPE Order SYSTEM "Order.dtd">

<Order partner="06-853-2535">
 <Date>2001-03-05</Date>
 <Item type="ISBN">0471404012</Item>
 <Quantity>22</order:Quantity>
 <Comments>None.<order:Comments>
 <ShippingMethod class="4th">USPS</ShippingMethod>
</Order>
.
250 DAA04905 Message accepted for delivery
QUIT
221 mail.yourhost.com closing connection

telnet mail.yourhost.com 110
+OK POP3 yourhost.com v4.47 server ready
USER user
+OK User name accepted, password please
PASS
+OK Mailbox open, 1 messages
LIST
+OK Mailbox scan listing follows
1 693
.
RETR 1
+OK 693 octets
Return-Path: <user@otherhost.com>
Received: …
Date: Mon, 01 Jan 2001 00:00:04 -0500
From: mike@wyeast.net
Message-Id: <200010261010.FAA21016@mail.yourhost.com>
Status:

<?xml version="1.0" encoding="iso-8859-1" ?>
<!DOCTYPE Order System "order.dtd">

<Order partner="06-853-2535">
 <Date>2001-03-05</Date>
 <Item type="ISBN">0471404012</Item>
 <Quantity>22</order:Quantity>
 <Comments>None.<order:Comments>
 <ShippingMethod class="4th">USPS</ShippingMethod>
</Order>
.
```

```
STAT
+OK 1 693
QUIT
+OK Sayonara
```

You can automate much the same operation with a Java program as shown next.

## Sending Documents via SMTP with Java

The Java program `SendSMTP.java` sends an XML document (an instance of `order.xml`) to an email address.

```
/*
//
// SendSMTP.java
//
// Sends an order (order.xml) to an email address.
//
*/

import java.io.*;
import java.net.*;
import java.util.*;
import java.text.*;

public class SendSMTP {

   public static void main(String arg[]) {

   // Random number for unique filename

   Random rn = new Random();

   // Formatted date for unique filename

   DateFormat today = new SimpleDateFormat("yyyy-MM-dd");

   // Name

   String fn = new String(today.format(new Date()) + "-" +
rn.nextInt(10000) + "-order.xml");

      try {

         // Test argument

         if (arg.length != 1)
```

```
            throw new IllegalArgumentException("You must specify an
email address where to send an order.");

        // Set mail host

        System.getProperties().put("mail.host", "mail.testb2b.org");

        // Ask the user for the from, to, and subject lines

        String mailfrom = "b2buser@testb2b.org";
        System.out.println("From: " + mailfrom);
        String mailto = arg[0];
        String mailsubject = fn;
        System.out.println("Subject: " + mailsubject);
        System.out.println();

        // Establish connection, output stream

        URL m = new URL("mailto:" + mailto);
        URLConnection mailer = m.openConnection();
        mailer.setDoInput(false);
        mailer.setDoOutput(true);
        mailer.connect();
        PrintWriter output =
         new PrintWriter(new
OutputStreamWriter(mailer.getOutputStream()));

        // Inform of connect

        System.out.println("Connecting to " +
System.getProperties().get("mail.host") + " as " + m);
        System.out.println();
        System.out.flush();

        // Write mail headers, blank line

        output.println("From: \"" + mailfrom + "\" <" + mailfrom +
            ">");
        output.println("To: " + mailto);
        output.println("Subject: " + mailsubject);
        output.println();

        // Set input stream, write order.xml

        BufferedReader input = new BufferedReader(new
            InputStreamReader(System.in));

        System.out.println("Fill in values (content) for " + fn);
        System.out.println();
        output.println("<?xml version=\"1.0\" encoding=\"iso-8859-1\"
            ?>");
```

```java
            output.println("<!DOCTYPE Order SYSTEM
\"http://testb2b.org/order/Order.dtd\">");
        output.println();
        System.out.print("Partner (DUNS, e.g., 06-853-2535): ");
        String partner = input.readLine();
        output.println("<Order partner=\"" + partner + "\"
            xmlns=\"http://testb2b.org/order\">");
        System.out.print("Date (e.g., 2001-01-01): ");
        String date = input.readLine();
        output.println(" <Date>" + date + "</Date>");
        System.out.print("Type (Title or ISBN): ");
        String itemType = input.readLine();
        System.out.print("Item (either a title or an ISBN): ");
        String item = input.readLine();
        output.println(" <Item type=\"" + itemType + "\">" + item +
            "</Item>");
        System.out.print("Quantity: ");
        String quantity = input.readLine();
        output.println(" <Quantity>" + quantity + "</Quantity>");
        System.out.print("Comments: ");
        String comments = input.readLine();
        output.println(" <Comments>" + comments + "</Comments>");
        System.out.print("Class (Express, 1st, Parcel, or 4th): ");
        String mailClass = input.readLine();
        System.out.print("Shipping method (e.g., USPS): ");
        String ship = input.readLine();
        output.println(" <ShippingMethod class=\"" + mailClass + ">"
            + ship + "</ShippingMethod>");
        output.println("</Order>");

        // Close stream

        output.close();

        // Confirm sent

        System.out.println();
        System.out.println(fn + " was sent to " + mailto);
        System.out.flush();

    }

    // Handle exceptions

    catch (Exception err) {
    System.err.println(err);
    System.err.println("Usage: java SendSMTP <emailaddress>");

    }
  }
}
```

### What's Going on in SendSMTP.java?

The program sets the mail host with `System.getProperties()` to `mail.testb2b.org` and writes header information, including the email address from the command-line argument. Then it establishes a connection with the server with `URL` and `URLConnection`, makes clear that it will be doing only output (`mailer.setDoOutput(true)`), and sets up an output stream (with `PrintWriter`).

The program sets the headers in the mail output stream and then reads output (with `BufferedReader`) from the console as content for the XML document `order.xml` that it is sending. Once it has written the last end-tag of the document, it closes the output stream and the message is sent.

You can exploit this simple program to write a more robust and sophisticated program. I should mention in addition that Sun's JavaMail product offers a variety of abstract classes for managing email systems.

## Moving on to Security

With these examples, you should have a fairly good grasp of the transport mechanisms of the Internet, all of which—from TCP/IP to MIME—are important components in the B2B integration model. With a little shell or Java program, you can automate these kinds of transfers with the ultimate goal of transporting B2B framework documents back and forth across the Internet quietly and seamlessly.

What if you want a little privacy in sending these documents around? You don't want your competition to know who your business partners are or how many sales you have made today, so we have to employ some measures to secure these transactions. That's the purpose of the next chapter.

# Security

Unfortunately, we live in a world in which we have to aggressively protect private information from miscreants who would like to trash our hard drives, swipe our credit card numbers, steal our identities, and snoop on our business transactions. Fortunately, although we are forced to protect ourselves from electronic hoodlums, reliable ways to do so are readily available.

With the potential of rapid, automatic exchange of documents between business enterprises, security measures are absolutely essential. This chapter outlines some of the options you have when implementing a security scheme for your B2B implementation. First of all, I'll discuss the basics of key systems, data encryption, and how to sign documents digitally. Then I'll talk about other related topics, such as digital certificates, XML Signature, authentication schemes, Pretty Good Privacy (PGP), Secure Socket Layer (SSL) and Transport Layer Security (TLS), firewalls, plus a lot more. I've also devoted a little space to directory services at the end of the chapter.

Internet security is a vast topic, one that I can't cover in one chapter. I'll tackle the basics, provide some examples, and point you in the general direction of some solutions, but I won't cover it all. And I leave it to you to implement the most appropriate security system for your needs.

# Data Encryption

In the electronic world, encryption allows you to turn readable message text into something pretty much unreadable. This is done by means of a patterned scheme or algorithm that can both encrypt (encipher) and decipher (decrypt) the text. One of the most common ways to encrypt electronic text today is with the use of keys.

## Keys

In the context of encryption, a *key* is a number produced by an algorithm in a program that encodes data from something an ordinary reader can understand into apparent gibberish. Think of a key as a secret combination that locks a cache of information. You know that my car key won't start your car, and your car key won't start mine. It's the same basic idea with encryption keys. They lock data by transforming it into something the ordinary reader can't comprehend, something that would take a powerful computer decades to figure out. If you don't have my keys, you can't drive my car and you can't unlock my data, but if you are a genuine, trustworthy friend, I'll hand my keys over to you without a blink.

The most basic key I can think of is a simple transformation of the English alphabet and Arabic numerals. Table 4.1 shows the 26 letters in the English alphabet and the 10 digits together in a continuous list, with a key that right-shifts the sequence by 10. (Uppercase and lowercase letters are considered equivalent.) It would be harder to fall off a log than to figure out this key, but I'll use it to illustrate a point.

Using this simple key, you can encipher the phrase "NCB 0N3 1S1" and then quickly decipher the phrase as "XML and B2B." Now you have the basic idea. As you can imagine, a simple algorithm could easily implement this key to both encipher and decipher text. Such a key is known as a *symmetric key* because the same key could both encrypt and decrypt a message.

For millennia, people have been encrypting messages in a similar fashion to keep private, secret information out of the hands of enemies and scoundrels. From Roman generals to Nazi commandants, one of the most common uses of encryption has been for military communications, where keeping a message secret is a deadly matter. On the other hand, one of the greatest security risks and time sinks has been getting the keys for deciphering those encrypted messages into the proper hands. Key distribution has been a daunting task, whether it was intercepted in Roman times on the business end of a Gallian spear or by someone in our time eavesdrop-

**Table 4.1** Simple Key

| LETTER/DIGIT | KEY | LETTER/DIGIT | KEY | LETTER/DIGIT | KEY |
|---|---|---|---|---|---|
| A | 0 | M | C | Y | O |
| B | 1 | N | D | Z | P |
| C | 2 | O | E | 0 | Q |
| D | 3 | P | F | 1 | R |
| E | 4 | Q | G | 2 | S |
| F | 5 | R | H | 3 | T |
| G | 6 | S | I | 4 | U |
| H | 7 | T | J | 5 | V |
| I | 8 | U | K | 6 | W |
| J | 9 | V | L | 7 | X |
| K | A | W | M | 8 | Y |
| L | B | X | N | 9 | Z |

ping on Internet transmissions. An important breakthrough in key distribution was the invention of the *public key*.

## Public and Private Keys

A public key is freely available; a private key is meant to be kept secret. The public and private keys are mathematically linked. A public key can be thrown around for all eyes to see because it is infeasible mathematically to derive a private key from a public key. These keys are called *asymmetric* because you do not use the same key for encryption and decryption. Under different circumstances, you might use either a public or private key for either decryption and encryption.

It is not altogether impossible to factor a public key in order to find a private key, but it would normally take a very, very long time—not that a public key is unbreakable, but given the time and computing resources required to crack a good one, by the time you found the answer, it wouldn't matter anymore. The message would no longer be timely or worthy of consideration, and you and I would both be retired anyway. Public and private key systems are not perfect, but they are a very good bet.

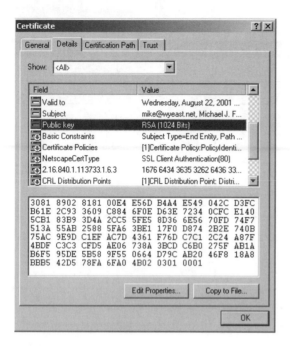

**Figure 4.1**  Example of a public key.

Figure 4.1 shows an RSA public key that is associated with my Microsoft Outlook 2000 mail client. You can see that it's just a bunch of digits in hexadecimal format, but a force to be reckoned with nonetheless. To see this dialog box in Outlook, assuming that you have a digitally signed message open, choose the File menu, then select Properties, then click the Security tab, click View Signing Certificate, and finally click the Details tab.

## The Diffie-Hellman-Merkle Solution

Perhaps you don't remember seeing any headlines about it, but its impact had enormous implications for the emerging Internet when in 1976, Whitfield Diffie, Martin Hellman, and Ralph Merkle came up with a way to exchange keys publicly. Diffie-Hellman, as it is called, is not an encryption algorithm, but a means to create and exchange keys that can be used as part of an encryption scheme. Let's say you and I wanted to exchange keys. This is how we would do it.

First, each of us would generate a pair of keys, one public, the other private. We would send each other our public keys. I would take your public key and my private key and compute a new key, and you, likewise, would take my public key and your private key and get the same result. It takes a few steps, but this process essentially eliminated the need to distribute symmetric keys in order to decipher messages.

## Rivest, Shamir, and Adelman (RSA)

The RSA algorithm was developed in 1977 by Ronald Rivest, with the help of fellow researchers Adi Shamir and Leonard Adelman (hence *RSA* for the first letters of their last names). RSA uses a one-way hash function, based on an a pair of extraordinarily large prime numbers, to compute a product for which it is very difficult to find factors, unless you have a key.

If I encrypt a message or document, such as an email message, with your public key and send it to you, the only way you can unlock it is with your private key. Remember, public-private key pairs are linked mathematically, and they rely on each other for decrypting messages. The way you can tell that a message decrypted correctly is that you can read it!

## Digital Signature Algorithm (DSA)

The Digital Signature Algorithm (DSA) is part of the Digital Signature Standard (DSS), a U.S. Federal Information Processing Standard (FIPS 186). DSS, which also includes RSA and Elliptic Curve DSA (ECDSA), defines methods for digitally signing documents that are approved for us by the U.S. federal government. DSA is also defined in ANSI X9.30.1-1997. Like RSA, this algorithm depends on a pair of large primes and also a random integer.

A brief Java program will help you see what the keys look like. The only point of this program is to give you an idea of what DSA public and private keys look like. Normally, you would keep the private key under wraps.

```
/*
//
// GetKeys.java
//
// Generate and display private and public keys.
//
*/
```

```
import java.security.*;
import java.io.*;
import java.lang.*;

public class GetKeys {

 public static void main(String arg[]) {

  try {

  // Convert argument to integer
  // Default modulus to 512 if no argument given

  int modArg = 512;
  if (arg.length != 0)
   modArg = Integer.parseInt(arg[0]);

  // Get key generator

  KeyPairGenerator kg = KeyPairGenerator.getInstance("DSA");
  SecureRandom rand = SecureRandom.getInstance("SHA1PRNG");
  kg.initialize(modArg, rand);

  // Get key private/public key pair

  KeyPair kp = kg.generateKeyPair();
  PrivateKey prv = kp.getPrivate();
  PublicKey pub = kp.getPublic();

  // Print private/public keys to stdout

  System.out.println("Public key: " + pub);
  System.out.println("Private key: " + prv);

  }

  catch (Exception err) {
   System.err.println(err);
   System.err.println("Usage: java GetKeys [modArg]");
  }
 }
}
```

## What's Going on in GetKeys.java?

This section is for folks who don't know Java well and want to know what is going on in this program. First of all, the program imports the java.security and java.io packages so that you can use all of the classes, types, and methods that are contained in these packages. As the program begins, you instantiate the integer variable modArg with a default value of 512.

If the command line has an argument, arg[0] is converted from a string to an integer (Integer.parseInt(arg[0])) so that it can be used to generate a parameter for the DSA algorithm. The method parseInt() is part of the Integer class from the java.lang package. You can access this method without importing the whole package by prepending the name of the class (Integer) to the method name.

Next the program uses a few classes and methods from java.security. It constructs an instance for a DSA key generator (keyGen) and gets a Secure Hash Algorithm (SHA-1) random number to use in the DSA algorithm (random), though only 64 of the 160 bits are used. *PRNG* stands for pseudo-random number generation. Then it initializes the key generator with these values. Then the program gets the keys and stores them in prv and pub. Finally, it prints the keys to stdout (your screen).

> **NOTE** Normally, you wouldn't just print out a private key or make it accessible at all, but this is just a demonstration. The private key won't be used for anything except enlightenment (I hope).

### Running GetKeys

You can find this program in the program archive available on this book's companion Web site. When you run the program, your output will vary depending on the modulus, which you can provide as an argument on the command line. If you do not give an argument, the modulus for the DSA algorithm will default to 512:

```
java GetKeys
```

You could add an argument on the command line that would set the modulus to 768:

```
java GetKeys 768
```

The valid arguments for this program are 512, 576, 640, 704, 768, 832, 896, 960, and 1024. If you chose the default modulus (512), the output of this program will look something like this:

```
Public key: Sun DSA Public Key
    Parameters:
    p:
```

```
    fca682ce 8e12caba 26efccf7 110e526d b078b05e decbcd1e b4a208f3 ae1617ae
    01f35b91 a47e6df6 3413c5e1 2ed0899b cd132acd 50d99151 bdc43ee7 37592e17
    q:
    962eddcc 369cba8e bb260ee6 b6a126d9 346e38c5
    g:
    678471b2 7a9cf44e e91a49c5 147db1a9 aaf244f0 5a434d64 86931d2d 14271b9e
    35030b71 fd73da17 9069b32e 2935630e 1c206235 4d0da20a 6c416e50 be794ca4
  y:
    7aa45905 ef93aadf b2450665 5a3d1fd6 9f69d204 2a825fff 38de38eb 4886407b
    75774bb3 f063e07e 716b5727 af9efb6d 5d0213f8 e06d6e66 477817ce 8e7be6c3

Private key: Sun DSA Private Key
parameters:
    p:
    fca682ce 8e12caba 26efccf7 110e526d b078b05e decbcd1e b4a208f3 ae1617ae
    01f35b91 a47e6df6 3413c5e1 2ed0899b cd132acd 50d99151 bdc43ee7 37592e17
    q:
    962eddcc 369cba8e bb260ee6 b6a126d9 346e38c5
    g:
    678471b2 7a9cf44e e91a49c5 147db1a9 aaf244f0 5a434d64 86931d2d 14271b9e
    35030b71 fd73da17 9069b32e 2935630e 1c206235 4d0da20a 6c416e50 be794ca4


x: 95d65ef05a66fdc392402ef318107e570e56356
```

Starting with the public key, the output shows the p or base parameter for the DSA algorithm, the q or prime parameter, and the g or subprime parameter. Finally, it shows y, which is the actually public key. Likewise, the output also shows the p, q, and g parameters for generating the private key, which are the same as for the public key, with x showing the actual private key. This private key is normally encoded and kept secret, but we're just having a show-and-tell here, so there you have it. It is never necessary to keep the p, q, and g parameters secret in order to conceal the keys.

## Digital Certificates

Figure 4.1, which shows a public key, also illustrates part of the information found in a digital certificate. You see a hint in the title of the dialog box. A digital certificate includes information about who the certificate is issued to, who is the certificate authority (CA), who issued the certificate (such as VeriSign), for how long the certificate is valid, your public key, and so forth. Secure Socket Layer (SSL), for example, uses information from a digital certificate to protect and authenticate Web documents— such as a document containing a credit card number. Figure 4.2 shows some general digital certificate information from Microsoft Outlook 2000.

**Figure 4.2**    General digital certificate information on Windows.

To see this dialog box in Outlook, from the File menu, select Properties, then click the Security tab, assuming that you have a digitally signed message open.

Digital certificates are based on the ITU-T standard X.509. X.509 defines an authentication framework with two levels: (1) a simple level that uses passwords for authentication and (2) a strong method with credentials coming from digital certificates. Digital certificates are often signed with digital signatures.

X.509 was first adopted in 1988, but it has been amended and expanded to encompass developments through 2000. It was originally defined to be part of the X.500 directory service, discussed later in this chapter in the section called *Directory Services: From X.500 to UDDI*. A directory can serve as a repository of public key information that can be accessed securely.

### Public Key Infrastructure (PKI) Management

The issuing of digital certificates by a CA such as VeriSign is part of key management. Distributing, storing, and generating public and private keys constitute key management. You can do it privately, or you can rely on a trusted CA to help you manage the keys necessary for your enterprise.

A CA can provide certificates not only for simple email, but also for SSL operations, Virtual Private Networks (VPNs), online payment systems, and so forth. In addition, you can go to a CA Web site and find digital certificate information based on an email address or a full name.

For example, let's say that your B2B partners have decided on Verisign as your CA. If you want to look up an individual partner to see if, for example, his or her digital ID (digital certificate for email) is still valid, follow these steps:

1. Access the site https://digitalid.verisign.com.
2. Click Personal IDs.
3. Click Search.
4. Enter the email address, full name, or serial number for the person you want to look up.

An example showing the results of a search is shown in Figure 4.3.

## Digital Signatures

A handwritten signature is a sign and seal that legally obligates the signer to, for example, a marriage or a mortgage or a will. A signed document is proof of the signer's identity. Likewise, a digital signature is a way to electronically sign a document so that a person receiving the document can verify indeed that it came from where it was supposed to come from.

You usually generate a digital signature by first creating a hash or digest of your message or document, then applying your private key to the digest. The result is a digital signature. A person on the receiving end can then verify your digital signature by using your public key.

### The Message Digest

By applying yet another algorithm, such as SHA-1 or MD5, you can create a message digest. A message digest is the result of hashing or, put simply,

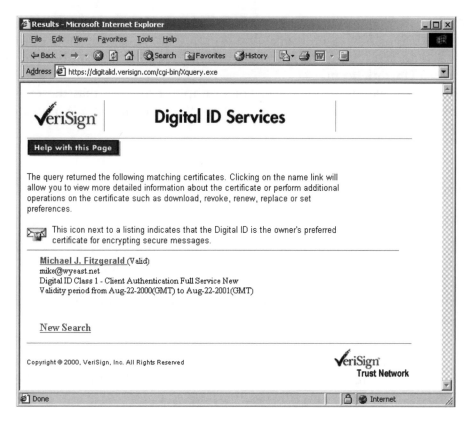

**Figure 4.3**    Search results for digital certificate information on Verisign.

converting text into a string of integers of preset length. A hash function transforms a data object such as a text file into a hash value or digest. A common algorithm for creating a message digest is MD5 (Message Digest version 5), another bit of code by Ron Rivest. Another algorithm is the Secure Hash Standard (SHA-1 for short), a U.S. Department of Commerce standard modeled after Rivest's MD4. RIPEMD-160 is yet another hashing algorithm.

How do you create a message digest? Programs such as mail clients can do it for you behind the scenes, but if you want to see how it's done and the code that makes it happen, here's one illustration. John Walker, founder of Autodesk, Inc., has written a little public domain MD5 program—based on Colin Plumb's earlier work—that converts input text into a hash value with the MD5 algorithm. The downloadable file (www.fourmilab.ch/md5/md5.zip) contains an executable program for a Windows environment and source code for those who prefer to compile and run the program on a Unix platform.

It has a simple-to-use interface. For example, provided that the executable md5.exe is in the path, if you type the following at a Windows command prompt:

```
md5 -d"Create a hash value from this text"
```

you get the following output:

```
E43759646528D710D45FA6B650856BE2
```

The command md5 is the name of the executable program. The -d switch is followed immediately with no intervening space by a quoted string. You must quote the string with double quotes ("). The output is a hash value. An MD5 hash is a continuous, fixed-length 128-bit string of hexadecimal values. You can shorten the input text:

```
md5 -d"Create a hash value"
```

The output string is then different, but it is still a 128-bit value. In the case of the shorter text string, the result is padded out to 128 bits.

```
EBD79CE5719B2C13D0E447054D3CDCAD
```

Let's push it a little further. With the download from John Walker's site, you'll get a local copy of Ron Rivest's RFC 1321, "The MD5 Message-Digest Algorithm." I'll do a hash on it and show you the result. The input to md5 is now a filename.

```
md5 rfc1321.txt
```

Here is the 128-bit result, the same length as the others, though the RFC is 21 pages long:

```
754B9DB19F79DBC4992F7166EB0F37CE
```

Hash values are one-way—that is, it is infeasible to invert them or to use the output value such as this 128-bit message digest to determine a possible input value such as a text file. Another feature of a reliable hash function is that it is collision-free or that two inputs cannot produce the same output. These qualities make message digests awfully difficult, expensive, and time-consuming to decipher.

You can also direct your output to a file rather than the screen as shown here:

```
md5 rfc1321.txt rfc1321.hash

type rfc1321.hash

754B9DB19F79DBC4992F7166EB0F37CE
```

### How Digital Signatures Work

Normally, for the sake of speed and compactness, you digitally sign a message digest rather than the actual message. When you apply your private key to a message digest, the computed result is the digital signature. Anyone who has access to your public key can apply that public key to your digital signature and determine that it was you who signed it and that the message was not altered. See *PGP* later in this chapter for an example.

Often, too, you send the original, unencrypted message along with the signed digest because the information in the message is not secret. In such a case, you may not need to keep the content of a message secret. You only want the recipient to be able to verify that you are the author of the message. After decrypting a digital signature, you can then apply the hash function such as MD5 to the unencrypted message to see if you get the same digest that was signed. Essentially, you then have two witnesses that the message is authentic: (1) you can decrypt the signature with a known public key, and (2) you get the same result when you perform a hash on the message or document. Verifying a digital signature is one form of authentication.

### Signing order.xml with Java

The following program, SignOrder.java, digitally signs the file order .xml so that a recipient of the file may verify the signature as coming from the expected party. Let's jump right into the code itself.

```java
/*
//
// SignOrder.java
//
// Digitally signs order.xml.
//
*/

import java.security.*;
import java.io.*;
```

```
public class SignOrder {

 public static void main(String arg[]) {

  try {

  // Convert argument to integer
  // Default modulus to 512 if no argument given

  int modArg = 512;

  if (arg.length == 1) {
   modArg = Integer.parseInt(arg[0]);
   System.out.println("Using " +modArg+ " bit strength...\n");
   System.out.flush();
  }
  else {
   System.out.println("No argument. Using default "+modArg+" bit strength...\n");
   System.out.flush();
  }

  // Get key pair

  KeyPairGenerator kg = KeyPairGenerator.getInstance("DSA");
  SecureRandom rand = SecureRandom.getInstance("SHA1PRNG");
  kg.initialize(modArg, rand);
  KeyPair kp = kg.generateKeyPair();
  PublicKey pub = kp.getPublic();
  PrivateKey prv = kp.getPrivate();

  // Get signature object, initialize with private key

  Signature dsa = Signature.getInstance("SHA1withDSA");
  dsa.initSign(prv);

  // Get order.xml

  FileInputStream fs = new FileInputStream("order.xml");
  BufferedInputStream bf = new BufferedInputStream(fs);
  byte[] buf = new byte[1024];
  int len;
  while (bf.available() != 0) {
   len = bf.read(buf);
   dsa.update(buf, 0, len);
   }
  bf.close();

  // Sign and save

  byte[] orderSig = dsa.sign();
```

```
FileOutputStream sf = new FileOutputStream("order.xml.signature");
sf.write(orderSig);
sf.close();
System.out.println("order.xml signed...\n");
System.out.println("DSA signature written to file order.xml.signature...\n");
System.out.flush();

byte[] key = pub.getEncoded();
FileOutputStream kf = new FileOutputStream("order.xml.publickey");
kf.write(key);
kf.close();
System.out.println("Public key written to file order.xml.publickey...\n");
System.out.flush();
System.out.println("SignOrder done. Use VerifyOrder to verify signature.");
System.out.flush();

}
catch (Exception err) {
 System.err.println("Usage: java SignOrder [modArg]");
 System.err.println(err);
}
}
}
```

### What's Going on in SignOrder.java?

Again, this section describes the program in some detail for those who aren't acquainted with Java. Like GetKeys.java, you can invoke the program with or without an argument:

```
java SignOrder
```

or

```
java SignOrder 1024
```

This is the bit strength for the modulus or first parameter for the DSA algorithm. By default, that is, if you don't use an argument, it will be 512 (int modArg = 512). The valid arguments are 512, 576, 640, 704, 768, 832, 896, 960, and 1024 (from 8 * 64 to 16 * 64). A value of 1024 is considered secure enough to withstand attacks for a number of years.

The command-line argument arg[0] is converted from a string to an integer (Integer.parseInt(arg[0])) so that it can be used to generate a parameter for the algorithm. Next the program uses the same code as the example GetKeys.java. It constructs an instance for a DSA key generator (kg) and gets a SHA-1 random number to use in the DSA algorithm (rand), though only 64 of the 160 bits are used. *PRNG* stands for pseudo-random number generation. Then it initializes the key generator with these values. The program then gets the keys and stores them in prv and pub.

Using a Signature object based on SHA-1 with DSA, the private key is initialized. The file order.xml is read in and signed (dsa.sign()) and written out to the file order.xml.signature in the current directory. Finally, the public key is also written out to order.xml.publickey, again in the current directory. These files will be used in the next example when you verify this signature.

### Verifying a Signature with Java

So what's the use of signing order.xml if we aren't going to use the digital signature to verify it? Here's a program that does that for you.

```
/*
//
// VerifyOrder.java
//
// Verifies a digital signature.
//
*/

import java.io.*;
import java.security.*;
import java.security.spec.*;

class VerifyOrder {

 public static void main(String arg[]) {

  try{

    // Get the public key file

    FileInputStream kf = new FileInputStream("order.xml.publickey");
    byte[] encode = new byte[kf.available()];
    kf.read(encode);
    kf.close();

    // Get X509 key

    X509EncodedKeySpec ks = new X509EncodedKeySpec(encode);
    KeyFactory dsakey = KeyFactory.getInstance("DSA");
    PublicKey pub = dsakey.generatePublic(ks);

    // Get signature file
```

```
FileInputStream sf = new FileInputStream("order.xml.signature");

byte[] sv = new byte[sf.available()];
sf.read(sv);
sf.close();

// Create signature object
// Initialize public key for verification

Signature sg = Signature.getInstance("SHA1withDSA");
sg.initVerify(pub);

// Read in and verify order.xml

FileInputStream fl = new FileInputStream("order.xml");

BufferedInputStream bf = new BufferedInputStream(fl);

byte[] buffer = new byte[1024];
int len;
while (bf.available() != 0) {
 len = bf.read(buffer);
 sg.update(buffer, 0, len);
}
bf.close();

boolean ver = sg.verify(sv);
if (ver)
 System.out.println("Signature for order.xml verified.");
else {|
 System.out.println("Verification failed!");
 }
}
catch (Exception err) {
 System.err.println("VerifyOrder failed. The files:");
 System.err.println("  order.xml");
 System.err.println("  order.xml.publickey");
 System.err.println("  order.xml.signature");
 System.err.println("Must be in the current directory.");
 System.err.println(err);
 }
}
}
```

### What's Going on in VerifyOrder.java?

You will most likely want to verify a signed file in a different location from
where it was signed. I am assuming that you will have copied the three files
order.xml, order.xml.publickey, and order.xml.signature
over a secure transport so that you can verify the signature elsewhere. The

bytecode class file `VerifyOrder.class` has to be in the same directory as well. You run the program with the command:

```
java VerifyOrder
```

First, this program imports an additional package, `java.security.spec.*`, which provides key and algorithm parameter specifications, such as class `X509EncodedKeySpec`. Then it reads in the file `order.xml.publickey` into the byte array `encode`.

This array is converted to the ASN.1 encoding of a public key with `X509EncodedKeySpec`. The `KeyFactory` class method `getInstance()` then generates an object that implements the DSA algorithm (`dsakey`). This, in turn, generates a public key based on the original input file `order.xml.publickey` and places it in `pub`.

Next the program reads in the signature file `order.xml.signature`, generates a Signature object that implements the DSA algorithm (`sg`), and initializes the public key for verification with that object (`sg.initVerify(pub)`). Last but not least, `order.xml` is read in, updated with the Signature object, and verified against the signature in `order.xml.signature` (`sg.verify(sv)`). If the program succeeds, you get the comforting message "Signature for order.xml verified."

### Using policytool

The JDK has yet another tool that enables you to establish a clear security policy for files, directories, programs, and signatures. It's called `policytool`, and it has a graphical interface, as shown in Figure 4.4.

You can do lots of things with `policytool`, but I'll mention only a few here. For example, you can grant permissions to read files or directories and then save this set of permissions in a policy file. You can grant permissions based on who has digitally signed a file, using a keystore file to reference who has valid signatures. The `policytool` can help you restrict access to files and entry to directories based on certain criteria.

If you have not used policytool before, by all means check out the tutorial at http://java.sun.com/docs/books/tutorial/security1.2/toolsign/index.html, where you will find details on how to set up your own policy.

## Authentication

Authentication is the process by which an operating system or some other piece of software determines that you are really the person you say you are

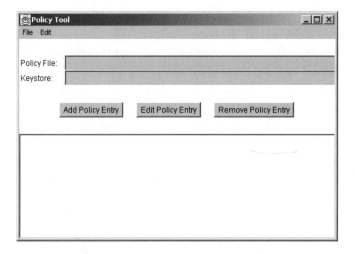

**Figure 4.4**    policytool dialog.

or that a process is really what it purports to be. For example, when you log in to a Windows NT/2000 or Unix system, you first need to authenticate who you are by presenting a valid user or login name and a password. Similarly, when you attempt to retrieve email from a mail server using POP3, you must also give a username and password. However you decide to transport your B2B documents, you will undoubtedly rely on some sort of authentication scheme to get or post documents.

Not all authentication schemes are created equal. Few systems claim to be perfectly impervious to intrusion, but some are more bulletproof than others. On the mushy side, if your system uses a simple username-password scheme with little restriction on passwords, you may wind up with passwords that can be easily cracked.

For example, if Jane Smith is permitted to use `jane.smith` as her username and `smith` as her password, her account will likely be vulnerable to attack. Because her password is common as well as lexical, a password-cracking program could pretty easily find this password and break in to her account.

Maybe the convenience of having an easy-to-remember password is worth the risk because if the username-password is simply protecting a private email account, well, few hackers will go to the trouble of busting in—unless Jane Smith is a CIA agent. If, for example, you are managing exchange documents for a U.S. Department of Defense secret weapons laboratory, perhaps you should step up security a bit.

On the other end of the scale are advanced, highly-secure systems that use two or more factors in the authentication process. In such systems, your password may change every minute and be provided to you via a handheld device, which is also password protected. Or you may be required to swipe a smart card that swings from a lanyard around your neck. Or your system may require you to place your thumb on a piece of glass, undergo voice analysis, or have your retina scanned.

Your choice of security systems depends on what you need to protect and how vulnerable your documents are to competition or, at worst, to real enemies. If you are exchanging documents about your glass telephone wire insulator collection, you may feel perfectly calm about a light authentication scheme, but if one of those insulators is rare and sitting on the fireplace mantel in your living room, perhaps you'll want to be more cautious about who has that information.

## Authentication versus Authorization

Authorization is different from authentication. Authentication is a process that figures out who you are. Authorization is a process that figures out what you can get away with. Let's say that you log in to a computer system successfully. You are authenticated. Now, what can you do?

Not surprisingly, you can probably copy, read, edit, and write files to your heart's content in your own home directory. You are authorized to do that. But if you try to do something that requires root or superuser privileges, such as edit a Unix `passwd` file or the Windows Registry, you are out of luck. You do not have the authority to do such things. That's the difference between authentication and authorization.

## Authentication on an Apache Server

The Apache Web server hosts more Web sites than any other server out there, so it makes sense to give an Apache authentication example. You can have directory-level control over server settings with what are called *directives*. These directives are placed in Apache plain-text configuration files, most commonly `access.conf`. Directives tell the server how to handle files, what kind of access to allow, how to handle authentication, and so on.

I tested this example against Apache 1.3.12; you might have an older or newer version, but I doubt you will have a problem.

The <Directory> directive may be placed in the access.conf file to control access to a directory and its subdirectories on the server, but commonly, the .htaccess file is used to apply local control over a directory. (The .htaccess file descended to us from the early WWW server NCSA HTTPd, which is no longer supported.) This file is placed in the directory where you want to limit access and require authentication. I'll show you how I set up such a file for a directory in a Unix environment on testb2b.org, called B2B-auth. (You won't have access to testb2b .org; you'll have to get access to another system.)

First I'll show you what the file looks like, then I'll tell you what it does.

```
AuthUserFile /usr/testb2b.org/web/B2B-auth/.htpasswd
AuthType Basic
AuthName "B2B Order Access"

require valid-user
```

In the first line in the file, the AuthUserFile directive provides the (fictitious) absolute path for a file that contains usernames and passwords for those that are authorized to access this directory and its subdirectories. The second directive, AuthType, identifies the authentication type, currently Basic or Digest. We are using Basic; Digest uses MD5 digest values to authenticate users (and requires a little more setup which I won't cover).

The AuthName directive indicates a string that identifies the realm. A realm is a domain or section on your server, such as a directory and its subdirectories—even a file—to which access is limited by authentication. The require valid-user directive indicates that access to this realm (the directory B2B-auth and below) requires a username and password that is stored in the file named by AuthUserFile.

To set up who can access this realm, you also need to create a password file with the following command:

```
/usr/local/apache/bin/htpasswd -c ./.htpasswd b2buser
New password:
Re-type new password:
Adding password for user b2buser
```

This command assumes that you installed Apache on a Unix machine under /user/local, as it commonly is. It may be installed elsewhere, as certainly it will be under Windows, such as under C:\program files\ apache group\apache.

This command invokes htpasswd and creates a new file (-c) in the current directory called .htpasswd. It accepts the username of b2buser and then prompts you to give it a password and then confirm the password. You know you have been successful when you get an Adding password... report. Now enter the following command:

```
cat .htpasswd
```

and you will see the contents of the file, which will be similar to this:

```
b2buser:bbaeHGkjZHB4o
```

Adding users to this password file is done with this command:

```
/usr/local/apache/bin/htpasswd ./.htpasswd mike
```

Each time you add a username and a password, they will be appended to the file.

```
b2buser:bbaeHGkjZHB4o
mike:bjWDhSngyepxI
robert:45HcJiwqv6iUw
floydene:4bOZQTRAt2xP.
```

This shows the content of the password file, which includes the username and encrypted password separated by a colon. The password in this example is encrypted using CRYPT, a Unix password encryption function based on the Data Encryption Standard (DES). You can also encrypt passwords with MD5 (-m) or the SHA-1 (-s).

I'll illustrate what happens if you issue an HTTP request directly to a protected directory:

```
GET /B2B-auth HTTP/1.1
Host: www.testb2b.org
```

Because this directory contains a .htaccess file, you will see the following HTTP challenge response:

```
HTTP/1.1 401 Authorization Required
Date: Mon, 01 Jan 2001 00:00:03 GMT
Server: Apache/1.3.12 (Unix) PHP/4.0.3RC1
WWW-Authenticate: Basic realm="B2B Order Access"
Content-Type: text/html; charset=iso-8859-1
```

The WWW-Authenticate header is specified in RFC 2617, "HTTP Authentication: Basic and Digest Access Authentication." If you were using a browser such as Netscape 6, you would be presented with a dialog box, as shown in Figure 4.5.

If you click Cancel or enter an incorrect username and password, you receive an HTTP/1.1 401 Authorization Required message. To gain entrance, enter b2buser as the username and b2buser as the password. In raw HTTP, you would send a message with the following header:

```
Authorization: Basic YjJidXNlcjpiMmJ1c2Vy
```

The field body of the header contains a string with the authentication scheme (Basic) and a base64-encoded username and password in the form username:password.

You can tweak .htaccess endlessly with all kinds of directives. For example, instead of allowing all valid users, as with:

```
require valid-user
```

you can further tighten down the bolts by allowing only specific users:

```
require user b2buser
```

Likewise, as you probably know, all users are assigned to groups by the operating system's authentication system. For example, there is usually a special group of users who all have administrator privileges on a given machine. You could likewise set up a group such as b2b and require that all local users belong to that group in order to gain access to the directory. Here are the added lines for .htaccess:

```
AuthGroupFile /usr/testb2b.org/web/B2B-auth/group
```

```
require group b2b
```

The directory listing is for files on a virtual or shared host, with web as the root directory of the virtual site. By HTTP, the directory would be available at www.testb2b.org/B2B-auth.

Once your username and password are offered, if you do not have an entry in the group file (or some other file) showing that you belong to the group b2b, you will be denied access. A text group file would contains entries like this:

```
b2b: b2buser mike robert floydene
```

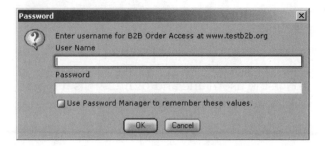

**Figure 4.5**   Netscape 6 authentication dialog box.

I think one that will be of use to you in setting up a B2B system is authentication from a certain IP address or domain, rather than from specific users. This is done with the following directive:

```
order deny,allow
deny from all
allow from testb2b.org
```

By default, the server figures out, first, to whom it will `allow` access and, second, to whom it will `deny` access. With the `order` directive, you change the order so that the server will first `deny`, then `allow`. Then you `deny` all comers from having any access (`deny from all`), but you open the door just a crack to allow anyone from `testb2b.org` or its IP address to have access to this directory. I like this method because you won't be bothered with an authentication challenge if you are from the right domain. In addition, as it is not the default, it improves security because it closes down access to all except those you explicitly accept, rather than the other way around, accepting from all except those you specifically deny.

## Other Authentication Schemes

There are many other authentication schemes that you could use for your B2B trust system, and though, I am sorry to say, I can't cover more than a handful, I'll mention PAM and Kerberos briefly. You have many choices, but while the system must be reliable, I would go for simplicity and openness. You could spend plenty of your hard-earned dollars to set up a robust, well-supported system, but as I say, why let them have all the fun?

### *Pluggable Authentication Modules on Linux*

The Linux-based Pluggable Authentication Modules, or PAM, allow you to have a flexible, broad-range means of authenticating users. PAM goes way beyond the traditional steps for checking a username and password against an /etc/passwd file. Rather than forcing you to rewrite common authentication applications, such as login, to accommodate new systems, you can attach PAM instead. PAM can support the simplest, most archaic authentication schemes, but it can also integrate newer systems such as smart cards. PAM comes standard with the most popular Linux distributions.

### *Kerberos*

Kerberos, as you might remember from Greek literature, is the three-headed dog that guards the entrance to Hades. It is also a network authentication system developed at MIT. Instead of authenticating the authorship of documents, Kerberos authenticates network requests by symmetric keys. Symmetric key cryptography employs the same key for both encryption and decryption and does not use digital signatures. Since the mid-1990s, some work has been underway to include public keys in Kerberos.

Kerberos relies on a trusted third party—a separate server—to administer secret keys and authenticate users. This might be a suitable approach for a B2B application, if the two or more parties exchanging documents can agree on which party will host the Kerberos server securely. This is a concern because if a Kerberos server is broken into, say by a disgruntled insider, the security of the document exchange could be compromised, and your business will be hurt. A public-key system works independently of a central server, not unlike the Internet itself; for this reason, it is not vulnerable to a single server attack. Nevertheless, Kerberos may be preferred by tight-knit partners, especially if the enterprises exchanging documents are within the same organization.

## S/MIME

S/MIME stands for Secure/Multipurpose Internet Mail Extensions. As you can guess, S/MIME extends MIME to provide security for messages sent in a MIME format. S/MIME provides the means to authenticate users, to affix digital signatures, and to encrypt messages.

S/MIME is not restricted for use with email: You can use it with a document format that uses regular, old MIME, such as BizTalk or the other B2B documents we have already transported via HTTP, FTP, or SMTP. A form of S/MIME is used when sending digitally signed messages, such as in this fragment.

```
Content-Type: multipart/signed;
    protocol="application/pkcs7-signature";
    micalg=SHA1; boundary="boundary";

--boundary
Content-Type: text/plain;
    charset="iso-8859-1"
Content-Transfer-Encoding: 7bit

This is a clear message (unencrypted) with a digital signature attached!

--boundary
Content-Type: application/pkcs7-signature;
    name="smime.p7s"
Content-Transfer-Encoding: base64
Content-Disposition: attachment;
    filename="smime.p7s"

MIAGCSqGSIb3DQEHAqCAMIACAQExCzAJBgUrDgMCGgUAMIAGCSqGSIb3DQEHAQAAoIIFzDCC
ApswggIEoAMCAQICAwOztTANBgkqhkiG9w0BAQQFADCBkjELMAkGA1UEBhMCWkExFTATBgNV
BAgTDFdlc3Rlcm4gQ2FwZTESMBAGA1UEBxMJQ2FwZSBUb3duMQ8wDQYDVQQKEwZUaGF3dGUx
HTAbBgNVBAsTFENlcnRpZmljYXRlIFNlcnZpY2VzMSgwJgYDVQQDEx9QZXJzb25hbCBGcmVl
bWFpbCBSU0EgMjAwMC44LjMwMB4

. . .
--boundary--
```

The MIME header `Content-Type` is not `multipart/related` or `multipart/mixed`, as in the previous examples, but it is `multipart/ signed`. This MIME type is for clear or unencrypted messages that are accompanied by a digital signature. This is followed by the MIME type `application/pkcs7-signature`, which is used as the type for the detached signature that follows in the second part (after the second boundary). The boundary for the parts is defined uncreatively as `boundary`.

This is followed by the Message Integrity Check algorithm (`micalg`) with a value of `SHA1` (Secure Hash Algorithm-1). It could also have the value of `MD5` (Message Digest 5); any others are considered unknown. This is the algorithm used in verifying the digital signature.

After the first boundary comes the clear message with familiar content (`text/plain`) and Latin-1 encoding (`iso-8859-1`). The transfer encoding (`7bit`) is suitable for US-ASCII, but not much else.

After that is another boundary, followed by some more headers for the signature. The content type for this part is again `application/pkcs7-signature`. This is followed by a filename, `smime.p7s`. The filename helps older systems and network gateways that don't understand S/MIME to pass information through to the destination host, which, of course, must know S/MIME.

For example, if a system does not understand `application/pkcs7-signature`, it may discard the type and replace it with `application/octet-stream`, thus tossing out important information. The filename will be passed through and will help the destination recover from the lost S/MIME information. The transfer encoding for this part of the message, labeled an attachment, is `base64`. This base64 encoding contains the signed hash of the message.

# XML Signature

A joint initiative is underway at W3C and IETF (Internet Engineering Task Force) to use an XML syntax to describe digital signatures. This syntax is called XML Signature, and it uses XML elements to encapsulate data for the encryption and signing of XML documents.

IBM alphaWorks has developed an implementation of XML Signature, a Java suite called the XML Security Suite (XSS) that provides security features for B2B activities. Some of these security features include digital signatures, access control, and encryption based on XML elements.

Let's look at an example using XSS. First you must download the latest version of XSS (www.alphaworks.ibm.com/tech/xmlsecuritysuite). Once installed on your system, perhaps in either the directory `c:\xml\xss` on Windows or `/home/mike/xml/xss` on Unix, you will almost be ready to run some sample programs.

But first, if you have never met, let me introduce you to `keytool`.

## Using keytool

If you have installed the Java Development Kit on your system, you also have a handy, free tool at your disposal for generating keys. It is called `keytool` (it replaces the earlier JDK tool called `javakey`). You can use keytool to generate keys for use with XSS. I'll show you how.

The `keytool` is installed when you install the JDK or the JRE, for example, in `C:\jdk1.3\bin` on Windows or perhaps `/home/mike/jdk1.3/bin` on a Unix system. The keytool must be in the path in order to use it at a command prompt without explicitly listing the full path (see *The Path Variable* section in Chapter 3, "Transport").

At a command prompt, type the following bold text, replacing the personal information with your own. This personal information is known as a *distinguished name*, and it is in a format that comes from the International Telecommunication Union-Telecom Standardisation (ITU-T) standard X.500 and is similar to that used by Lightweight Directory Access Protocol (LDAP).

```
keytool -genkey -alias orders -storepass mystrpasswd -keypass
mykeypasswd
What is your first and last name?
  [Unknown]:  Mike Fitzgerald
What is the name of your organizational unit?
  [Unknown]: Writing Department
What is the name of your organization?
  [Unknown]:  Wy'east Communications
What is the name of your City or Locality?
  [Unknown]:  West Linn
What is the name of your State or Province?
  [Unknown]:  OR
What is the two-letter country code for this unit?
  [Unknown]:  US
Is <CN=Mike Fitzgerald, OU=Writing Department, O=Wy'east Communications,
L=West Linn, ST=OR, C=US> correct?
  [no]:  y
```

What have you just done? In your home directory, in a file named .keystore, you stored a pair of keys, one public and one private. The .keystore file is protected with the password mystrpasswd while the private key stored in the file is protected by the password mykeypasswd. Of course, you'll want to use more imaginative passwords than those, but you get the idea. If you do not provide the passwords on the command line, you will be prompted to give them later.

Let's extract the public key and have a look at it. Enter the bold text:

```
keytool -export -alias orders -file order.cer -storepass mystrpasswd
Certificate stored in file <order.cer>
```

You have now exported to the file order.cer, stored in the current directory, a digital signature, which includes, among other things, a public key. To look at the file order.cer, type this line:

```
keytool -printcert -file order.cer
```

While the fingerprints will be quite different, you should see output similar to this:

```
Owner: CN=Mike Fitzgerald, OU=Writing Department, O=Wy'east
     Communications, L=West Linn, ST=Oregon, C=US
Issuer: CN=Mike Fitzgerald, OU=Writing Department, O=Wy'east
     Communications, L=West Linn, ST=Oregon, C=US
Serial number: 3a2d4e84
Valid from: Tue Dec 05 12:22:28 PST 2000 until: Mon Mar 05 12:22:28 PST
     2001
Certificate fingerprints:
     MD5:  1C:A3:4D:B8:D1:B2:12:62:B1:5A:44:A4:58:4B:3A:17
     SHA1: 2C:8E:20:6A:8E:70:8F:6C:79:49:42:EA:F7:DE:FA:46:53:7D:51:8B
```

This is just a sampling of what you can do with `keytool`. If you implement keys and certificates for your B2B system, you can use `keytool` to manage your store of keys and certificates. Some of the tasks involved include managing a store of keys and certificates, establishing a relationship with a certificate authority (CA), such as VeriSign, Inc., so that you can establish a trusted chain of digital certificates, importing certificates for a CA, and exporting a certificate for your public key.

Now that you have stored some keys with `keytool`, you can use the key store to run an XSS example.

## Running the XSS Example SampleSign2

At a command line, run the sample program with this:

```
java -classpath "xerces.jar;xalan.jar;xss4j.jar;xss4j\samples"
SampleSign2 orders mystrpasswd mykeypasswd -embxml
http://testb2b.org/B2B/order.xml > signature.xml
```

You will see output similar to this:

```
Key store: C:\Documents and Settings\mike.WYEAST\.keystore
Sign: 5427ms
```

The file `.keystore` that XSS uses is in your home directory, so the actual output will depend on the location of your own home directory.

As usual, for simple illustration, I have placed the necessary JAR files in the current directory and then included them in the classpath, with `xerces.jar` first (this is important). In order to use XSS successfully, you must have the `xerces.jar` from Xerces 1.2 (or later), the `xalan.jar` file from Xalan 1.2 (or later), as well as the `xss4j.jar` file that comes with XSS. (Replace semicolons with colons in the classpath if you are on a Unix system.)

You should set up your `classpath` according to your preferences, as explained previously in Chapter 2, "The XML Foundation," and in the section called *The Classpath Variable* in Chapter 3. This classpath contains not only JAR files but also a directory, that is, `xssj4\samples`. I am running the program from the directory just above `xss4j\samples`. The location of the `samples` directory will be different on your system, depending on where you unzipped the archive.

`SampleSign2` is the name of the program stored in the directory `xssj4\samples`. It takes the following as input on the command line:

**orders.** The alias for the key store file `orderstore`.

**mystrpasswd.** Your password, which I hope is different from this cheesy one, for accessing the key store `orderstore`.

**mykeypasswd.** The password for access to your private key.

**-embxml http://testb2b.org/B2B/order.xml.** The URL for the file you want to sign. The option –embxml means that the URL will be embedded in the resulting signature, indiscernibly in the XML Signature file.

**> signature.xml.** The greater-than sign (>) redirects the output of the program to the file `signature.xml`.

If this example runs successfully, the contents of `signature.xml` will appear similar to the following:

```
<?xml version='1.0' encoding='UTF-8'?>
<Signature xmlns="http://www.w3.org/2000/09/xmldsig#">
  <SignedInfo>
    <CanonicalizationMethod Algorithm="http://www.w3.org/TR/2000/WD-xml-
c14n-20000119"/>
    <SignatureMethod Algorithm="http://www.w3.org/2000/09/xmldsig#dsa-
sha1"/>
    <Reference URI="#Res0">
      <Transforms>
        <Transform Algorithm="http://www.w3.org/TR/2000/WD-xml-c14n-
20000119"/>
      </Transforms>
      <DigestMethod Algorithm="http://www.w3.org/2000/09/xmldsig#sha1"/>
      <DigestValue>V1fRYnODJjNNYM9JTnEM1DmzUUw=</DigestValue>
    </Reference>
  </SignedInfo>
  <SignatureValue>
    SWh6aI6CnXNdDZsSXQD5x6zFOD+H89W5sTzIdOyZQFqw3lJ/BL/ouw==
  </SignatureValue>
  <KeyInfo>
    <KeyValue>
      <DSAKeyValue>
<P>/X9TgR11EilS30qcLuzk5/YRt1I870QAwx4/gLZRJmlFXUAiUftZPY1Y+r/F9bow9subV
WzXgTuAHTRv8mZgt2uZUKWkn5/oBHsQIsJPu6nX/rfGG/g7V+fGqKYVDwT7g/bTxR7DAjVUE
1oWkTL2dfOuK2HXKu/yIgMZndFIAcc=</P>
<Q>l2BQjxUjC8yykrmCouuEC/BYHPU=</Q>
```

```
<G>9+GghdabPd7LvKtcNrhXuXmUr7v6OuqC+VdMCz0HgmdRWVeOutRZT+ZxBxCBgLRJFnEj6
EwoFhO3zwkyjMim4TwWeotUfIOo4KOuHiuzpnWRbqN/C/ohNWLx+2J6ASQ7zKTxvqhRkImog
9/hWuWfBpKLZl6Ae1UlZAFMO/7PSSo=</G>
<Y>owLoIOjP+ajQJNSBBTbZWTc/W1gx+d39FVhpVFDUlOoc7SMeywAymdL8WfAaY3J1w6Q9h
OchUKQenmreDJZemsPmRzUFV2l1pRNDfzCPghjwl5N1273CeKKFBkMO5FdIOx7rgWzYx+tBr
ahZ7LygmNZWENpJOot2nW30BczHm8U=</Y>
  </DSAKeyValue>
 </KeyValue>
 <X509Data>
 <X509SubjectName>CN=Mike Fitzgerald, OU=Writing Department, O=Wy'east
 Communications, L=West Linn, ST=Oregon, C=US</X509SubjectName>
 <X509Certificate>
 MIIDSzCCAwkCBDotVaAwCwYHKoZIzjgEAwUAMIGKMQswCQYDVQQGEwJVUzEPMA0GA1UECBMG
 T3J1Z29uMRIwEAYDVQQHEwlXZXN0IExpbm4xHzAdBgNVBAoTF1d5J2Vhc3QgQ29tbXVuaWNh
 dGlvbnMxGzAZBgNVBAsTEldyaXRpbmcgRGVwYXJ0bWVudDEYMBYGA1UEAxMPTWlrZSBGaXR6
 Z2VyYWxkMB4XDTAwMTIwNTIwNTIOOFoXDTAxMDMwNTIwNTIOOFowgYoxCzAJBgNVBAYTAlVT
 MQ8wDQYDVQQIEwZPcmVnb24xEjAQBgNVBAcTCVdlc3QgTGlubjEfMB0GA1UEChMWV3knZWFz
 dCBDb21tdW5pY2F0aW9uczEbMBkGA1UECxMSV3JpdGluZyBEZXBhcnRtZW50MRgwFgYDVQQD
 Ew9NaWtlIEZpdHpnZXJhbGQwggG4MIIBLAYHKoZIzjgEATCCAR8CgYEA/X9TgR11EilS30qc
 Luzk5/YRt1I870QAwx4/gLZRJmlFXUAiUftZPY1Y+r/F9bow9subVWzXgTuAHTRv8mZgt2uZ
 UKWkn5/oBHsQIsJPu6nX/rfGG/g7V+fGqKYVDwT7g/bTxR7DAjVUE1oWkTL2dfOuK2HXKu/y
 IgMZndFIAccCFQCXYFCPFSMLzLKSuYKi64QL8Fgc9QKBgQD34aCF1ps93su8q1w2uFe5eZSv
 u/o66oL5V0wLPQeCZ1FZV4661FlP5nEHEIGAtEkWcSPoTCgWE7fPCTKMyKbhPBZ6i1R8jSjg
 o64eK7OmdZFuo38L+iE1YvH7YnoBJDvMpPG+qFGQiaiD3+Fa5Z8GkotmXoB7VSVkAUw7/s9J
 KgOBhQACgYEAowLoIOjP+ajQJNSBBTbZWTc/W1gx+d39FVhpVFDUlOoc7SMeywAymdL8WfAa
 Y3J1w6Q9h0chUKQenmreDJZemsPmRzUFV2l1pRNDfzCPghjwl5N1273CeKKFBkMO5FdIOx7r
 gWzYx+tBrahZ7LygmNZWENpJOot2nW30BczHm8UwCwYHKoZIzjgEAwUAAy8AMCwCFDOHyxAG
 yq7+UJnoihB4EJKKJRa1AhQ3A/t7ztUVi6DHHGS8Ey4lSjZ/2g==
 </X509Certificate>
 </X509Data>
 </KeyInfo>
 <dsig:Object Id="Res0" xmlns=""
 xmlns:dsig="http://www.w3.org/2000/09/xmldsig#">
 <Order partner="06-853-2535">
  <Date>2001-03-05</Date>
  <Item type="ISBN">0471404012</Item>
  <Quantity>22</Quantity>
  <Comments>None.</Comments>
  <ShippingMethod class="4th">USPS</ShippingMethod>
 </Order>
 </dsig:Object>
</Signature>
```

Just by glancing at this document, you can make some pretty reasonable guesses about what is going on in it. This is one of the beauties of XML, which, if designed and written thoughtfully, describes itself merely by its element names, thus providing incidental metadata.

The root element, as you might predict, is `Signature`. `SignedInfo` contains information about algorithms for canonicalization, signature, and digest methods.

CanonicalizationMethod and Transform contain information about the canonicalization algorithm. Canonical XML is a W3C initiative that, using a set of rules, converts an XML document to a strict, canonical, physical form to ease or improve processing by applications. Even though two perfectly legal XML documents may at first blush appear different, after canonicalization, they are deemed equivalent. Some examples are these: All canonical XML documents use UTF-8 encoding, their empty elements are converted to have start-tag/end-tag pairs, and all attributes are delimited with double rather than single quotes. (Even though Canonical XML has been updated, at the time of writing, XSS still uses the form found in the January 2000 working draft. The SignatureMethod algorithm is used for generating and validating the signature—DSA with SHA-1, which is part of DSS. DigestMethod states that SHA-1 is the digest algorithm, with the actual digest result stored in DigestValue. The URI attribute in Reference refers to the embedded reference (#Res0) to the document stored in the certificate (http://testb2b.org/B2B/order.xml). SignatureValue contains the base64-encoded digital signature.

KeyInfo holds key information that a recipient may use to validate a signature. The DSAKeyValue is broken into the parts: P for the base (modulus) parameter, Q for the prime parameter, and G for the subprime parameter. Y is for the resulting public key.

X509Data contains X.509 information. X509SubjectName holds the distinguished name of the subject of the certificate. Following that is the actual X.509 certificate in X509Certificate. Finally, the Object element's content represents the signed document, order.xml, found at http://testb2b.org/B2B/order.xml.

### Verifying the Signature File with VerifyGUI

You can now verify your signature file with VerifyGUI. At a command line, type the following:

```
java -classpath "xerces.jar;xalan.jar;xss4j.jar;xss4j\samples" VerifyGUI
< signature.xml
```

Using the same classpath as in the previous example, you invoke VerifyGUI, using the less-than sign (<) to direct the contents of the file signature.xml as input to the program. The console output of this program will look something like this:

```
The signature has a KeyValue element.
The signature has one or more X509Data elements.
```

```
Checks an X509Data:
  It has 1 certificate(s).
  Certificate Information:
  Version: 1
  Validity: OK
  SubjectDN: CN=Mike Fitzgerald, OU=Writing Department,
  O=Wy'east Communications, L=West Linn, ST=Oregon, C=US
  IssuerDN: CN=Mike Fitzgerald, OU=Writing Department, O=Wy'east
  Communications, L=West Linn, ST=Oregon, C=US
  Serial#: 976049568
Time to verify: 240 [msec]
```

The program recognizes the `KeyValue` and `X509Data` elements and checks the X.509 data. It discovers that the file contains a single X.509 certificate and confirms its validity. It also reports the distinguished names for the subject of the certificate, as well as the issuer, which are both the same in this instance, and the certificate's serial number.

VerifyGUI, as its name suggests, also outputs a simple graphical status box, as shown in Figure 4.6, confirming the validity of the certificate.

# IPSec

Internet Protocol Security (IPSec) goes a little deeper by applying cryptographic techniques to the IP packets themselves and is fast becoming a de

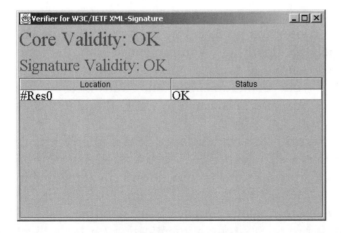

**Figure 4.6**   The XSS VerifyGUI graphical output.

facto standard. Under IPSec, both the IP packets' header and payload are secured. There are facilities for encryption, authentication, data integrity, and even key management. You can use IPSec as you would IP, where data is transported from host to host, but protected with IPSec's security features. You can also use IPSec in a tunneling mode where nonsecure data is encapsulated with IPSec.

## IPSec and VPNs

IPSec is frequently implemented in Virtual Private Network (VPN) schemes. Rather than setting up the expensive infrastructure for a private network, a VPN is a less expensive solution. Basically, a VPN uses the existing Internet to create a virtual network that is protected by encryption and other security measures. IPSec is being used in place of traditional PPTP and L2TP. Point-to-Point Tunneling Protocol (PPTP), a Microsoft child, is a vehicle that allows good, old Point-to-Point Protocol (PPP) to tunnel across an IP connection. L2TP (Layer 2 Tunneling Protocol), the offspring of Cisco Systems, blends the features of PPTP and Cisco's earlier Layer 2 Forwarding (L2F). Now these protocols seem to be on their way out as IPSec is on its way in.

SSH Communications Security, a Finnish company, offers an SDK for IPSec development called SSH IPSec Express. This C toolkit offers a TCP/IP interface and libraries to help your application use HTTP and LDAP.

## SSH

Secure Shell (SSH) is a protocol that allows you to log in to a remote computer with your network connection protected by encryption, such as by the IDEA, DES, or Triple-DES algorithms. You can run it from the command line or a GUI. It looks similar to a regular `telnet` session with password authentication, but your communication and transmissions are shielded from snooping or intrusion. You can also use FTP under SSH as well as SCP (Secure Copy).

SSH Communications Security, which developed SSH in the first place back in the mid-1990s, offers a client called SSH Secure Shell that runs on both Unix and Windows. Figure 4.7 shows the Windows client logging in to `testb2b.org`.

SSH provides replacement technology for such Unix standbys as `telnet`, `rlogin`, and FTP. It provides strong authentication for both client

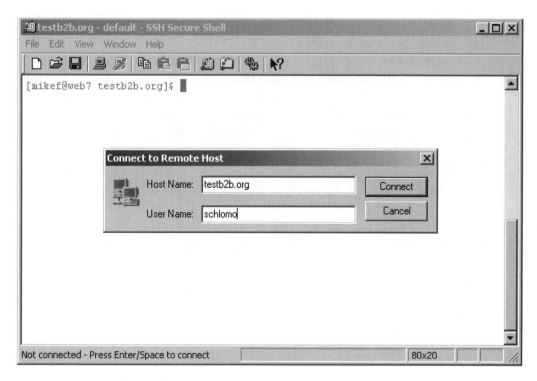

**Figure 4.7**   SSH Secure Shell from SSH Communications.

and server, including password, public key, and host-based methods. A variety of encryption methods are available, such as Triple-DES (3DES) and Blowfish, plus public-key schemes such as DSA and Diffie-Hellman. It also provides tunneling. Secure FTP (SFTP) for Unix is also available.

# PGP

Phil Zimmerman's Pretty Good Privacy (PGP) incorporates a variety of cryptographic techniques to achieve quite good security for both email and files. PGP uses message digests and digital signatures as well as document encryption and key transport. A variety of standard algorithms are part of

PGP, such as MD5 and SHA-1 for message digests. It also uses ZIP technology for compressing data.

You can download the latest version of a free PGP distribution from MIT (http://web.mit.edu/network/pgp.html). You can also buy a distribution, but you should try it out first. You can get packages for both Windows and Unix, which have both graphical and command-line interfaces or a command-line-only interface. I'll demonstrate a few command-line examples.

After you have downloaded and installed the software, type at a command line:

```
pgp -kg
```

This will allow you to generate a key pair. A typical session follows. User responses are shown in bold:

```
Choose the public-key algorithm to use with your new key
1) DSS/DH (a.k.a. DSA/ElGamal) (default)
2) RSA
Choose 1 or 2: 1
Choose the type of key you want to generate
1) Generate a new signing key (default)
2) Generate an encryption key for an existing signing key
Choose 1 or 2: 1
Pick your DSS "master key" size:
1)  1024 bits- Maximum size (Recommended)
Choose 1 or enter desired number of bits: 1
Generating a 1024-bit DSS key.

You need a user ID for your public key.  The desired form for this user
ID is your name, followed by your E-mail address enclosed in <angle
brackets>, if you have an E-mail address.
For example:  John Q. Smith <jqsmith@nai.com>
Enter a user ID for your public key: Mike Fitzgerald <mike@wyeast.net>

Enter the validity period of your signing key in days from 0 - 10950
0 is forever (the default is 0): 0

You need a pass phrase to protect your DSS secret key.
Your pass phrase can be any sentence or phrase and may have many words,
spaces, punctuation, or any other printable characters.

Enter pass phrase:
Enter same pass phrase again:

PGP will generate a signing key. Do you also require an
encryption key? (Y/n) y
Pick your DH key size:
```

```
1)   1024 bits- High commercial grade, secure for many years
2)   2048 bits- "Military" grade, secure for foreseeable future
3)   3072 bits- Archival grade, slow, highest security
Choose 1, 2, 3, or enter desired number of bits: 1

Enter the validity period of your encryption key in days from 0 - 10950
0 is forever (the default is 0): 0

Note that key generation is a lengthy process.

PGP needs to generate some random data. This is done by measuring the
time intervals between your keystrokes. Please enter some random text on
your keyboard until the indicator reaches 100%.
Press ^D to cancel
100% of required data
Enough, thank you.
.*******  ..........................................*******  .
Make this the default signing key? (Y/n) y
.........*******  ...................................*******
Key generation completed.
```

As you can see, you are prompted to choose a number of options. The first option is the type of key, either DSS and Diffie-Hellmann (DH) or RSA. The default is DSS/DH because one of PGP's neat tricks is how it exchanges keys. DH is a key exchange system for symmetric keys—that is, a system that uses a single key to both encrypt and decrypt messages—but it uses DSS—an asymmetric key system—to encrypt the key with the message. Pretty clever.

Other options include choosing the bit strength for the keys, a user ID and password, and a validity period for the keys. PGP then uses random numbers, generated by your keystroke intervals (or mouse movement with the graphical interface) to set up the parameters for the key. Again, pretty clever.

PGP's security is so good that Phil Zimmerman got into a bit of trouble over it. It seems that the U.S. Attorney General and the FBI went after him for exporting technology that could help enemies of the United States transmit information that could not be deciphered, at least not within any of our lifetimes. The case was finally dropped in 1996, but it has remained a subtle endorsement for the power of PGP. U.S. export restrictions remain, however. If you live outside the United States, you can still get strong encryption, just not legally in coded form from a U.S. source. Well, you can get it from a book or scientific paper, just not in digital form. Nonetheless, if you live outside the United States, you can get PGP from international sources in digital form, circumventing American entanglements. America is an interesting place to live.

By default, your keys are stored locally in the file `secring.skr`. You can view the contents of this file with a command such as:

```
pgp -kvv mike@wyeast.net
```

Here you enter your own email address, as suggested by the prompt when you generated the key. The `-kvv` option indicates that you want to view the keys and signature on your key ring, as it's called. Your output will appear somewhat like this:

```
Looking for user ID "mike@wyeast.net".
Type bits    keyID         Date          User ID
DSS  1024    0xABA698A5    2000/12/16
 DH  1024    0xABA698A5    2000/12/16 *** DEFAULT SIGNING KEY ***
                           Mike Fitzgerald <mike@wyeast.net>
sig          0xABA698A5    Mike Fitzgerald <mike@wyeast.net>
1 matching key found.
```

To simply encrypt a copy of the file `order.xml`:

```
pgp -c order.xml
```

This command will encrypt a file and save it to `order.xml.pgp`. You could also encrypt the file as US-ASCII (what appears to be base64) by adding the `-a` switch.

```
pgp -ca order.xml
```

This would save the file as `order.xml.asc`, and the encrypted output would be:

```
-----BEGIN PGP MESSAGE-----
Version: PGP 6.5.8

pOIcDaCXti/zjxwJBqW5kOfXK9k1MQ9FB/Aap7RYQBhqio2fQY+fBMbC5uLsxvgzJbQBT67G
ssp/BL1GkYIS07bSFfA1gGM5dueyOi9HZNt60YjIrJ2qALvscdMZvLJwG4FBM72cc2tuYfTv
drWE7lnFfqQB7AFixDnUD0maEm2q94cJ5/6Q1F1klOKq4O1CqBse7N6Hx0PmjHn7sQm0eRLB
SAL3pQFHbnyrpBaoJmhrIgHJP94WkmFLcIKxUKmO6xpnd03KmJiK/nG6LJpQzdkLK2X4taRC
o4kRsmi8k6zNCJwo=vkRo
-----END PGP MESSAGE-----
```

Say that you are going to send a signed file to a known recipient, `schlomo@testb2b.org`. Schlomo has a key on my system (you won't have a key for Schlomo as this is just an illustration).

```
pgp -kvv schlomo@testb2b.org
```

On my system the key produces this result:

```
Looking for user ID "schlomo@testb2b.org".
Type bits      keyID       Date        User ID
DSS  1024      0x2E7F76E9  2000/12/07
 DH  1024      0x2E7F76E9  2000/12/07  schlomo@testb2b.org
sig            0x2E7F76E9              schlomo@testb2b.org
1 matching key found.
```

Provided that you have Schlomo's public key, you can encrypt the file with this public key and sign it with your private key. Now generate another key with `pgp -kg` and then use the new key's ID to issue the next command:

```
pgp -ea order.xml schlomo@testb2b.org
```

`schlomo@testb2b.org` is replaced by whatever ID you used in generating the key. The output for this command on my system tells the story of what happens next:

```
Recipients' public key(s) will be used to encrypt.

Key for user ID: schlomo@testb2b.org
1024-bit DSS key, Key ID 0x2E7F76E9, created 2000/12/07
Key can sign.

Ciphertext file: order.xml.asc

type order.xml.asc

-----BEGIN PGP MESSAGE-----
Version: PGP 6.5.8
qANQR1DBwE4DJ2Pj+pUSCPEQBACWKDHd6T+Xz2Q/y9CVb1UH9M5Cx2X4pgSVt9X1tzLObWX8
BS1TDbIEcNjKWH962zOfdP7MGsDr72DamzS2c33xSPfxyrtg4I11mNEVVG907f3zBIOkV2SC
DVwRIUzC3Dl7xt3hOnO8p1tscXAlCxxs6GKaAq5e2bvhxkqSuPH8uwP+MrpFUZiIrJD5ToeW
fRrMmxFUvFzqbzrcnINexShIbUrsEdLiIy5iLMhZcEh+PSBoRFVT/tyO2zbjUy3T+GNMHzIS
avRYC7Az5o5p4P81POSe0KosMoVHO2vZ1J3G9umJ+FztGF5I+EcLXvTjWN57AOU6r6DAm7pv
heSIe/cw6qfJwCPiQPJqQW/6FJNVutfsZK6ZkhHvpsJGH1ZiPQ/tuZQH4jJYVZRMM9JO6CP2
HPrrVUbLjBhIr6tojk1NC9xgr/OFzu32/SYp43MU2gc/M5LNJBPhyvKv9rxdTngHVKRHuwLI
oGFC3HgSXCNU0KpcGJnqQjNnifSvllUAUWyVvlhT01sO8uK8/zTG8tQNFgl+/JxpGZWmo/Iy
hZazIyzySF4QtXuO7K1ExUm5OAHWuzjY++wSChFQMH7qCXU8mZ5g7y7mUrCC/DlPdiS9QxnT
By7RfGfRL0E1uPBGZTmUu3xgtM+nkg===3PzC
-----END PGP MESSAGE-----
```

You can now transport this text file by HTTP, SMTP, FTP, whatever, and Schlomo (or whomever) can then decrypt it with his private key. He enters:

```
pgp order.xml.asc order.xml
```

`order.xml.asc` is the encrypted input file and `order.xml` will be the decrypted plain XML. (You could use a different file name than `order.xml`

to avoid a naming conflict when decrypting it in the same directory.)
Schlomo (or whomever) will be prompted to give his password for his private key:

```
File is encrypted. Secret key is required to read it.

Key for user ID: schlomo@testb2b.org
1024-bit DSS key, Key ID 0x2E7F76E9, created 2000/12/07
Key can sign.
You need a pass phrase to unlock your secret key.

Enter pass phrase: xxxxxxxx

Plaintext filename: order.xml
```

The decrypted, plain text file is proof that this file was signed by someone who used Schlomo's public key.

On the Windows platform, you could sign and transport the files in one shot with the following script, pgpcmds.bat:

```
pgp +batchmode -ea order.xml schlomo@testb2b.org
ftp -n -s:pgpcmds.txt testb2b.org
```

The addition of the +batchmode flag to the pgp command line turns off some interactive questions. This line encrypts order.xml with Schlomo's public key and writes the encrypted file in US-ASCII to the file order.xml.asc.

The ftp command turns off auto-login (-n) so that you can submit a user name and password in the script file (-s:pgpcmds.txt). After connecting to testb2b.org, the FTP commands in pgpcmds.txt are executed:

```
user b2buser
xxxxxxxx
ascii
cd web/B2B
lcd c:\pgp
put order.xml
put order.xml.asc
bye
```

The script logs in as b2buser and then submits a password. It sets the mode to ascii for good measure because it's about to transfer text files. It changes directories on the destination host to web/B2B, and it changes directories on the local host to c:\pgp. Then it puts the files order.xml and `order.xml.asc` on `testb2b.org` and closes the session with a polite `bye`.

After the PGP debacle in the mid-1990s, Phil Zimmerman founded PGP, Inc., which was later acquired by Network Associates, Inc. Network Associates now offers a PGP software development kit for implementing PGP in your software. Cryptix, an international organization, offers open-source PGP software tools and libraries, such as a Java implementation of OpenPGP. See the end notes for links to these tools.

## Secure Socket Layer (SSL)

If you look back at Figure 4.3, you will see a little padlock at the bottom right of the browser pictured. You can also see at the top of the window that transport protocol is `https` rather than `http`. The `https` protocol scheme and the padlock visually indicate that the browser is connected to the Web site through a Secure Socket Layer (SSL) connection. If your server has a digital certificate in place, using `https` activates SSL.

SSL (now at version 3) was first developed by Netscape and has evolved into a widely accepted standard. It uses certificates to authenticate servers and clients. The term *layered* comes from the fact that the technology uses a layer between the protocol HTTP—or FTP, SMTP, or Telnet, for that matter—and the TCP/IP layers.

Digital certificates authenticate the transactions conducted under SSL. SSL's handshake protocol helps the client and server to negotiate what algorithm they will use to encrypt data that they will send back and forth, plus it exchanges keys so that the transmitted data can be decrypted. Authentication is done with public or asymmetric keys, while secret or rather symmetric keys are used to encrypt for transmitted data.

Though SSL has a wide base of acceptance, it may be superceded by TLS.

## Transport Layer Security (TLS)

Like SSL, TLS provides privacy and security between communicating applications over the Internet. The key advantage of TLS over SSL is that it doesn't specify exactly how security is implemented, leaving decisions about how to authenticate with certificates and so forth up to application designers. TLS is based on SSL, but the two don't interoperate.

As mentioned earlier, Netscape invented SSL and now owns a patent on it. It offers its technology royalty-free, but the patent does present some problems when you would like to improve or extend the technology. IETF started developing TLS with several aims. One of its chief aims is to improve on performance by permitting session caching, thus reducing the number of fresh connections that are necessary and inciting less network activity. Another important goal is to make the standard extensible to allow for improved algorithms and key mechanisms.

Sun's Java Secure Socket Extension (JSSE) supports TLS as well as SSL. If you are developing a Java B2B application, you will no doubt want to be familiar with and probably implement the features available in JSSE (http://java.sun.com/products/jsse/).

SSH Communications has published a paper comparing TLS with IPSec. It's worth a look (see it at www.ssh.com/tech/techie/article11101999.html).

## The Firewall

Last but not least, no discussion of Internet security would be complete without a discussion—however brief—of firewalls. Firewalls are implemented on Web servers to help keep the riff-raff out, but if your riff-raff happens to be internal (inside the walls of your company or organization), firewalls may not be effective. Internal riff-raff, though, is a problem for almost any security system. Who can you trust, anyway?

You have many options with firewalls, and there is no such thing as a standard firewall. Firewalls are often a concoction of software and hardware that discourages and, we hope, foils would-be infiltrators. Probably the simplest firewall consists of a network router that performs packet filtering. Packet filtering denies access to any port under 1024 except those granted conventional access for relatively secure activities, such as HTTP (port 80), SMTP (port 25), or POP (port 110).

Another common method for creating a firewall is by placing a bulwark server between external and internal networks, with packet filtering on both sides. This takes a little longer to set up, costs a little more, and may reduce performance, but it is certainly more secure than packet filtering alone.

Proxy servers can force everything that is pushed or pulled across the network to pass between a straw-man server before touching the real server. Filtering can be performed on the proxy, and if things really go haywire, a proxy can "pull the plug," so to speak, before the real server is penetrated. Application gateways manage the activities of certain applications, such as FTP. Such gateways can crush suspicious or clandestine FTP activity before it ruins a system administrator's day.

Combinations of these schemes are surely possible, and no server dedicated to the exchange of B2B documents should go without the added security of a firewall, on top of data encryption and other measures. If you are setting up a firewall on a Linux or OpenBSD system, try *Building Linux and OpenBSD Firewalls* by Wes Sonnenreich and Tom Yates (John Wiley & Sons, 2000).

## A Plug for CERT

The Computer Emergency Response Team Coordination Center (CERT CC) (www.cert.org) is a great place to get the latest information on computer virus alerts, security risks, software vulnerabilities, or anything related to security attacks. CERT was first started by the Defense Advanced Research Projects Agency (DARPA) in 1988. CERT, which is managed by Carnegie Mellon University in Pittsburgh, Pennsylvania, also provides training for response teams and helps coordinates teams that must respond to large-scale incidents.

## Directory Services: From X.500 to UDDI

ITU-T X.500 is a standard for a directory service. An X.500 directory is something like a database system, but not quite, as it is expected to be queried more often than updated, and it is often used as a way to find and store resources across a network. Some of those resources are what is known as a distinguished name, a person, a printer, a fax number, an email address, an application, or most importantly in regard to this discussion, a digital certificate, as set out by X.509.

Directories can be distributed across a number of systems on a network as well as replicated to improve access. A typical X.500 hierarchical tree (distinguished name) is organized along the lines of locality, as shown in Figure 4.8. You also saw an example of a distinguished name when I discussed `keytool` earlier in this chapter.

The first item after the root is the country (c), next is the organization (o), then a common name (cn) and an email address (mail) associated with the common name.

As originally set down in the X.500 standard, accessing information in the directory is done through Directory Access Protocol (DAP) with communications handled through Open Systems Interconnection (OSI) networking. OSI is a full-fledged International Standards Organization (ISO)

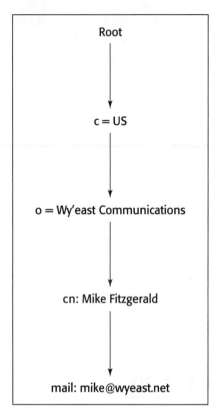

Root

c = US

o = Wy'east Communications

cn: Mike Fitzgerald

mail: mike@wyeast.net

**Figure 4.8** X.500 distinguished name.

standard networking protocol, which, although thoughtfully designed, has been passed over largely in favor of TCP/IP.

## LDAP

Because implementing DAP has a somewhat high cost of entry, some folks at the University of Michigan created the Lightweight Directory Access Protocol, or LDAP. LDAP servers do many of the same things as DAP, but through its use of TCP instead of OSI, LDAP avoids some session and presentation overhead. In addition, it encodes many data elements with ordinary, human-readable strings.

LDAP clients allow you to search, retrieve, and modify entries in the directory as well as other commands. The relationship between DAP and LDAP reminds me of the relationship between SGML and XML: The first is a heavy-duty, no-holds-barred solution, while the second trims down its predecessor to a more manageable interface and lightens a developer's load.

An LDAP server stores information in the form of a Lightweight Directory Interchange Format (LDIF) file, which has the following format. This is an example of only part of such a file.

```
dn: o=wyeast.net, c=us
o: Wyeast Communications
objectclass: organization
dn: cn=Mike Fitzgerald, o=wyeast.net, c=us
cn: Mike Fitzgerald
sn: Fitzgerald
mail: mike@wyeast.net
objectclass: person
```

It's not hard to see what is being expressed here. You haven't seen sn yet, but you probably already figured out that it stands for surname. Might all this be better expressed in XML? Try DSML on for size.

## DSML

Directory Services Markup Language (DSML) is an XML vocabulary for defining, reading, and writing LDAP content. DSML takes advantage of XML while also leaning on the strengths of LDAP, such as security and scalability.

Sun Microsystems is implementing DSML with its Java Naming and Directory Interface (JNDI) API (http://java.sun.com/products/jndi/index.html). This API provides Java applications with the ability to use directory services. You can use JNDI DAP and LDAP, plus other naming and directory services, such as DNS and Network Information Service (NIS), formerly Yellow Pages (YP).

A DSML document looks like this:

```
<?xml version="1.0" encoding="iso-8859-1" ?>
<!DOCTYPE dsml SYSTEM "dsml.dtd">

<dsml xmlns="http://www.dsml.org/DSML">
 <directory-entries>
  <entry dn="c=us,o=wyeast.net,ou=writing">
   <attr name="cn"><value>Mike Fitzgerald</value></attr>
   <attr name="mail"><value>mike@wyeast.net</value></attr>
   <attr name="cacertificate">
    <value encoding="base64">7aa45905ef93aadfb24506655a3d1fd
69f69d2042a825fff38de38eb4886407b75774bb3f063e07e716b5727af9
efb6d5d0213f8e06d6e66477817ce8e7be6c3
    </value>
  <entry>
 <directory-entries>
</dsml>
```

This little XML document represents the data you saw earlier descending from X.500 and LDAP. The root element `dsml` can contain either a schema for a directory (`directory-schema`, not shown) or directory entries (under `directory-entries`). The element entry has a CDATA attribute for containing the distinguished name (`dn`), including country (`c`), organization (`o`), and organizational unit (`ou`). The three instances of the child element `attr` each have a value, each labeled by a `name` attribute: common name (`cn`), email address (`mail`), and a public key from a CA certificate, given in `base64`.

DSML is a good start for an XML implementation of directory services, but whether it will be a dominant vocabulary remains to be seen. UDDI, on the other hand, is getting a lot of attention and is coming on strong.

## UDDI

Universal Description, Discovery, and Integration (UDDI) is a database-like framework for discovering or finding business partners and otherwise sharing information in a global, platform-independent registry. Big hitters like Intel, IBM, Microsoft, and Hewlett-Packard, and a deep bench of other industry names are all behind UDDI. It appears on the surface to be similar to X.500 and LDAP, but it goes beyond them with its nifty XML/SOAP-based APIs. Here is an example of a UDDI API message, embedded in a SOAP message, that has a method call. The HTTP method and headers are included in the example as well. (Sorry, `testb2b.org` is not really a UDDI operator site, so this example is for illustration only.)

```
POST /find_business HTTP/1.1
Host: www.testb2b.org
Content-Type: text/xml; charset="utf-8"
Content-Length: 419
SOAPAction: "http://www.testb2b.org/uddi-intent"

<?xml version="1.0" encoding="UTF-8" ?>

<Envelope xmlns="http://schemas.xmlsoap.org/soap/envelope/">
 <Body>
  <find_business generic="1.0" xmlns="urn:uddi-org:api">
   <name>Wy'east</name>
  </find_business>
 </Body>
</Envelope>
```

This example uses the HTTP POST method to submit a simple search to a UDDI operator site. An operator site is one that hosts traffic to and from a UDDI registry. The `find_business` element marshals a method call to the program /find_business on the host www.testb2b.org, submitting by name the partial search string *Wy'east* to the registry. A response message containing information about Wy'east Communications would be sent back in a form similar to the following:

```
HTTP/1.1 200 OK
Date: Fri, 01 Dec 2000 00:00:01 GMT
Server: Apache/1.3.12 (Unix) PHP/4.0.3RC1
Content-Length: 676
Content-Type: text/xml

<?xml version="1.0" encoding="UTF-8" ?>

<Envelope xmlns="http://schemas.xmlsoap.org/soap/envelope/">
 <Body>
  <businessList generic="1.0" operator="some-operator-id"
   truncated="true" xmlns="urn:uddi-org:api">
   <businessInfos>
    <businessInfo
      businessKey="28a9fe51-00e3-ed9d-4e9b-cefb19a7aa77">
     <name>Wy'east Communications</name>
     <description>Freelance writing with emphasis on XML
      technologies, including B2B.</description>
    </businessInfo>
   </businessInfos>
  </businessList>
 </Body>
</Envelope>
```

The response comes in a SOAP envelope, too, with some information tucked in a businessInfo element, including a name and description of the company, plus the UDDI key value associated with the business.

Unfortunately, UDDI does not appear to provide a data structure for storing and discovering public keys for businesses. Not yet, anyway.

The ebXML framework, discussed in the next chapter, has its own registry system integrated into it.

## On to Vocabularies and Protocols

This is the end of Part I, where I explored foundational technologies for a B2B system, such as XML, transport mechanisms, such as HTTP, and security schemes, such as PGP. In Part Two, I'll discuss vocabularies for defining XML documents or data and protocols for packaging them. The first we'll discuss is ebXML.

# Vocabularies, Frameworks, and Protocols

Part Two is dedicated to the XML vocabularies and protocols that you may use to create and package B2B documents. The OASIS-UN/CEFACT joint effort to create a global B2B standard, Electronic Business XML (ebXML), is discussed in Chapter 5. Chapter 6 reviews Commerce One's vocabulary XML Common Business Library or xCBL. Ariba's Commerce XML (cXML) is covered in Chapter 7. Chapter 8 examines Simple Object Access Protocol (SOAP), a messaging envelope for packaging documents. Chapter 9 investigates BizTalk, Microsoft's SOAP implementation and B2B engine.

Unfortunately, RosettaNet is not brought to light in these chapters because this book went into production just before version 2.0 of the RosettaNet Implementation Framework was to be released. Nevertheless, you can learn about RosettaNet on the book's companion Web site, www.wiley.com/compbooks/fitzgerald. Because things can change quickly, it's a good idea to regularly check the companion site for updates on all these rapidly evolving technologies.

I confess that I'm a believer in the open software movement. I look at it this way: If you throw a few hundred very smart people at one operating system or application, and you throw a few thousand very smart people at another operating system or application, which one is going to wind up more robust? OK, some could argue that a closed team can get more done, and granted, it takes a lot longer to consider the input and suggested changes of a vast hoard of engineers, but I'll keep rooting for open software projects. Linux is a good example of what can come of such an effort, and I have a strong hunch Electronic Business XML (ebXML) will be, too.

ebXML is a joint project of OASIS and UN/CEFACT. OASIS is the Organization for the Advancement of Structured Information Standards, a nonprofit, international standards body whose roots started with SGML and who is now host to a variety of XML-related standards work. OASIS invites all comers to participate in ebXML committee work. Corporations have to pay a healthy fee to join OASIS, but an individual can join for a relatively small fee.

UN/CEFACT is the United Nations Center for Trade Facilitation and Electronic Business, which helps states who are UN members participate in and develop recommendations or standards that encourage international trade, cooperation among businesses, and the growth of commerce. UN/ CEFACT works within the United Nations Economic Commission for Europe (UN/ECE), which reports to the Economic and Social Council of the United Nations (ECOSOC).

EbXML is intended to become an open framework or infrastructure, all based on XML, that will lay down global standards for business and communications. It won't be a single, monolithic model, but a series of standards whose main objective will be to remove barriers and make those standards readily available to not only the big players but also small and medium-sized businesses in both developed and developing nations.

Another concern of the ebXML folks is to not leave behind those who have considerable investments in EDI. I mentioned EDI in Chapter 1, "Getting Down to Business-to-Business." I won't be saying much about it in this book, only that the UN has had ties to EDI through its previous UN/EDIFACT standard efforts (United Nations Electronic Data Interchange for Administration, Commerce, and Transport). EDI is perceived by many to have a high barrier of entry, not unlike SGML. I think XML is to SGML what ebXML will be to EDI: a lowering or removing of barriers so that these standards are available to just about everyone. EbXML will not toss EDI aside, but it will build on its foundation.

I might sound a little idealistic about this, but imagine the economic impact of simple, readily accessible standards on the life and well-being of crafts people in Suriname, who, with the help of ebXML, could more effectively sell their products to a distributor in New York. I don't doubt that having a long reach is part of the reason why the UN is involved in international business standards. A good economy goes a long way to reduce the threat of poverty and war, and even the Internet can help solve those problems.

Personally, I think OASIS and UN/CEFACT have a really good thing going with ebXML. First, these bodies have high respect and are not directly tied to any one corporation, sector, or vendor, so their motivations are ostensibly more pure than those of parties who may be creating standards to draw business to themselves. Jon Bosak of Sun Microsystems, who is widely respected as the "Father of XML," has a role with the requirements team, and he is no doubt having a good influence. Under his leadership, XML became a W3C recommendation in about 20 months. His presence portends good things for ebXML.

The ebXML inaugural meeting was held in November 1999; early on the project was estimated to take about 18 months, reaching completion by May 2001. At the time of this writing, the estimated time of completion is March 2001, a couple of months ahead of schedule.

**NOTE** At the time of this writing, ebXML is not yet a well-established standard. Work is moving forward quickly with a variety of specifications under the ebXML umbrella, but nothing is chiseled in marble, and things tend to change quickly. It is not possible for me to present the entire standard in final form in a single chapter because the work on ebXML, which covers a lot of territory, is not complete. As updates become available, nonetheless, I will post them on this book's companion Web site at www.wiley.com/compbooks/fitzgerald.

## The ebXML Effort

The overall ebXML effort is divided into a number of specifications, each with its own committee. You can break the ebXML standards work down into the following areas:

**Requirements.** The general requirements of the ebXML standard is essentially a set of guidelines that describes what the standard will consist of, how it will be used, and how to create applications that comply with the standard. The *ebXML Requirements Specification* was published in May 2000.

**Technical architecture.** A fairly mature draft of the ebXML technical architecture document is already available. The architecture gives you the lay of the land—that is, how all the components of ebXML actually work together. This includes the use of existing standards, such as XML, URIs, HTTP, and so forth, as well as registries, repositories, and the like.

**Transport, routing, and packaging.** This part defines the ebXML message, which consists of a communication envelope, such as HTTP, a message envelope using MIME, then header and payload envelopes, also using MIME. ebXML's message envelope is similar to SOAP.

**Registry and repository.** An ebXML registry will provide a way to look up and discover trading partner profiles, business processes, and so forth. It will most likely be able to map to other popular registry formats. (You read about other registries in Chapter 4.)

**Business processes.** An ebXML team is dedicated to modeling business processes so that they can be represented in the form of exchangeable XML documents. The business processes (BP) and core components (CC) teams work together.

**Core components.** This part of the standard focuses on the basic components that can be used over and over again through the ebXML frame-

work. Some examples of these basic components include regional classifications, based on ISO 3166, and product and services classifications, based on United Nations Standard Product and Service Code
(UNSPSC).

**Trading or collaborative partner agreements.** IBM independently developed Trading Partner Agreement Markup Language (tpaML) and
submitted it to OASIS. EbXML later adopted IBM's work and will
incorporate it into the ebXML infrastructure. I won't be surprised
when other B2B developers fall in with the ebXML brigade. (I've
heard rumors, but I'm not saying anything yet.)

Besides those mentioned, several other committees are at work to
promote and develop ebXML, such as the marketing, quality, and proof-
of-concept (POC) committees. The POC committee is charged with demonstrating how all the ebXML parts fit together, and they do so on a regular
basis at conferences, for all eyes to see. I don't know about you, but that
impresses me. I think they are serious about what they are doing.

> **NOTE**    EbXML will include facilities for managing security, such as the ability
> to digitally sign a business document. Digital signatures are mentioned in
> several places, but as of this writing, based on the documents available at
> present, I am not certain how ebXML will handle encryption or security,
> whether in an ebXML-compliant application or as part of a business document.

## ebXML Architecture

Based on the Open-EDI Reference Model (ISO/IEC 14662), ebXML uses
two general views to describe or model its basic architecture: the Business
Operational View (BOV) and the Functional Service View (FSV).

The BOV deals with the semantics of business transactions, agreements
and the obligations that go along with them, and the conventions or architecture for conducting business transactions. The realm of the BOV in
ebXML includes the core component or basic properties and processes that
are incorporated into a business object or process.

On a lower level, a core component is described by a lexicon or dictionary in ebXML. An example of this is a component that identifies the countries and regions where parties do business, all based on ISO 3166. That
core component can be incorporated into a higher-level document, such as
one describing a business process like the issuance of a purchase order. All
together, the collection of business processes and objects are said to be
stored in a library.

Business Operational View

Functional Service View

**Figure 5.1**    ebXML's BOV and FSV.

The FSV covers things such as the protocols, interfaces, and functional capabilities of the services that support the BOV. An ebXML-compliant application, such as a browser that can fully handle ebXML content, is an example of an interface within the FSV. Other tools in the FSV box include XML, a tool to edit XML into an ebXML document, and a protocol such as HTTP to transport an ebXML document. Furthermore, a registry and repository, with the interfaces that access them, also fit into the FSV.

Figure 5.1 shows an interpretation of the relationship between BOV and FSV steps and process in ebXML.

## How ebXML Works

Let's walk through a scenario to see how ebXML works. I'll call your company Software Discounters, Inc., or SDI. You are in the business of reselling top software products in large quantities, with online-only distribution of executables, source, and documentation. You don't actually write software: You just resell it.

My new company, Millennia Megaware Corporation (MMC), has written a new software package that can retrieve, parse, and store B2B documents written in ebXML, RosettaNet, cXML, xCBL, SOAP, and whatever other new-fangled B2B vocabulary that comes along. The software, called B2B Trader, is selling quite well, and you'd like to get in on the rush. You are an ebXML user, but you don't know if I am. What's your first step?

## Registry and Repository

Because you are an ebXML user, you are also aware of some of the ebXML facilities that are available. The first place you go knocking is at an ebXML registry and repository (RR). On the surface, the RR is a Web site with links and a search engine, just like any old Web site, but it also offers ways to discover other companies that use ebXML and are potential trading partners. The RR site also offers ebXML specifications to help anyone write ebXML-compliant software and links to sites that sell shrink-wrapped ebXML software.

By contacting the registry client on the RR site, you are able to discover the names, addresses, phone and fax numbers, e-mail addresses, and so forth of all the registered companies that write and sell software. One of those ebXML-ready companies is MMC.

In addition to the basic information you are able to obtain from the RR, you are also able to obtain something called a Trading Partner Profile (TPP). MMC's TPP tells all about what ebXML processes it supports and what it does not support. With this data in your hands, you at SDI send a message to me at MMC, asking if I'd like to do business with you. With the potential of selling 10,000 more software licenses per month through SDI, the answer is yes, of course.

## Trading or Collaborative Partner Agreements

Through a series of exchanges we know what business processes the other supports, such as purchase orders, inventory inquiries, and so forth, so we know we will get along swimmingly. The next step is to execute a trading partner agreement (TPA)—or as it is now called, a collaborative partner agreement (CPA)—which is a legally binding set of documents, electronically executed, that spells out the ground rules for how we will do business. TPAs came to us originally from the world of EDI.

EbXML's TPA/CPA data structures come from IBM's tpaML, which ebXML has adopted. By data structures I simply mean the XML elements, attributes, and other structures that compose a TPA/CPA document. A TPA/CPA document articulates and exposes, in electronic form, the business processes and interactions of the agreeing parties.

I am not going to show you an entire TPA/CPA document (they are kind of long), but I will show a piece of one, just to give you an idea of what it contains. TPA is the root element (but this may change).

```
<TPA>
.  .  .
<Member IdCodeType="01" MemberId="86-757-8317">
 <PartyName Partyname="wyeast">
  Wy'east Communications
 </PartyName>
 <CompanyTelephone>503.555.9999</CompanyTelephone>
 <Address>
  <AddressType>location</AddressType>
  <AddressLine>Wy'east Communications</AddressLine>
  <AddressLine>P.O. Box 537</AddressLine>
  <City>West Linn</City>
  <State>OR</State>
  <Zip>97068-0537</Zip>
  <Country>USA</Country>
 </Address>
 <Contact Type="primary">
  <LastName>Fitzgerald</LastName>
  <FirstName>Michael</FirstName>
  <MiddleName>J.</MiddleName>
  <Title>VP, Outdoor Activities</Title>
  <ContactTelephone Type="primary">
   503.555.9999
  </ContactTelephone>
  <ContactTelephone Type="secondary">
   503.555.9997
  </ContactTelephone>
  <EMail Type="primary">mike@wyeast.net</EMail>
  <Fax>503.555.9998</Fax>
 </Contact>
</Member>
.  .  .
</TPA>
```

This gives you only a hint of the information that is exchanged in a TPA/CPA. Other information that can be included in a TPA/CPA is the protocol used for transactions, role definitions (such as buyer/seller), arbitrators, and lifetime or duration, to name a handful.

Now we are all set up. We have accepted a TPA/CPA, and we know what business processes the other supports and have found them compatible. It is time to do business.

## Click and Mortar

Your company, SDI, is a click-and-mortar operation and distributes bytes only—products in the form of binaries, source code, and documentation, all transported over the Internet alone, with no CD-ROM, DVD, or printed products. You don't have the headache of physical inventory and fulfill-ment. You simply make copies of the products you sell and license the copies at a stupendous discount. It's the wave of the future. Catch it and hang 10 as soon as you can.

Because of the way you do business, I am not going to be sending you shrink-wrapped boxes complete with CD-ROM, perfect-bound manual, and coupons for 1000 free hours with a certain national Internet service provider that shall remain unnamed. No, our transactions will consist of MMC authorizing SDI to sell a quantity of licenses, including such things as payment methods and amounts.

Those transactions will take place by means of ebXML messages, sent back and forth between the companies. The ebXML messaging specifica-tion is not yet complete but is nearly operational. In the following section of the chapter, I will discuss ebXML messages and how they work.

## The ebXML Message

An ebXML message is an envelope within an envelope within an envelope, as shown in Figure 5.2. The ebXML message envelope, by the way, has a remarkable resemblance to SOAP, which will be discussed in Chapter 8, "Simple Object Access Protocol."

The first envelope, or the outer shell, is the transport or communication protocol envelope. This layer consists of the protocol such as HTTP, SMTP, FTP, or whatever else you can dig up to move files or data streams. The transport layer is handled by software outside of the strict ebXML defini-tion, and you won't see it represented here.

As customary, let's look at a simple example before we go any further. The first part of an actual ebXML message is a MIME header.

```
Content-Type: multipart/related;
type="application/vnd.eb+xml";
version="0.8";
boundary="ebXML_boundary"
Content-Length: xxx

--ebXML_boundary
Content-ID: 2343.6733@sdi-b2b.com
Content-Length: xxx
Content-Type: application/vnd.eb+xml;
version="0.8"; charset="utf-8"

<?xml version="1.0" encoding="utf-8"?>
<!DOCTYPE ebXMLHeader SYSTEM "level1-10122000.dtd">
<ebXMLHeader
```

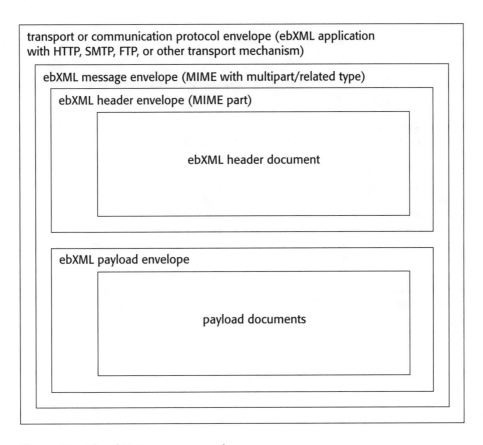

**Figure 5.2**   The ebXML message envelope.

```
xmlns= "http://www.ebxml.org/namespaces/messageHeader"
Version="1.0"
MessageType="Normal">
<Manifest>
 <DocumentReference>
  <DocumentLabel>ItemCreate</DocumentLabel>
  <DocumentId><CID:2343.6733@sdi-b2b.com></DocumentId>
  <DocumentDescription>Creates an item.</DocumentDescription>
 </DocumentReference>
</Manifest>
<Header>
 <From>
  <PartyId context="DUNS">068532535</PartyId>
 </From>
 <To>
  <PartyId context="DUNS">867578317</PartyId>
 </To>
 <TPAInfo>
  <TPAId context="tpadb">
   /068532535/867578317/ItemCreate
```

```
   </TPAId>
   <ConversationId context="ItemCreate">
    2343.6733.5@sdi-b2b.com
   </ConversationId>
   <ServiceInterface>ItemAlignmentBuyer</ServiceInterface>
   <Action>receiveItemCreate</Action>
  </TPAInfo>
  <MessageData>
   <MessageId>2343.6733@sdi-b2b.com</MessageId>
   <TimeStamp>2001-01-01T00:00:43.593Z</TimeStamp>
  </MessageData>
  <ReliableMessagingInfo DeliverySemantics="OnceAndOnceOnly"/>
 </Header>
 <RoutingHeader>
  <SenderURI>http://sdi-b2b.com/servlet/service</SenderURI>
  <ReceiverURI>http://mmc-b2b.com/servlet/service</ReceiverURI>
  <ErrorURI>http://sdi-b2b.com/servlet/errors</ErrorURI>
  <Timestamp>2001-01-01T00:00:43.593Z</Timestamp>
  <SequenceNumber>1</SequenceNumber>
 </RoutingHeader>
</ebXMLHeader>

--ebXML_boundary--
```

I'll briefly explain what each part of the message means.

## The MIME multipart/related Type

Next you have the ebXML message envelope that consists of a MIME `multipart/related` composite type. EbXML recommends the use of `multipart/related` as the `Content-Type` (MIME type) over `multipart/mixed` or `multipart/form-data` because `multipart/related` is more generic. A compliant header must also contain a `type` of `application/vnd.eb+xml`. This is based on RFC 2376.

The `version` parameter identifies the version for the ebXML envelope header, which, at this writing, is 0.8. Nevertheless, you can expect this version number to change. The `version` parameter is optional here, but you must use it in any following MIME headers, as you will see.

The MIME boundary is set to `ebXML_boundary`, only as an example. The boundary string or value must not match any value that has the slightest chance of appearing in the message as something other than a boundary. The boundary, therefore, must be unique and probably more creative than what I have offered here.

The meaning of `Content-Length` is fairly obvious. What you might not know is that the length is calculated from the first octet after the CR/LF following the first MIME header and ending with the octet right before the last boundary, which is the one that ends with a pair of hyphens (--ebXML_boundary--).

# The ebXML Header Envelope

After the initial MIME header comes the header for the ebXML header envelope. This envelope holds header information in an XML document. It begins with a boundary marker. A boundary marker always begins with a pair of hyphens (--ebXML_boundary). Following that is a Content-ID MIME header. This defines a unique ID for this part of the message. This is then followed by the Content-Length and the Content-Type.

You recognize the media type application/vnd.eb+xml and the version parameter. The version parameter must be used in all but the first MIME header. A charset parameter of utf-8 is recommended for compatibility. UTF-8 is not mandated for ebXML, but it is currently the most commonly used encoding in ebXML. The XML declaration states that the encoding is utf-8 as well. The document type declaration points to an early DTD. The final name for the DTD will probably be something different.

### The ebXMLHeader Element

This element has three attributes. The namespace attribute declares the namespace for this element, with http://www.ebxml.org/namespace/messageHeader required. Without a prefix, this becomes the default namespace. This value is fixed in the DTD.

The Version attribute tracks the current version of the messaging specification. The Version is also fixed as the default in the DTD. The MessageType attribute can be one of Normal, Error, or Acknowledgment. This value indicates what kind of message this is. You've got three choices. You will see an acknowledgment message in the example. The ebXML messaging specification provides facilities for error reporting (see section 7.13).

### The Manifest Element

Every instance of ebXMLHeader must contain an instance of Manifest. This element may contain a list of references to other parts of the message, such as in the payload portion of the message. This element can contain zero or more occurrences of DocumentReference.

DocumentReference makes it easier to extract a document that is part of the message or is associated with it. It has three children. DocumentLabel and DocumentID are required; DocumentDescription, the third, is not required.

A DocumentLabel is a bit of text that allows a human reader or software reading the file to determine what the document is without dereferencing it. DocumentId provides a URL to the Content-ID of a MIME body part. It can point to a part, later in the message, that holds payload data, or it can point to a remote URL that is an external resource. The optional DocumentDescription element provides additional textual information about the document or resource referenced. If present, it must use an xml:lang attribute to specify the language of the description (such as en-US for United States English).

### Header and Its Children

Header must contain one instance each of From, To, TPAInfo, Message-Data, and ReliableMessagingInfo. From and To each contain a single instance of PartyID. The context attribute of PartyID identifies what kind of ID it is, such as a DUNS number or a URI.

TPAInfo provides information relating to the trading partner agreement or collaborative partner agreement (TPA/CPA) under whose auspices this document is sent. It has four of its own children, all required. With a URI TPAId identifies the TPA/CPA associated with the message. The context attribute notes the context within which the content has meaning, that is, tpadb, ostensibly a database of TPA/CPA information. The content is the DUNS number for the requester (068532535), the DUNS number for the receiver (867578317), and the document label or type of transaction.

Likewise, ConversationID identifies a conversation, a group of messages related to this message or transaction, conducted between two parties. The context is the document label or the type of transaction.

The ServiceInterface element identifies a service interface that may process the message's payload, that is, ItemAlignmentBuyer. Finally, Action identifies a particular process within the service interface. The current specification admits that it does not address service interfaces at this writing, so it is unwise to wander too far away from camp in order to explain it. You can guess that it might have something to do with a proposed function or feature of the processing software.

### What's in a Message?

The MessageData element is also required. It holds identifying information about the message at hand. It must come right after TPAInfo, and it has three children. The first two, MessageID and TimeStamp, are required, but RefToMessageID is not always required, but is required under certain circumstances.

MessageID holds a unique identifier using the Content-ID (CID: or MID:) type of URL. This is based on RFC 2392. TimeStamp is an ISO 8601-style date and time using Coordinated Universal Time (UTC), also called Greenwich Mean Time (GMT), without an offset. RefToMessageID is a reference to a previous MessageID. It is optional in a Normal message, which the example is. In the case of an Acknowledgment or Error message, it must reference the MessageID of the message being acknowledged or in error, whichever is the case.

### *Message Reliability*

The empty element ReliableMessagingInfo has two possible values for its attribute DeliverySemantics. BestEffort means that reliable delivery is not specified. This means that a sending service—a program that sends messages using a transport mechanism of some sort—will not be notified in case a message fails to be delivered, and so forth. The other value, OnceAndOnlyOnce, means that a failure message will be sent if warranted, among other specific behaviors.

The OnceAndOnlyOnce attribute value indicates that reliable messaging is in force. This means that two message services will engage in reliable messaging semantics. So what does that mean? It means that the sending and receiving messaging services (programs that manage messages) must behave in a reliable way.

This is how it will go. First, the sender tucks away a copy of the message it is about to send out in what is called *persistent storage*. The message is then sent with both a MessageID and a SequenceNumber (see the upcoming section *Reliability and the SequenceNumber Element*). The receiving site stores the one copy of the message in its own persistent storage, and it sends an acknowledgment back to the sender, even for duplicate messages. The sender may then discard the confirmed message from its persistent storage, if the sender so chooses.

Also built into the service program should be several parameters. Timeout indicates how long the sender will wait for an acknowledgment before assuming the message failed. Retries and RetryInterval set how many times the service will resend a message and how long it will wait to resend a message. Upon failure, the sending service will perform a lost message recovery sequence (see section 7.12 of the specification).

### *RoutingHeader*

At the end of the message, a single instance of RoutingHeader comes directly after the Header element. RoutingHeader must contain one each of the following elements in order: SenderURI, ReceiverURI, ErrorURI, and Timestamp. Zero or one of the optional SequenceNumber element may also be used.

SenderURI is the URI for the sender's messaging service handler, while ReceiverURI is the URI for the receiver's messaging service handler. ErrorURI is the sender's designated URI for error reporting. Timestamp is the date and time of when the RoutingHeader was created, in 8601 format. (By the way, the URIs in the example are well formed but are all bogus. You won't be able to get them to do anything.)

### *Reliability and the SequenceNumber Element*

If ReliableMessagingInfo's attribute DeliverySemantics is set to OnceAndOnlyOnce, you must use SequenceNumber. This element is simply a sequential integer value that is incremented by 1 in the range 1 through 999,999,999. This sequence is yet another way to keep track of how many messages were sent.

## Handling Errors

The messaging system must also be equipped to generate and send errors if any are detected. The following code is a valid fragment of a message showing the ErrorHeader element. An explanation follows that.

```
<ebXMLError>
 <ErrorHeader>
  <ErrorCode>UnableToParse</ErrorCode>
  <Severity>Error</Severity>
  <Description xml:lang="en-US">
   Parsing error in namespace URI
  </Description>
  <SoftwareDetails>ErrWare v0.4; build 253</SoftwareDetails>
 </ErrorHeader>
 <ErrorLocation>
  <RefToMessageId>2343.6733@sdi-b2b.com</RefToMessageId>
  <Href>http://mmc-b2b.com/B2B/2001-01-01-2343.6733.xml</Href>
 </ErrorLocation>
</ebXMLError>
```

The element ebXMLError is the root. It must contain exactly one ErrorHeader and only zero or more of ErrorLocation. ErrorHeader contains one each of ErrorCode and Severity. Some valid values for ErrorCode are UnableToParse, ValueNotRecognized, NotSupported, and Inconsistent. The two valid values for Severity are Warning or Error.

The optional Description contains a bit of human-readable explanation for the error, and SoftwareDetails reports a few facts about the software that generated the error.

ErrorLocation passes on the ID for the message in RefToMessageID plus the location (Href) of the message in error (fictitious in this example).

For more details on handling messages, see section 7.13 of the messaging specification.

## An Acknowledgment Message

After successfully sending a message containing ItemCreate, the receiving service—the ebXML-aware server—will send back a receipt or acknowledgment that will look like this (sans the MIME headers):

```
<?xml version="1.0" ?>
<!DOCTYPE ebXMLHeader SYSTEM "level1-10122000.dtd">
<ebXMLHeader xmlns=
 "http://www.ebxml.org/namespaces/messageHeader"
  Version="1.0"
  MessageType="Normal">
 <Manifest>
  <DocumentReference>
    <DocumentLabel>
     ItemCreateAck
    </DocumentLabel>
    <DocumentId>
     <CID:2343.6733@sdi-b2b.com>
    </DocumentId>
  </DocumentReference>
 </Manifest>
 <Header>
  <From>
   <PartyId context="DUNS">867578317</PartyId>
  </From>
  <To>
   <PartyId context="DUNS">068532535</PartyId>
  </To>
```

```
<TPAInfo>
 <TPAId context="tpadb">
  /867578317/068532535/ItemCreateAck
 </TPAId>
 <ConversationId context="ItemCreateAck">
  2343.6733.5@sdi-b2b.com
 </ConversationId>
 <ServiceInterface>ItemAlignmentSupplier</ServiceInterface>
 <Action>receiveItemCreateAck</Action>
</TPAInfo>
<MessageData>
 <MessageId>2343.6733@sdi-b2b.com</MessageId>
 <TimeStamp>2001-01-01T00:00:43.593Z</TimeStamp>
</MessageData>
<ReliableMessagingInfo DeliverySemantics="OnceAndOnceOnly"/>
</Header>
<RoutingHeader>
 <SenderURI>http://sdi-b2b.com/servlet/service</SenderURI>
 <ReceiverURI>http://mmc-b2b.com/servlet/service</ReceiverURI>
 <ErrorURI>http://sdi-b2b.com/servlet/errors</ErrorURI>
 <Timestamp>2001-01-01T00:00:43.593Z</Timestamp>
 <SequenceNumber>2</SequenceNumber>
</RoutingHeader>
</ebXMLHeader>
```

This won't always be the case, but if this acknowledgment looks similar to the message sent in the last example, then you are pretty observant. I'll note a few differences.

The service interface is an example. It was `ItemAlignmentBuyer` but now is `ItemAlignmentSupplier`. The `ConversationID` context is now `ItemCreateAck`, *not* `ItemCreate`.

## Patient Confidence

In this chapter, I have attempted to give the airline pilot's view of ebXML. In a few months, about the time this book is on the shelves, ebXML will be much further along than it is now, so I recommend that you take a look at the book's companion Web site for updates (www.wiley.com/compbooks/fitzgerald).

In spite of its current state, I still have a lot of confidence in the ebXML project, if only because OASIS and UN/CEFACT are managing it. I don't always get it right, but I think I've spotted a trend. One of the main reasons I am so confident about ebXML is that I believe it is the best positioned of the B2B collections, the best positioned to reach the far corners of the world, and because of its openness, the best positioned to overcome technical obstacles and win the support of the everyday engineer who has to make this B2B work happen.

If in six months to a year, if ebXML doesn't unfold as I predict, you are welcome to walk up to me at an XML conference and say, "I told you so!" I don't think you will be able to, though.

# CHAPTER 6

Commerce One's XML vocabulary for B2B information exchange is called the XML Common Business Library, or xCBL. This collection, now at version 3.0, makes up one of the largest libraries of XML components for B2B documents available. Many coded values from the EDI world (EDIFACT and X12) are represented by XML in xCBL. This is a convenience to those who are already up to their ear lobes in EDI and want to find a way to integrate EDI with an XML solution.

You can validate documents from the xCBL library against DTDs or with schema written in Schema for Object-oriented XML (SOX) or in XML Data Reduced (XDR). SOX is Commerce One's schema language, while XDR comes to us primarily from Microsoft, with a little help from others. SOX and XDR are offered freely as a solution to the limitations of DTDs. When you have an aching need, such as the need to validate XML documents precisely, why not solve it yourself, especially when an official solution from W3C may take several years to reach recommendation status?

So what is Commerce One's motive here? It has generously offered xCBL to the world for free, in part as a fulfillment of its vision for a world of ecommerce built on universal building blocks. Where better to start than XML? But xCBL also makes it easy for folks to use and integrate with Commerce One's software offerings, such as MarketSet. I can't imagine any corporation would give away its property unless it accrued some business benefit from so doing, but I can't be the judge. It's kind of Commerce One to provide xCBL, no matter the motive. I'll simply say thanks and refrain from impugning the company.

Even if you are not going to purchase or use Commerce One products, xCBL gives you a wide range of choices for defining business documents in XML, including some choices that other vocabularies don't offer you, such as auctions and schedule planning. Also, xCBL is a good choice based on its ties to EDI, if that matters to you. For that that matter, it is also supported by Microsoft's BizTalk.

One other thing of interest to note is that xCBL uses relatively few attributes compared to the number of elements. I believe this is strictly a matter of preference. In other words, some developers would prefer to use child elements to further distinguish a parent element. Others will just add an attribute to an element to help distinguish that element. The advantages or disadvantages of an element-intense solution, such as this:

```
<Date>
 <Day>01</Day>
 <Month>January</Month>
 <Year>2001</Year>
</Date>
```

over an attribute-intense solution, such as this:

```
<Date Day="01" Month="January" Year="2001" />
```

could take hours, even days, to debate, if you like to debate. I'll leave the debate to those of a squabbling ilk and just move right on ahead.

> **NOTE**   As usual, I have to offer a little disclaimer here. You will get a general overview of xCBL in this chapter, but not a comprehensive treatment. I will not, in other words, laboriously rehash all the document types and elements offered by xCBL. I'll let the official xCBL documentation do that. I hope, though, that by the end of the chapter, you have a general but clear idea of what xCBL is and what it can do.

## Namespaces and xCBL

Strangely, xCBL does not implement XML namespaces as you would normally expect, that is, as outlined in the "Namespaces in XML" specification that appeared early in 1999. I think this is because Commerce One was ahead in the XML game and implemented its own namespace strategy. As you will see in the SOX example that follows, an xCBL namespace is declared in the `uri` attribute of a `schema` element, the root of a SOX schema document. The URI in this attribute is for an appropriate DTD.

Frankly, I am a little surprised that xCBL did not fall in line with the W3C namespace recommendation when it came out with its latest release (v3.0) just as this book was going into production. But then again, maybe I shouldn't be surprised. The semantics of XML namespaces, as they stand in the 1.0 version of the spec, are shrouded with controversy and the subject of numerous debates on the XML-DEV mail list.

Essentially, the debate is over whether a URL namespace identifier, such as `http://www.w3.org/1999/XSL/Transform`, should be considered merely a uniquely identifying string or whether, as its traditional semantics suggest, it should dereference or link to an actual resource, such as a schema, that actually defines the elements, attributes, and so forth that inhabit the namespace.

Enough on namespaces. Now back to our regularly scheduled xCBL programming.

## A Few Words about SOX

In Chapter 2, "The XML Foundation," you learned about the differences between DTDs and XML Schema documents. It's appropriate for this chapter to introduce a few things about SOX, Commerce One's proprietary schema language. To start off, I'll hark back to the DTD way of doing things and create a simple content model:

```
<!ELEMENT Invoice (InvoiceHeader, InvoiceDetail, InvoiceSummary?)>
```

You might recall all this, but just for drill, I'll explain what is going on here. This DTD declaration is for the element `Invoice`. `Invoice` has the following content model: In the order shown, `Invoice` shall contain a single instance of the element `InvoiceHeader`, followed immediately by a single instance of `InvoiceDetail`, followed by zero or one instance of `InvoiceSummary`. The zero or one instance business is determined by the occurrence operator `?`. The absence of an occurrence operator means that the element shall appear once and only once. A + means one or more occurrences, and a * means zero or more.

Here is what the SOX schema document that defines `Invoice` and its children, plus a few other nice things, looks like.

```
<?xml version="1.0"?>
<!DOCTYPE schema SYSTEM "urn:x-
commerceone:document:com:commerceone:xdk:xml:schema.dtd$1.0">

<schema uri="urn:x-
commerceone:document:com:commerceone:XCBL30:XCBL30.sox$1.0">
```

```
<intro>
 <h1>Invoice</h1>
 <p>Copyright Notice</p>
 <p>XML Common Business Library 3.0</p>
 <p>Copyright 2000 Commerce One, Inc.</p>
 <p>Permission is granted to use, copy, modify and distribute
     the DTD's, schemas and modules in the Commerce One XML
     Common Business Library Version 3.0 subject to the terms
     and conditions specified at
<tt>http://www.commerceone.com/xml/cbl/docs/copyright.html</tt>
 </p>
 </intro>

<elementtype name="Invoice" >
 <model>
  <sequence>
   <element type="InvoiceHeader" />
   <element type="InvoiceDetail" />
   <element type="InvoiceSummary" occurs="?" />
  </sequence>
 </model>
</elementtype>

</schema>
```

The schema element is the root element of the SOX document, just as it is for XML Schema. This element declares a namespace using a uri rather than an xmlns attribute. The namespace is a canonical URN defined by Commerce One. The intro element that follows schema provides a place to include HTML tags for documentation purposes or, as is the case here, copyright information.

The SOX elementType element defines element types or structures for XML documents. The model element sets off the content model, with sequence indicating the sequence in which the elements that follow will occur, that is, InvoiceHeader first, InvoiceDetail next, followed by InvoiceSummary. Each element declaration in the sequence is declared to have a named type, which ostensibly is defined elsewhere.

The occurs attribute associated with InvoiceSummary has a value of ?, which means, as you remember, zero or one occurrence of the element is allowed.

If you defined the same elements in XML Schema, the following schema document would represent a fair translation.

```
<?xml version="1.0"?>

<schema xmlns="http://www.w3.org/2000/08/XMLSchema">
```

```
<annotation>
 <documentation>
  Invoice. Copyright Notice. XML Common Business Library 3.0.
  Copyright 2000 Commerce One, Inc. Permission is granted to
  use, copy, modify, and distribute the DTDs, schemas, and
  modules in the Commerce One XML Common Business Library
  Version 3.0 subject to the terms and conditions specified at
  http://www.commerceone.com/xml/cbl/docs/copyright.html
 </documentation>
</annotation>

<complexType name="Invoice" >
 <sequence>
  <element ref="InvoiceHeader" />
  <element ref="InvoiceDetail" />
  <element ref="InvoiceSummary" minOccurs="0" maxOccurs="1" />
 </sequence>
</complexType>


 .  .  .


</schema>
```

Rather than being enclosed in an `intro` element, the copyright information is held in a `documentation` element, which is a child of `annotation`. The `elementType` element now becomes `complexType`. Say good-bye to the `model` element because it is gone, but `sequence` remains. The `ref` attribute refers to element declarations elsewhere (not shown). The SOX `occurs` attribute, and its values of ? or * or +, has been replaced with a pair of attributes, `minOccurs` and `maxOccurs`, which have numerical values. By default, `minOccurs` and `maxOccurs` both have a value of 1 and are assumed, so they are not shown.

## The XML Development Kit

Along with xCBL, Commerce One also offers you its XML Development Kit (XDK), free for the taking. It has a command-line parser `cxp` that can validate documents based on both SOX and DTDs. It also has an XSLT engine, `cxsl`, for transforming documents. These are actually batch files for use in Windows, so you might have a little retooling to do if you are working solely on a Unix platform.

The XDK is written in Java and is based on James Clark's `xp` and `xt`. The XDK also supports SAX (Simple API for XML), a Java interface for event-based XML parsing and a de facto standard for XML processing. SAX was developed by David Megginson along with members of the XML-DEV mail list community. SAX was discussed near the end of Chapter 2, in the section titled *Document Object Model (DOM) and Simple API for XML (SAX)*.

# xCBL Documents

The xCBL vocabulary makes it possible for you to author a number of XML documents suitable to a particular need, especially for day-to-day B2B use. A general list of the kinds of xCBL documents and features available includes the following:

- Catalogs
- Order management
- Invoicing
- Payment
- Shipping management
- Planning
- Security
- Statistics
- Forecasting
- Trading partner information
- Auction
- Request for quote
- Price, availability, and order checks
- Changes to previous documents
- Message acknowledgment

I'll choose a few documents from among this rather long list and explain them fully. First, I'll discuss a simple order, then an invoice; finally, for something a little different, I'll go through an auction example.

**NOTE** With so many elements in xCBL, it won't do for me to fully explain each one, not even all the ones in the examples. If you download the software package from www.xcbl.org, you will get good HTML reference documentation along with it. That's the best place to discover the purposes, meanings, and nuances for each xCBL element.

# A Simple Order

What could be more basic to business than a purchase order? Here is one scenario that shows how a purchase order could flow based on the xCBL vocabulary:

1. A buyer makes a purchase inquiry.

2. The supplier responds by issuing an `OrderRequest`.

3. Once this `OrderRequest` is approved or accepted through a requisitioner, an `Order` is placed by the buyer and sent to the seller. (The `OrderRequest` step is not mandatory for placing an order.)

4. When a seller receives and processes the order, the seller sends back an `OrderResponse` message. (While an `OrderResponse` is good practice, it too is not mandatory.)

5. If a buyer desires to make a change to an order, the buyer can send a `ChangeOrder` document to the seller that references a previous order. (This step also is not mandatory.)

Following is a simple purchase order document written with xCBL elements. After showing you the example, I'll step through the document and discuss its points of interest.

**NOTE** Only the `Order` document is used in this example. Steps that are not mandatory—`OrderRequest`, `OrderResponse`, and `ChangeOrder`—are not shown. (The documentation that comes with xCBL provides sample documents demonstrating each of these elements. Where each element is documented you will find a link to a sample document that uses the element.)

```
<?xml version="1.0"?>
<!DOCTYPE Order SYSTEM "XCBL30.dtd">

<Order>
 <OrderHeader>
  <OrderNumber>
   <BuyerOrderNumber>PO-2001-00001</BuyerOrderNumber>
   <SellerOrderNumber>i000001-2001-01-01</SellerOrderNumber>
   <ListOfMessageID>
    <MessageID>
     <IDNumber>9-9984-8333-7234</IDNumber>
     <IDAssignedBy>
      <IDAssignedByCoded>
       AccountsPayableOfficer
      </IDAssignedByCoded>
     </IDAssignedBy>
```

```xml
    </MessageID>
   </ListOfMessageID>
 </OrderNumber>
 <OrderIssueDate>20001230T09:30:00</OrderIssueDate>
 <Purpose>
  <PurposeCoded>Original</PurposeCoded>
 </Purpose>
 <OrderCurrency>
  <Currency>
   <CurrencyCoded>USD</CurrencyCoded>
  </Currency>
 </OrderCurrency>
 <OrderLanguage>
  <Language>
   <LanguageCoded>en</LanguageCoded>
  </Language>
 </OrderLanguage>
 <OrderParty>
  <BuyerParty>
   <Party>
    <PartyID>
     <Identifier>
      <Agency>
       <AgencyCoded>Other</AgencyCoded>
       <AgencyCodedOther>
        Wy'east Communications
       </AgencyCodedOther>
      </Agency>
      <Ident>US-WST-OR-326</Ident>
     </Identifier>
    </PartyID>
    <NameAddress>
     <Name1>Wy'east Communications</Name1>
     <POBox>P.O. Box 537</POBox>
     <PostalCode>97068-0537</PostalCode>
     <City>West Linn</City>
     <Region>
      <RegionCoded>USOR</RegionCoded>
     </Region>
     <Timezone>
      <TimezoneCoded>-08.00</TimezoneCoded>
     </Timezone>
    </NameAddress>
   </Party>
  </BuyerParty>
  <SellerParty>
   <Party>
    <PartyID>
     <Identifier>
```

```
      <Agency>
       <AgencyCoded>Other</AgencyCoded>
       <AgencyCodedOther>TestB2B.org</AgencyCodedOther>
       <CodeListIdentifierCoded>
        AssignedBySender
       </CodeListIdentifierCoded>
      </Agency>
      <Ident>US-WST-OR-327</Ident>
     </Identifier>
    </PartyID>
   </Party>
  </SellerParty>
 </OrderParty>
</OrderHeader>
<OrderDetail>
 <ListOfItemDetail>
  <ItemDetail>
   <BaseItemDetail>
    <LineItemNum>
     <BuyerLineItemNum>1023</BuyerLineItemNum>
     <SellerLineItemNum>653</SellerLineItemNum>
    </LineItemNum>
   </BaseItemDetail>
  </ItemDetail>
 </ListOfItemDetail>
</OrderDetail>
<OrderSummary>
 <NumberOfLines>2</NumberOfLines>
 <TotalTax>
  <MonetaryAmount>0.00</MonetaryAmount>
  <Currency>
   <CurrencyCoded>USD</CurrencyCoded>
  </Currency>
 </TotalTax>
 <TotalAmount>
  <MonetaryAmount>24.99</MonetaryAmount>
  <Currency>
   <CurrencyCoded>USD</CurrencyCoded>
  </Currency>
 </TotalAmount>
 <SummaryNote>No sales tax in Oregon!</SummaryNote>
</OrderSummary>
</Order>
```

There you have it. Let's go over some of the finer points of the xCBL purchase order.

## Purchase Order IDs

Order is the root element. It has three immediate children, OrderHeader, OrderDetail, and OrderSummary. BuyerOrderNumber is a unique identification number, of the buyer's choosing, that identifies this particular purchase order. The same goes for SellerOrderNumber, only this unique ID comes from the seller. Both are children of OrderNumber.

IDNumber, a child of MessageID, is a unique, user-assigned ID for the message itself. This ID was purportedly assigned by the Accounts-PayableOfficer. This is just one possibility for the content of IDAssignedByCoded. Many other possible values are available, all based on EDIFACT (3035) and X12 (98) party identifier codes.

OrderIssueDate provides a date and time for the issuance of the order, based on the ISO 8601 standard.

The PurposeCode element indicates the purpose or function of the order document. It can contain one of the following codes as content: Other, Cancellation, Replace, Confirmation, Duplicate, Original, Change, or InformationOnly. This list of codes comes from EDIFACT (1225) and X12 (353). If the value of the content is Other, you must explain yourself by adding the PurposeCodedOther element (child of Purpose, as is PurposeCode). The content of PurposeCodedOther should then be a user-defined string explaining the purpose of the purchase order.

The OrderCurrency is United States dollars (USD), and the Order-Language is English (en).

## The Parties

The OrderParty element has, among other child elements, both Buyer-Party and SellerParty. These elements contain readily discernable information that identifies either buyer or seller. Because AgencyCoded contains Other, AgencyCodedOther must follow with a string of the issuer's choosing that describes the agency. This *Other* pattern is repeated throughout xCBL. The identifier US-WST-OR-326 in Ident is also a user-defined code.

The information in NameAddress is pretty obvious. The Region information is taken from the subdivision code of the 1998 draft of ISO 3166, where US (United States) is the country code and OR (Oregon) is the region code. Kind of a handy notation, don't you think?

TimezoneCoded is the offset from Coordinated Universal Time (UTC), also called Greenwich Mean Time (GMT). UTC is eight hours ahead of the time on the West Coast of Canada and the United States, or Pacific Standard Time (PST), as it is known.

`SellerParty` contains some information similar to `BuyerParty`. `CodeListIdentifierCoded` is an identifier code (`AssignedBySender`) that is derived from EDIFACT (1131) and X12 (1270).

## Details of the Order

The `BuyerLineItemNum` and the `SellerLineItemNum` both list unique identifying numbers that indicate what the purchase order is all about. Line items can refer to documents on either the buyer or seller side that describe, in whole or in part, a transaction or something associated with a transaction. The line items in this order could very well deal with a purchase item and the ledgers that account for them. What these documents are depends on your application of xCBL.

## In Summary

Finally, you wrap up with the `OrderSummary` element. It notes the `NumberOfLines` that deal with line items (2), taxes (`TotalTax`), if any, and the total amount of the order (`TotalAmount`). An optional `SummaryNote` allows you room to leave free-text notes about the order, a sort of catch-all for anything not covered by the other elements. There are so many of them, you won't likely have a lot of need for `SummaryNote`, but it is there for the taking.

# A Simple Invoice

Now that a buyer has processed an `Order`, it is time for the supplier to send an `Invoice` to collect monies that are due.

In the SOX example given earlier in the chapter, you saw how SOX defined `Invoice` compared to a DTD and XML Schema.

The following is a simple invoice that will illustrate the use of these elements:

```
<?xml version="1.0" ?>
<!DOCTYPE Invoice SYSTEM "XCBL30.dtd">

<Invoice>
 <InvoiceHeader>
  <InvoiceNumber>
   <Reference>
```

```
  <RefNum>PO-2001-00001</RefNum>
 </Reference>
</InvoiceNumber>
<InvoiceIssueDate>20010101T00:00:22</InvoiceIssueDate>
<InvoicePurpose>
 <InvoicePurposeCoded>Original</InvoicePurposeCoded>
</InvoicePurpose>
<InvoiceType>
 <InvoiceTypeCoded>CommercialInvoice</InvoiceTypeCoded>
</InvoiceType>
<InvoiceLanguage>
 <Language>
  <LanguageCoded>en</LanguageCoded>
 </Language>
</InvoiceLanguage>
<InvoiceParty>
 <BuyerParty>
  <Party>
   <PartyID>
    <Identifier>
     <Agency>
      <AgencyCoded>Other</AgencyCoded>
      <AgencyCodedOther>
       Wy'east Communications
      </AgencyCodedOther>
     </Agency>
     <Ident>US-WST-OR-326</Ident>
    </Identifier>
   </PartyID>
   <NameAddress>
    <Name1>Wy'east Communications</Name1>
    <POBox>P.O. Box 537</POBox>
    <PostalCode>97068-0537</PostalCode>
    <City>West Linn</City>
    <Region>
     <RegionCoded>USOR</RegionCoded>
    </Region>
    <Country>
     <CountryCoded>US</CountryCoded>
    </Country>
   </NameAddress>
  </Party>
 </BuyerParty>
 <SellerParty>
  <Party>
   <PartyID>
    <Identifier>
     <Agency>
      <AgencyCoded>Other</AgencyCoded>
      <AgencyCodedOther>TestB2B.org</AgencyCodedOther>
      <CodeListIdentifierCoded>
       AssignedBySender
```

```
          </CodeListIdentifierCoded>
        </Agency>
        <Ident>US-WST-OR-327</Ident>
      </Identifier>
    </PartyID>
  </Party>
 </SellerParty>
</InvoiceParty>
<InvoiceTermsOfDelivery>
 <TermsOfDelivery>
  <TermsOfDeliveryFunctionCoded>
   CollectedByCustomer
  </TermsOfDeliveryFunctionCoded>
  <ShipmentMethodOfPaymentCoded>
   Account
  </ShipmentMethodOfPaymentCoded>
 </TermsOfDelivery>
</InvoiceTermsOfDelivery>
</InvoiceHeader>
<InvoiceDetail>
 <ListOfInvoiceItemDetail>
  <InvoiceItemDetail>
   <InvoiceBaseItemDetail>
    <LineItemNum>
     <BuyerLineItemNum>1023</BuyerLineItemNum>
     <SellerLineItemNum>653</SellerLineItemNum>
    </LineItemNum>
    <TotalQuantity>
     <Quantity>
      <QuantityValue>1</QuantityValue>
      <UnitOfMeasurement>
       <UOMCoded>C62</UOMCoded>
      </UnitOfMeasurement>
     </Quantity>
    </TotalQuantity>
   </InvoiceBaseItemDetail>
   <InvoicePricingDetail>
    <ListOfPrice>
     <Price>
      <UnitPrice>
       <UnitPriceValue>24.99</UnitPriceValue>
      </UnitPrice>
     </Price>
    </ListOfPrice>
    <InvoiceCurrencyTotalValue>
     <MonetaryValue>
      <MonetaryAmount>24.99</MonetaryAmount>
      <Currency>
       <CurrencyCoded>USD</CurrencyCoded>
      </Currency>
     </MonetaryValue>
    </InvoiceCurrencyTotalValue>
```

```
      <ActualPaymentStatus>
       <ActualPaymentStatusCoded>
        PaidInFull
       </ActualPaymentStatusCoded>
      </ActualPaymentStatus>
     </InvoicePricingDetail>
    </InvoiceItemDetail>
   </ListOfInvoiceItemDetail>
  </InvoiceDetail>
  <InvoiceSummary>
   <InvoiceTotals>
    <NetValue>
     <MonetaryValue>
      <MonetaryAmount>24.99</MonetaryAmount>
     </MonetaryValue>
    </NetValue>
    <GrossValue>
     <MonetaryValue>
      <MonetaryAmount>24.99</MonetaryAmount>
     </MonetaryValue>
    </GrossValue>
    <PrepaidAmount>
     <MonetaryValue>
      <MonetaryAmount>24.99</MonetaryAmount>
     </MonetaryValue>
    </PrepaidAmount>
   </InvoiceTotals>
   <InvoicePaymentStatus>
    <InvoicePaymentStatusCoded>
     PaidInFull
    </InvoicePaymentStatusCoded>
   </InvoicePaymentStatus>
   <SummaryNote>Free shipping.</SummaryNote>
  </InvoiceSummary>
 </Invoice>
```

It may be long, but none of this is too scary. Let's go over it.

## Invoice Header Information

Of course, `Invoice` is the root. It has `InvoiceHeader`, `InvoiceDetail`, and `InvoiceSummary` (optional) as children. Remember `Order`'s children? They are `OrderHeader`, `OrderDetail`, and `OrderSummary` (optional). This is a predictable pattern you will see throughout xCBL.

`RefNum` (descendant of `InvoiceNumber`) contains the `BuyerOrderNumber` from the `Order` document. This helps keep track of workflow. The `InvoiceIssueDate` contains an ISO 8601 date and time.

The `InvoicePurposeCoded` content is one of three possible values: `Original`, `Duplicate`, or `Other`. These are derived from EDIFACT (1225) and X12 (353 and 587). A value of `Other` triggers an `InvoicePurpose-CodedOther` element, a common pattern you have seen before, which would hold user-defined information about the purpose of the invoice.

`InvoiceTypeCoded` (child of `InvoiceType`) contains `Commercial-Invoice`. Other possible values could be `CreditInvoice`, `Corrected-Invoice`, or `DebitInvoice`. The language of the invoice is English (en).

The children of `InvoiceParty`, `BuyerParty` and `SellerParty`, both contain easy-to-understand information that is very similar to what you saw in `Order`, so I won't discuss it again here.

The `InvoiceTermsOfDelivery` includes descendants such as `Terms-OfDeliveryFunctionCoded` and `ShipmentMethodOfPaymentCoded`. `TermsOfDeliveryFunctionCoded` contains the value `CollectedBy-Customer`. This means that the customer is to pick up the goods from the supplier and take care of the transportation of the goods. This and other values come from EDIFACT (4055).

From EDIFACT 4215 and X12 146 come values for `ShipmentMethod-OfPaymentCoded`. `Account` means that the charges will be placed on account. Other possible values are `CollectOnDelivery` and `Service-Freight-NoCharge`.

## Invoice Details, Details

Under `InvoiceItemDetail` comes `BuyerLineItemNum` and `Seller-LineItemNum`, which borrow their line item numbers from the preceding `Order`.

There is a quantity value of 1, and the unit of measurement (`UOMCoded`) is C62, which means *One*, *Piece*, or *Unit*. This and a parcel of other codes are from the United Nations Economic Commission for Europe (UN/ECE) Recommendation 20 and X12 (355).

The `InvoicePricingDetail` subelements include unit price (see `UnitPriceValue` under `ListOfPrice`), invoice total (see `Monetary-Amount` under `InvoiceCurrencyTotalValue`), and payment status. `ActualPaymentStatusCoded` contains the value `PaidInFull`, which has obvious meaning. Other possible values are `PartPaid`, `NotPaid`, `OverPaid`, `FreeOfCharge`, and `Other`.

## Summarizing the Invoice

Finally, in the `InvoiceSummary`, you can recap the `Invoice` with such elements as `NetValue`, `GrossValue`, and `PrepaidAmount`. `Monetary-Amount` in each instance contains a value of type `Decimal21_6`. A value of this type can have up to 21 digits. This includes up to 15 on the left side of the decimal point and up to 6 on the right side of the decimal point. The value in `MonetaryAmount` could be expressed as `000000000000024.990000`.

`InvoicePaymentStatus` is similar to `ActualPaymentStatus`, but the difference is that `ActualPaymentStatus` is for a line item and `InvoicePaymentStatus` covers the whole invoice. The `SummaryNote` element again is a place for free text from the user.

## Setting Up an Auction

Auctions provide a way to sell goods or services at a variable price. Languishing in the back corner of your warehouse, you have a pallet stacked high with last year's Christmas blockbuster that now has been passed over in favor of the next gizmo. Short of writing the inventory off, you can use xCBL to set up an auction and get at least some revenue for the product while moving it out of precious warehouse space.

The xCBL auction model follows this pattern in a Commerce One environment:

1. You, the initiator, set up an auction with an AuctionCreate document and send it to a server that can handle auction services. An example of an auction services portal or server is the Commerce One Auction Services platform.

2. Through the auction services, e-mail messages are sent to notify potential buyers of the auction. (This is done by the auction services, not the `AuctionCreate` document.)

3. An `AuctionCreateResponse` message is sent from auction services to notify you that the auction creation was successful.

4. The potential buyers can now become participants in the auction by checking a Web interface provided by auction services.

5. After the auction plays out and auction services determines, for example, a high bidder, auction services sends you an `Auction-Result` document to which you respond with an `AuctionResult-Response` document.

**NOTE** Example documents for `AuctionCreate`, `AuctionCreateResponse`, `AuctionResult`, and `AuctionResultResponse` are all provided with the xCBL reference documentation that you can download from the www.xcbl.org site. These documents can be lengthy, so I will list only an example of an `AuctionCreate` document in this chapter. This example should be sufficient to give you a feel for how auction documents work.

You can see from the auction steps that the Commerce One Auction Services platform does a lot of the work. If you use xCBL's free auction facilities, you are not forced to use a Commerce One solution, but you have to use some sort of intermediary services to help manage auction documents. If you have the resources to program your own auction services, you will probably save yourself some money (which, in the first place, is the intent of this book).

Even though these topics are outside the scope of this book, I'll just say that you could write such a program with JavaScript, ASP, Java, or some other language. The services or suite of programs would have to cover these steps:

1. You first write a program that can use the HTTP POST method to post data to a URI. This program can be something as simple as a JavaScript Web page with an HTML form that has a browser interface.

2. You post an `AuctionCreate` document to a program. Supposedly this program is on a server that is available on the Internet. This program also sends back to your browser an `AuctionCreateResponse` document to let you know the status of the auction so far. This program also evaluates the `AuctionCreate` document so that it can set up a secure Web page and notify by email the possible participants in the auction.

3. Participants interact with the Web page to view the product and make bids. When the time for the auction expires, or when the program is triggered in some other way, it sends an `AuctionResult` document back to you. This might be in the form of an email notification giving you a URI for where you can access the `AuctionResult`.

4. On the Web page showing the `AuctionResult` document, you could also include some script that will send an `AuctionResultResponse` back to the program that sent the `AuctionResult`.

The steps look simple and straightforward, but, of course, the actual programming is not trivial. These are not all the precise steps you would have to account for with your own auction services, but they convey the general idea of what is required.

## An AuctionCreate Example

Here is the `AuctionCreate` example document I promised. After the listing, you can find explanations of what is going on.

```
<?xml version="1.0"? >
<!DOCTYPE AuctionCreate SYSTEM 'XCBL30.dtd'>

<AuctionCreate>
 <AuctionCreateHeader>
  <AuctionCreatePurpose>
   <Purpose>
    <PurposeCoded>Original</PurposeCoded>
   </Purpose>
  </AuctionCreatePurpose>
  <AuctionCreateIssueDate>
   20010101T08:19:00
  </AuctionCreateIssueDate>
  <AuctionCreateID>AuctionNo-2001-1</AuctionCreateID>
  <ForwardAuctionIndicator>true</ForwardAuctionIndicator>
  <AuctionValidityDates>
   <ValidityDates>
    <StartDate>20010101T09:00:00</StartDate>
    <EndDate>20010131T09:00:00</EndDate>
   </ValidityDates>
  </AuctionValidityDates>
  <DecisionDate>20010202T09:00:00</DecisionDate>
  <RulesProfile>
   <BidRuleCoded>EnglishForward</BidRuleCoded>
   <WinRuleCoded>HighestBidWins</WinRuleCoded>
  </RulesProfile>
  <AuctionParticipants>
   <InitiatingParty>
    <Party>
     <PartyID>
      <PrimaryID>
       <Agency>
        <AgencyCoded>Other</AgencyCoded>
        <AgencyCodedOther>
         Wy'east Communications
        </AgencyCodedOther>
       </Agency>
       <Ident>US-WST-OR-AUCTION-23</Ident>
      </PrimaryID>
     </PartyID>
     <NameAddress>
      <Name1>Wy'east Communications</Name1>
      <POBox>P.O. Box 537</POBox>
      <PostalCode>97068-0537</PostalCode>
      <City>West Linn</City>
      <Region>
       <RegionCoded>USOR</RegionCoded>
      </Region>
      <Country>
```

```
    <CountryCoded>US</CountryCoded>
   </Country>
  </NameAddress>
  <CorrespondenceLanguage>
   <Language>
    <LanguageCoded>en</LanguageCoded>
   </Language>
  </CorrespondenceLanguage>
 </Party>
</InitiatingParty>
<ListOfAuctionPartners>
 <AuctionPartners>
  <PartyID>
   <PrimaryID>
    <Agency>
     <AgencyCoded>Other</AgencyCoded>
      <AgencyCodedOther>
       Bud's Auction Central
     </AgencyCodedOther>
    </Agency>
    <Ident>US-WST-OR-AUCT-1</Ident>
   </PrimaryID>
  </PartyID>
  <GroupIndicator>true</GroupIndicator>
 </AuctionPartners>
</ListOfAuctionPartners>
</AuctionParticipants>
<Language>
 <LanguageCoded>en</LanguageCoded>
</Language>
</AuctionCreateHeader>
<AuctionCreateDetail>
<AuctionItem>
 <AuctionItemID>234-569</AuctionItemID>
 <AuctionItemName>0471416207</AuctionItemName>
 <ListOfAuctionCategory>
  <AuctionCategory>
   <AuctionCategoryName>Books</AuctionCategoryName>
   <AuctionCategoryLevel>1</AuctionCategoryLevel>
  </AuctionCategory>
 </ListOfAuctionCategory>
 <AuctionItemHierarchyLevel>1</AuctionItemHierarchyLevel>
  <AuctionQuantity>
   <Quantity>
    <QuantityValue>1</QuantityValue>
    <UnitOfMeasurement>
     <UOMCoded>EA</UOMCoded>
    </UnitOfMeasurement>
   </Quantity>
```

```
      </AuctionQuantity>
     </AuctionItem>
  </AuctionCreatDetail>
  <AuctionCreateSummary>
   <TotalNumberOfAuctionItems>1</TotalNumberOfAuctionItems>
  </AuctionCreateSummary>
</AuctionCreate>
```

`AuctionCreate` is the root element. It is followed by an `AuctionCre-ateHeader`, an `AuctionCreateDetail`, and optionally an `Auction-CreateSummary`.

## Auction Header Information

`PurposeCoded` is used here as in the `Order` document. It indicates the purpose or function of the document and contains one of the following: `Other`, `Cancellation`, `Replace`, `Confirmation`, `Duplicate`, `Original`, `Change`, or `InformationOnly`. This list comes from EDIFACT (1225) and X12 (353). As you have already seen, if the value is `Other`, you must also use the `PurposeCodedOther` element. The content of `PurposeCodedOther` is a user-defined string that explains the purpose of the document.

`AuctionCreateIssueDate` is obviously an 8601 date and time, and the `AuctionCreateID` is a unique ID of your choosing, just as you have already seen.

A `ForwardAuctionIndicator` indicates if the auction is a forward (`true`) or a reverse (`false`) auction. In a forward auction, you post a product or service you have to sell; in a reverse auction, you post the products and services you want to buy.

`ValidityDates` state in 8601 the date and time when an auction begins (`StartDate`) and when it ends (`EndDate`). `DecisionDate` provides a date and time when the winner will be selected. It must be later than `EndDate`.

The `RuleProfile` element contains `BidRuleCoded` and `WinRule-Coded`. `EnglishForward` means that the price is raised with each bid until the auction closes. Other options are `EnglishReverse`, `YankeeForward`, `DutchForward`, and so forth. `HighestBidWins` is, well, high bidder takes all. Other rules include `YankeeRule` or `LowestBidWins`, among others.

## Who's Involved?

The auction participants include `InitiatingParty` and `ListOfAuctionPartners`. The information in the `InitiatingParty` element is familiar territory, just like the contents of `PartyID` elements you have seen in other documents.

`ListOfAuctionPartners` provides a list of trading partners that will be participating in the auction. This element contains one or more instances of `AuctionPartners`. This document lists only one partner, Bud's Auction Central, but this partner is not an individual but a group of partners, as indicated by a `true` in `GroupIndicator`.

The language of the auction is English (en).

## What Are You Selling?

`AuctionCreateDetail` provides the space to spell out what it is that you are auctioning. The `AuctionItemID` and the `AuctionItemName` identify the item to be auctioned. These numbers are provided by the auction initiator and are meaningful in context—that is, both the initiating partner and the other participants will have local records that carry the meanings. For example, the participants at Bud's will know that `0471416207` is an International Standard Book Number (ISBN).

The `AuctionCategoryName` is `Books`, so at least we have a meaningful label for what is offered for sale. The `AuctionCategoryLevel` is a way to categorize interconnected or more complex items, but it is of little use in this auction. Likewise, the `AuctionItemHierachyLevel` is not of much use when you are just auctioning off one book, but it helps when you are auctioning items at the component level, such as computer hardware.

`AuctionQuantity` (`QuantityValue` of 1) is simple enough to understand, as is `UnitOfMeasurement` with a `UOMCoded` value of EA (each), which is based on UN/ECE Recommendation 20.

## Wrap Up

`AuctionCreateSummary` is an optional element that can contain one `TotalNumberOfAuctionItems` and one `TotalNumberOfPartici-pants` or one each of both. That's it. This auction summary shows only that there is 1 auction item.

# xCBL Is Big

If you have already downloaded xCBL, you have noticed that it is big. The DTD version of the online reference manual is over 2 megabytes and documents nearly six hundred elements. It would take a thick and hefty reference book to document all the xCBL elements and probably another book to explain how the elements all work together. So, in a single chapter, all I am able to do is to introduce xCBL to you and to help you make a decision about whether to use it.

You may want to go with xCBL if you are moving from the EDI world into XML because xCBL relies heavily on EDI (both EDIFACT and X12) type date for element content. Also, if you are creating auctions, xCBL is the only freely available XML vocabulary that offers auction infrastructure. XCBL comes with its own free parser for both SOX and DTDs. No other B2B vocabulary can boast that. If you are supporting a wide variety of B2B documents—not just purchase orders, but shipping management, planning, and statistical documents, to name a few—then xCBL is probably a good choice for you. Finally, if you are using Commerce One software products such as MarketSet somewhere in your supply chain, xCBL should be a hands-down choice.

# cXML

Commerce XML (cXML) is an XML collection or vocabulary brought to you by Ariba Technologies, Inc. It is a fairly stable specification (version 1.1), so that even though it is associated with a private company, because it is based on XML and other open standards, just about anyone can use the cXML vocabulary.

Like xCBL, the cXML vocabulary is the product of what is known as a vendor consortium. It is not the creation of a separate standards body, such as the W3C or OASIS, but represents the combined efforts of a variety of companies, such as Microsoft, Cisco Systems, FedEx, and Hewlett-Packard, to name a few (Microsoft's BizTalk supports cXML, by the way; see Chapter 9, "BizTalk"). Sometimes big players involve themselves in vendor consortia for more than just charitable reasons. Perhaps they use consortia to avoid appearing like a monopoly and to circumvent potential anti-trust action. Nevertheless, when divergent parties, including competitors, come together to forge agreements on ground rules for integration and interaction, everyone benefits, even if the motives of the parties are not purely humanitarian.

Ariba "grants . . . a perpetual, nonexclusive, royalty-free, worldwide right and license to use the cXML specification." Pretty generous, don't you think? A cXML buy-in means that it will be easier for third parties to integrate with Ariba's products. This is a suitable if not worthy aim of vendor consortia, and, to tell you the truth, it helps more than it hurts.

Ariba offers a number of B2B-related applications that support cXML. All of them are part of the Ariba B2B Commerce Platform. I don't have the inside scoop on this, but I'll go out on a limb and say that third-party integration support is one of the main reasons why Ariba offers cXML to the public. You may very well want to integrate your B2B application with Ariba's applications. Using cXML is essential if that is your plan. But, honestly, you could use cXML without getting near an Ariba application, and cXML alone will save you a lot of trouble.

Briefly, some of the current, main products offered with the Ariba platform are these:

**Ariba Buyer.** This is Ariba's procurement application. It allows whole enterprises to buy goods and services, track expenses, and analyze spending.

**Ariba Marketplace.** This is a market maker's application for deploying information to online marketplaces, from simple procurement to fully blown commodity exchanges.

**Ariba Dynamic Trade.** Here is Ariba's auction/exchange application. It offers dynamic pricing schemes and can handle lists of approved vendors, even multitier relationships.

**Ariba Commerce Services Network (CSN).** Essentially, Ariba's CSN is a server that integrates the activities of the platform's other applications while including security, routing with various protocols, and third-party integration.

As you already know, I can't cover everything about the cXML 1.1 specification here, nor will I attempt to completely rehash it. But I will provide an overview of how it works, through examples, of course. If you wind up implementing cXML, you can't avoid reading the spec for yourself. The spec is more than a hundred pages, but I'll cover the basics in far less space than that, which is lucky for both of us.

> **NOTE** The examples in this chapter will work as described if you have a transport mechanism, that is, an Ariba network server product, such as Ariba.com Network version 1.0 or Ariba Commerce Services Network (CSN). Nevertheless, you can still create, process, and transport cXML examples using your own tools. The cXML specification tells you enough about the processes that you could, if you are a programmer, use to create your own server or add a module to an existing server that performs as required. It all depends on whether you have more time than money or more money than time—or more curiosity than sense. (This is where I usually get in trouble.)

# What You Can Do with cXML

So what can you do with cXML, and how is it different from other similar B2B vocabularies? If you plan to use Ariba products as part of your B2B infrastructure, of course, using cXML will make your life a lot easier. The same is true if you have trading partners who use Ariba. The cXML specification provides some Active Server Pages (ASP) programming help if you want to implement some pages on your Web site that will interact with cXML documents, even if you are not using Ariba software on your side.

As with any XML vocabulary, you can use a cXML DTD without using Ariba products, especially because the Ariba license is so liberal. After reading this chapter, if you see elements that are useful to you, then there is nothing stopping you from using them, no matter how you throw your B2B system together.

A few highlights of cXML include the following:

- Online catalog management
- Supplier information management
- Punchout sessions that allow you to download portions of catalogs as needed rather than the whole kit and caboodle
- Purchase order management

**NOTE** If cXML doesn't seem right for you, I'd suggest skipping to the next chapter. This chapter will be helpful to folks who want to implement cXML, as it explores the DTD and sheds light on why you will use the elements and attributes that it contains. But if you are not actually creating something, it will come across as a dull explication. I don't think it's dull at all, but that's because I've got my hands busy doing something.

# No cXML Namespace?

Oddly, cXML, like xCBL, makes no mention of namespaces in either its user's guide or its DTD. I don't know why this is so, but I'll guess that the folks at Ariba are thinking this through. I wouldn't be surprised that because they have a controlled vocabulary, if an element, attribute, entity, or whatever is not in the current cXML DTD, the document is rejected as invalid, so who needs a namespace if there is no chance of mixing vocabularies?

Maybe namespaces will show up in the next release of cXML, but that remains to be seen. The original namespace specification has been the subject of a lot of controversy, so perhaps Ariba is waiting for W3C to straighten out namespaces before proceeding.

## A Simple Example: A Profile Transaction

In cXML, a profile transaction requests information from a server about its cXML capabilities, including what version of cXML it uses, what requests the server will honor, and so on. The following profile transaction consists of two simple examples that show what a cXML document looks like. The first document includes an empty `ProfileRequest` element while the second provides a `ProfileResponse` with several child elements. The example assumes that the document is submitted to an Ariba-aware server.

```xml
<?xml version="1.0" encoding="utf-8"?>
<!DOCTYPE cXML SYSTEM
"http://xml.cXML.org/schemas/cXML/1.1.009/cXML.dtd">

<cXML payloadID="9788@testb2b.org" xml:lang="en-US"
      timestamp="2001-01-01T00:00:19-08:00">
 <Header>
  <From>
   <Credential domain="B2B Order Access">
    <Identity>mike@wyeast.net</Identity>
   </Credential>
  </From>
  <To>
   <Credential domain="B2B Order Access">
    <Identity>schlomo@testb2b.org</Identity>
   </Credential>
  </To>
  <Sender>
   <Credential domain="B2B Order Access">
    <Identity>mike@wyeast.net</Identity>
     <DigitalSignature type="PK7 self-contained"
      encoding="Base64">
      T2ghIFlvdSBjYXVnaHQgbWUhIFRoaXMgaXMgYSBmYWtlIGRpZ2l0YWwwgc
      21nbmF0dXJlIHdyaXR0ZW4gaW4gYmFzZTY0Lg==
     </DigitalSignature>
   </Credential>
   <UserAgent>Mozilla/4.0 (compatible; MSIE 5.0;
    Win32)</UserAgent>
  </Sender>
 </Header>
 <Request deploymentMode="test">
  <ProfileRequest />
```

```
</Request>
</cXML>
```

UTF-8 encoding is the norm in cXML documents, as you can see in the XML declaration, and the document type declaration assumes that you validate your cXML document against the most recent version of the cXML DTD. At this writing it's version 1.1.009.

> **NOTE** This document type declaration, by the way, points to a SYSTEM identifier, not a PUBLIC identifier, as you can tell by the absence of the PUBLIC keyword and a legal public ID string.

Now let's tear into this example to get a better understanding of it.

## The cXML Element

The cXML element—the root element—must contain a single instance of either a Header element (followed then by either Request or Message) or a Response element. That's simple enough. This example contains only an instance of the Request element. The cXML element has four attributes: version, payloadID, timestamp, and xml:lang. Both payloadID and timestamp are required.

The payloadID attribute is a unique identifier for the document. It is used for logging purposes to identify documents as unique, thus avoiding duplicates. Once assigned, this value must not change. The format datetime.processid.randomnumber@hostname is recommended, though one of datetime, processid, or randomnumber will do—for example, 9788@testb2b.org where 9788 is a random number will do fine for most of us.

The timestamp attribute is a date and time the message was sent, in ISO 8601 format. This value also must not change after it is set for a document. The ISO 8601 format is in the form YYYY-MM-DDThh:mm:ss[-/+]hh:mm. The value is 2000-02-04T18:39:09-08:00 in our example. The last part of the value, -08:00, is the difference (minus) from Coordinated Universal Time (UTC) or, more traditionally, Greenwich Mean Time (GMT), for Greenwich, England, through which the prime or zero meridian runs. Minus eight hours is the difference between UTC and Pacific Standard Time (PST). The Pacific time zone covers the Yukon Territory and British Columbia in Canada, and in the United States, Washington, northern Idaho, Oregon, California, and Nevada.

The `version` attribute has a default value that is embedded in the DTD and depends on the version of the DTD you are using. For example, if your document type declaration points to the DTD at `http://xml.cxml .org/schemas/xCML/1.1009/cXML.dtd`, the version number will be 1.1.009, as defined in the entity `&cxml.version;`. The attribute `xml: lang`, if used, indicates the language of the document. It provides a language code, such as `de` (Deutsch or German) or `fr` (French), or a language and country code combination as described in RFC 1766, such as `en-US` (English-United States) or `en-GB` (English-Great Britain).

## To, From, and Sender

A `Header` element contains one each of `From`, `To`, and `Sender`. `From` and `To` contain one or more `Credential` elements. The `Sender` element must also contain an instance of `UserAgent`. The `UserAgent` element contains a string of parsed character data that represents the user agent such as a browser used in the transaction, such as `Mozilla/4.0 (compatible; MSIE 5.0; Win32)`. It is similar to the HTTP header `User-Agent`.

## Who Are You?

The element `Credential` must hold an `Identity` element and may contain an authentication element, either `SharedSecret` or `DigitalSignature`. `Credential` also has two attributes, `domain` and `type`; `domain` is required while the optional `type`, if used, must have a value of `marketplace`. You can use the type attribute to differentiate those who are associated with a marketplace and those who are not.

The `Identity` element may have an optional `lastChangedTimestamp` attribute, which, if used, holds the date and time when the object was last changed. `Identity` can have ANY content, but you can expect something like a DUNS number or an email address. If the content is a DUNS number, the `domain` attribute in `Credential` should have the value DUNS.

In the preceding example, `mike@wyeast.net` is who the message is from and `schlomo@testb2b.org` is the intended recipient of the message. The actual sender of the message is also `mike@wyeast.net`, who also authenticates himself with a digital signature in RSA's PKCS #7 message syntax.

You have two choices for authentication. The `SharedSecret` element is just that, a shared secret, usually a password or a username/password combination passed through a secure transport channel such as SSL or

TLS. DigitalSignature contains a digital signature. It has two attributes: type, whose default value is "PK7 self-contained," and encoding, whose default is "Base64." (The content in the example is not a real PK #7 signature.)

> **NOTE** If it contains a clear password, you will want to avoid exposing the SharedSecret element content if it will be read by a browser, unless it is sent under a digital certificate, such as with SSL or TLS. The scheme name https:// signals to the browser to use the digital certificate.

## The Request Element

The Request element has one attribute, deploymentMode, which can have a value of either production or test, with production as the default. In the previous example, the content of Request is an empty element ProfileRequest. Before we look at a ProfileRequest example, you should know that there are several other requests you can make with cXML, some with specific responses.

### Other Requests and Responses

Request may contain one instance of any of the following elements. This should be answered by a message containing a Response element, which must contain an instance of Status. Most request elements are paired with matching response elements.

**OrderRequest.** This element serves up purchase order content, such as the amount, tax, payment method, and so forth. This is often done in conjunction with a punchout session. See the section titled *Purchase Orders*, later in this chapter.

**PunchOutSetupRequest.** In the cXML framework, when a user logs in to a procurement application and finds a desired item and selects it, a punchout request is made by calling this element, with appropriate content. The response comes in a PunchOutSetupResponse element.

**StatusUpdateRequest.** This request processes information about changes in the status of an earlier order, such as the forwarding of an order request (OrderRequest) to another server.

**GetPendingRequest.** This grabs messages that are waiting, returning the oldest messages first, based on timestamp. It holds one or more

`MessageType` elements, which indicate the message types (in the form of element names) that you are looking for. It can discard messages that are too old. The response comes in a `GetPending-Response` element, which returns one or more messages that are waiting. See page 96 of the cXML specification for an example.

**`SubscriptionListRequest`.** This is an empty element that requests a buyer's list of catalog subscriptions. A `SubscriptionList-Response` returns a list of the current catalog subscriptions.

**`SubscriptionContentRequest`.** This requests the content of a catalog. The catalog may be in regular cXML format or in Catalog Interchange Format (CIF). The `SubscriptionContentResponse` returns the catalog content in one of three subelements in a `Subscription-Content`: `CIFContent`, `Index`, or `Contract`. `CIFContent` indicates a CIF file in base64. You can see what the `Index` element contains in the section titled *A Punchout Index Catalog*, later in this chapter. For information on `Contract`, see page 88 of the cXML specification.

**`SupplierListRequest`.** This empty element requests a list of suppliers that the buyer has a trading relationship with, while the `SupplierListResponse` element returns the requested list of suppliers.

**`SupplierDataRequest`.** This element requests available information about a supplier. The `SupplierDataResponse` element replies with the information, such as `PostalAddress`, `Phone`, `Fax`, and so forth.

## The ProfileResponse Element

The response to a `ProfileRequest` is returned in a `ProfileResponse` element by a server or script (not shown). You could then expect a message like this in a response.

```
<?xml version="1.0" encoding="utf-8"?>
<!DOCTYPE cXML SYSTEM
"http://xml.cXML.org/schemas/cXML/1.1.009/cXML.dtd">

<cXML payloadID="9788-14@testb2b.org" xml:lang="en-US"
      timestamp="2001-01-01T00:12:49-08:00">
 <Response>
  <Status code="200" text="OK"/>
   <ProfileResponse effectiveDate="2000-01-01T00:00:01-08:00">
    <Transaction requestName="OrderRequest">
     <URL>http://orders.testb2b.org/servlets/orders</URL>
    </Transaction>
    <Transaction requestName="PunchOutSetupRequest">
     <URL>http://orders.testb2b.org/servlets/punchouts</URL>
    </Transaction>
```

```
      </ProfileResponse>
     </Response>
 </cXML>
```

### What's the Status?

A `Status` element in a `Response` element has three attributes. The first, `code`, is required and represents an HTTP status code, such as `200`. The second, `text`, is also required and contains the accompanying text of the status code, such as `OK`. It can also have an `xml:lang` attribute, but this is optional. `Status` can be empty, or it can contain additional enlightening information expressed in parsed character data.

### The Response

As you can see, the `ProfileResponse` element has an `effectiveDate` attribute, which gives the ISO 8601 date and time when the listed services first became available. The `ProfileResponse` start-tag is followed by several `Transaction` elements, each containing a single URL. This is required. The URL is the address of a service, such as a Java servlet or CGI program, provided by the queried site. The URLs in the example are illustriously fake.

A `ProfileResponse` can also contain `Option` elements, with a required `name` attribute, though no options are defined in the current version of cXML. In the future, you might expect `Option` elements to feed information at the machine level, perhaps Booleans to switch options on and off or to provide some other system data. Here is an example of a fragment that employs user-defined `Option` elements.

```
<Transaction requestName="OrderRequest">
 <URL>http://orders.testb2b.org/servlets/orders</URL>
 <Option name="sale">1</Option>
 <Option name="homedir">/home/b2b/orders</Option>
</Transaction>
```

A value of `1` in the `Option` named `sale` indicates that the ordered or requested item is on sale. The `Option` named `homedir` provides the local home directory, on a Unix machine, where cXML documents are stored. (The URL is not real.)

## The Message Element

If a `Header` element does not have a `Request` child element, it must contain a `Message` element instead. `Message` has two attributes. The first, deploymentMode, can have a value of either production or test, with production as the default. The other, inReplyTo, is an optional string value that specifies the Message to which this Message will respond. The value of inReplyTo is the payloadID of an earlier Message element. It can also be a reference to the payloadID of an earlier cXML element. A Message that includes a ProfileResponse element might also have an inReplyTo attribute with the payloadID of the ProfileRequest that preceded it.

A Message element may contain zero or one instance of Status. If a Status element is not present, the following is assumed:

```
<Status code="200" text="OK" />
```

Whether or not you use Status, a Message element must hold one of the following elements (either as a child of Status, when present, or a direct child of Message):

**PunchOutOrderMessage.** This element sends the contents of a shopping cart to a procurement application.

**SubscriptionChangeMessage.** This element lets the recipients know how a catalog they subscribe to has changed.

**SupplierChangeMessage.** This sends information about changes in a supplier's data.

Here is an example of the Message element with Subscription-ChangeMessage as a child.

```
<?xml version="1.0" encoding="utf-8" ?>
<!DOCTYPE cXML SYSTEM
"http://xml.cXML.org/schemas/cXML/1.1.009/cXML.dtd">

<cXML payloadID="9444@testb2b.org" xml:lang="en-US"
      timestamp="2001-01-02T12:00:01-08:00">
 <Header>
  <From>
   <Credential domain="B2B Order Access">
    <Identity>mike@wyeast.net</Identity>
   </Credential>
  </From>
  <To>
   <Credential domain="B2B Order Access">
    <Identity>schlomo@testb2b.org</Identity>
   </Credential>
  </To>
  <Sender>
   <Credential domain="B2B Order Access">
```

```
    <Identity>mike@wyeast.net</Identity>
   </Credential>
   <UserAgent>Opera 5.01</UserAgent>
  </Sender>
 </Header>
 <Message>
  <SubscriptionChangeMessage type="new">
   <Subscription>
    <InternalID>97557899584</InternalID>
    <Name>Summer Specials</Name>
    <Changetime>2001-05-01T00:00:01-08:00</Changetime>
    <SupplierID domain="DUNS">86-757-8317</SupplierID>
    <Format version="2.1">CIF</Format>
    <Description>Upcoming specials, Summer 2001.</Description>
   </Subscription>
  </SubscriptionChangeMessage>
 </Message>
</cXML>
```

You should already be familiar with the `Header` element and its contents; the `Message` element is what we'll focus on. The child of `Message` is `SubscriptionChangeMessage`, which, as mentioned earlier, conveys information on how a catalog has changed.

## A Word on Subscriptions

If you're like me, you get a stack of catalogs in the mail nearly every month. Once you purchase even the cheapest item from a company, it seems, you are their friends for life. The company will send you a catalog until you move or send in a request that it cease all mailings. Maintaining, printing, and mailing catalogs is a costly enterprise, but a worthwhile one if it generates revenue to cover those costs. Perhaps that's why companies are moving their catalogs to Internet-based commerce sites.

A subscription is an arrangement in cXML whereby a buyer can subscribe to catalog information from a supplier. You can subscribe to catalogs and retrieve the contents of those catalogs. Besides `Subscription-ChangeMessage`, the other elements specific to subscriptions are as follows:

**`SubscriptionListRequest`.** This asks for a list of your current subscriptions; `SubscriptionListResponse` kicks back the requested list.

**`SubscriptionContentRequest`.** This asks for the contents of a catalog that you have subscribed to; `SubscriptionContentResponse` responds with the requested content.

### The SubscriptionChangeMessage Element

This element contains a Subscription element and its children. The InternalID element is an internal, unique ID, and Name is the name of the subscription, that is, Summer Specials.

ChangeTime gives the date and time in ISO 8601 when the subscription last changed. SupplierID is the ID—a DUNS number in the example—for the supplier of the catalog. Format gives the format of the catalog: Ariba's Catalog Interchange Format. This is optional (zero or one only), as is Description, which gives you the space to provide a description for the catalog.

Description has mixed content, that is, parsed character data mixed with a child element, in any order. The one element Description may contain is ShortName. Though the DTD allows you to freely mix Short-Name elements and #PCDATA, the purveyors suggest that, if you use it, you place ShortName at the beginning or end of the content in Description. A ShortName element is intended to be a brief description of the item or transaction or whatever it is. This ShortName will appear in detail views in Ariba applications.

### Catalog Interchange Format

Catalogs are stored in Ariba's Catalog Interchange Format, or CIF. You need Ariba infrastructure to read files in CIF. An example of a CIF document follows:

```
CIF_I_V2.1
LOADMODE: F
CODEFORMAT: SPSC
CURRENCY: USD
DUNS: TRUE
DATA
867578317,0471416207,0471416207,"XSL Essentials",
55101509,35.99,EA,2,John Wiley & Sons,http://www.wyeast.net,
http://www.wiley.com,44.99
ENDOFDATA
1/12/01 18:10:53
ITEMCOUNT: 1
```

The first line is the version number of the CIF file. LOADMODE can be either F for full replace or I for incremental replace. CODEFORMAT is SPSC, which stands for the United Nations Standard Products and Service Codes, a code sponsored by the UN and Dun & Bradstreet for classifying products and services. CURRENCY is USD (United States dollars). DUNS: TRUE means that the first value in the data will be a DUNS number.

DATA consists of a comma-delimited list of information about the catalog item. Items are separated by a single CR/LF. ENDOFDATA, of course, ends the catalog data. Next is a date and timestamp in the form MM/DD/YY HH:MM:SS, which does not conform strictly to ISO 8601. The final entry, ITEMCOUNT, is the number of catalog items separated by CR/LFs in DATA.

The DATA section consists of the following information, separated by commas:

```
Supplier-ID-or-DUNS,Supplier-Part-ID,Manufacturer's-Part-ID,"Item-
Description",SPSC-Code,Unit-Price-Rate,Units-of-Measure,Lead-
Time,Manufacturer's-Name,Supplier-URL,Manufacturere-URL,Market-Price
```

# Suppliers

The cXML vocabulary also allows you to manage information about the people who supply the products and services in the catalogs. Following are the elements that help you manage supplier information. You saw some of these earlier, in a different context, but I repeat them here for convenience.

**SupplierListRequest.** This element requests a list of suppliers with which you have a trading relationship. The SupplierList-Response element returns the requested list of suppliers.

**SupplierDataRequest.** This element asks for data about a specific supplier, and SupplierDataResponse responds with the data. See the example that follows for an example of this kind of response.

**SupplierChangeMessage.** This element requests a change to be made in supplier information. You saw this element in use in an earlier example. This element has a type attribute, which is required. Its value can be new, update, or delete. The element has as content one or more Supplier elements.

## A SupplierDataResponse Example

A Supplier element holds all kinds of information about a supplier, such as name, address, email addresses, URLs, and so on. The following example shows a Supplier element returned as part of a SupplierData-Response.

```
<?xml version="1.0" encoding="utf-8"?>
<!DOCTYPE cXML SYSTEM
```

```
     "http://xml.cXML.org/schemas/cXML/1.1.009/cXML.dtd">

     <cXML payloadID="435267@testb2b.org" xml:lang="en-US"
           timestamp="2001-01-01T00:03:01-08:00">
      <Response>
       <Status code="200" text="OK"/>
        <SupplierDataResponse>
         <Supplier>
          <SupplierID domain="private">030-0001</SupplierID>
           <SupplierLocation>
            <Address>
             <Name xml:lang="en-us">TestB2B.org</Name>
              <PostalAddress>
              <Street>P.O. Box 537</Street>
              <City>West Linn</City>
              <State>Oregon</State>
              <PostalCode>97068-0537</PostalCode>
              <Country isoCountryCode="us">United States</Country>
             </PostalAddress>
            </Address>
          <OrderMethods>
           <OrderMethod>
            <OrderTarget>
             <URL>http://testb2b.org/B2B/orders/cXML</URL>
            </OrderTarget>
           </OrderMethod>
           <Contact>
            <Name xml:lang="en-us">Schlomo</Name>
            <Email>schlomo@testb2b.org</Email>
            <Phone>(503)555-9999</Phone>
            <Fax>(503)555-9990</Fax>
           </Contact>
          </OrderMethods>
         </SupplierLocation>
        </Supplier>
       </SupplierDataResponse>
      </Response>
     </cXML>
```

Now let's take a closer look at the elements in this cXML document.

## The Supplier Element

A supplier of goods and services is identified by a Supplier element. This element must include one Name element, one or more SupplierID elements, and an optional SupplierLocation (zero or more).

Supplier also has two optional elements. A corporateURL is a URL for a Web site that provides information about the supplier, and a store-

`FrontURL` is a URL for a shopping site associated with the supplier. `Name` simply provides an identifying name to help describe the function of the supplier or whatever else you want to say about the supplier. It can also have an optional `xml:lang` attribute.

A `Comment` is an optional element that can provide descriptive information in the context of the `Supplier`. This is a mixed content element that can include one or more `Attachment` elements along with parsed character data, preferably at the beginning or end of the `Comment` content. `Comment` can also take an `xml:lang` attribute.

An `Attachment` element contains a single `URL` element. This URL will reference a `Content-ID` header in a multipart MIME part in the cXML document. In this context, the URL must use the CID format outlined in RFC 2111. A URL element may include a `name` attribute at your option. (An example of `Attachment` can be found in the section titled *An Order-Request Document: A Complete Example,* later in this chapter.)

### The SupplierID and SupplierLocation Elements

A `SupplierID` element identifies a supplier by means of a special ID, such as a DUNS number or a private ID scheme agreed upon by vendors, as noted in the required `domain` attribute. You can provide one or more `SupplierID` elements.

An optional `SupplierLocation` element provides information about the location of the supplier, especially the physical location. This element must contain one `Address` element and one `OrderMethods` element.

### The Address Element

An `Address` holds the following elements in order:

**Name.** This is an identifying string with optional `xml:lang` attribute.

**PostalAddress.** A `PostalAddress` has fairly predictable content describing a physical location (it may have a `name` attribute as well). It has zero or more `DeliverTo` elements, one or more of `Street`, exactly one `City`, zero or one of `State`, zero or one of `PostalCode`, and exactly one `Country`. `DeliverTo` is part of the address such as a person's name or a department name. The remaining elements, all #PCDATA, have obvious meanings. A `PostalCode` is a ZIP Code if you are in the United States. The `Country` element has a required attribute, `isoCountryCode`, which contains a two-letter ISO 3166 country code.

**Email.** An Email address is parsed character data with an optional name attribute. The email address should conform to the normal email address format, but the DTD cannot enforce it.

**Phone.** This element contains a single TelephoneNumber, and it may have a name attribute. A TelephoneNumber contains an international phone number: CountryCode, AreaorCityCode, Number, and zero or one of Extension. CountryCode is a 1–3 digit country code (Germany, for example, is 49). This element must also have an isoCountryCode attribute that contains an ISO 3166 country code (Germany, again, is de). This is followed by an area or city code (such as 30 for Berlin or 40 for Hamburg) in AreaOrCityCode. The local phone number is carried in Number. Extension is an optional extension.

**Fax.** A Fax can contain a TelephoneNumber, a URL, or an Email, depending on how a fax is implemented by your supplier. It can also have a name attribute.

**URL.** This contains a string representation for a URL, which can also have an optional name attribute.

Only one Name element is allowed, but you can have zero or one of the remaining elements. If you wish, Name can contain the optional attributes isoCountryCode, an ISO 3166 country code, and an addressID that contains a string to help link up an address with another ID in the document.

## The OrderMethods and OrderMethod Elements

OrderMethods lists the methods—one or more OrderMethod elements—you can use to order from a supplier. While the cXML DTD cannot enforce this, the intent is that the OrderMethod elements be listed in the order of supplier preference, with the first being most preferred and so on down the line. A Contact element may also be included to identify a technical contact who should be available to help with ordering.

OrderMethod must contain a single OrderTarget element, which may be followed by zero or more OrderProtocol elements. OrderTarget holds one of the following elements: Phone, Email, Fax, URL, or OtherOrderTarget. An OtherOrderTarget element contains any other address mechanism that is not already listed. The name attribute is optional. The OrderProtocol element simply states the protocol method—such as cXML—for communicating orders to suppliers. It contains only parsed character data.

### *The Contact Element*

Contact, an optional element, holds information about a communication contact. It may also have a role attribute that describes a person or department, such as buyer or agent. A Contact has these elements as content: a single Name and zero or more of PostalAddress, Email, Phone, Fax, and URL.

# The Punchout Site

One of the key functionalities of cXML is the punchout Web site. A punchout site can help a buyer to accesses products and services from a supplier on a local, item-by-item basis. The site can allow you to select one or more items from a catalog, so rather than sending a whole catalog at once, it sends the requested catalog items in short files. A punchout site also allows suppliers to control their catalogs locally. Central commerce servers or hubs, such as Ariba Network or Ariba CSN, help authenticate and negotiate the requests and responses between the buyer and supplier.

A punchout session can be broken down into several steps. Consider yourself the buyer or user in this example. An intermediate hub or server monitors everything.

1. Using a local procurement application, you first pick a supplier from which you want to purchase something. As you make a selection, your local application, such as Ariba Buyer, makes a request to the hub.

2. The hub authenticates you and opens up a secure session, perhaps using SSL, with the supplier's site.

3. You now find products or services on the supplier's site.

4. When you are ready to make your purchase, the hub helps process your request and sends the selected items to your local application.

5. After your final approval, the selected items are fed back through the hub to the supplier's site.

Here are the elements and documents that are part of a punchout session.

**Punchout Index Catalog files.** These files point to a punchout Web site and list supplier and catalog items. These files are associated with step 1 of the punchout session.

**PunchOutSetupRequest.** When a user selects a punchout item, the underlying application creates a PunchOutSetupRequest document and sends it to a hub site, which in turn sends it to a punchout Web site. Or you can do it yourself with a cXML launch page. An example of Active Server Pages (ASP) code for a launch page is provided on page 28 of the cXML spec. This is also part of step 1.

**PunchOutSetupResponse.** After getting a PunchOutSetupRequest document, the punch out site will send back a PunchOutSetupResponse. This document indicates if the PunchOutSetupRequest was successful and provides a redirect URL for the punchout StartPage; it also provides state information that will bind data to a session. The ASP launch page example starting on page 28 of the cXML specification includes a PunchOutSetupResponse. It also includes a URL for a StartPage. See step 3.

**PunchOutOrderMessage.** This message sends the content of the shopping cart to an application for checkout. You can see an ASP example of a sender's page on page 32 of the specification. See step 4. A PunchOutOrderMessage contains a BuyerCookie, a PunchOutOrderMessageHeader, and an ItemIn. BuyerCookie is discussed under *Cookies* near the end of this chapter. A PunchOutOrderMessageHeader has a required attribute, operationAllowed, whose value can be one of create, inspect, or edit. Its children are one of Total, and zero or one of ShipTo, Shipping, and Tax. (You'll see discussions of these elements later, though in different contexts.)

**OrderRequest.** When the punchout session wraps up, the local application sends a purchase order to the supplier in the form of an OrderRequest. An OrderResponse confirms the order. See step 5.

## A Punchout Index Catalog

A punchout index document updates the goods and services listed in a local procurement application, like Ariba Buyer or your own homegrown application. (Sorry, instructions on writing such an app are outside the scope of this book.) This is from step 1 of a punchout session. Following is a short example of an index document.

```
<?xml version="1.0" encoding="utf-8"?>
<!DOCTYPE Index SYSTEM
"http://xml.cXML.org/schemas/cXML/1.1.009/cXML.dtd">
```

```
<Index>
 <SupplierID domain="DUNS">86-757-8317</SupplierID>
  <SearchGroup>
    <Name xml:lang="en">XML books</Name>
    <SearchAttribute name="xsl" type="string"/>
  </SearchGroup>
  <IndexItem>
   <IndexItemAdd>
    <ItemID>
     <SupplierPartID>0471416207</SupplierPartID>
    </ItemID>
    <ItemDetail>
     <UnitPrice>
      <Money currency="USD">44.99</Money>
     </UnitPrice>
     <Description>XSL Essentials</Description>
     <UnitOfMeasure>EA</UnitOfMeasure>
     <Classification domain="UNSPSC">55101509</Classification>
     <ManufacturerName>John Wiley & Sons</ManufacturerName>
     <URL>http://www.wiley.com/compbooks/fitzgerald</URL>
    </ItemDetail>
    <IndexItemDetail>
     <LeadTime>180</LeadTime>
     <EffectiveDate>2001-05-21</EffectiveDate>
    </IndexItemDetail>
   </IndexItemAdd>
  </IndexItem>
  <IndexItem>
  <IndexItemPunchout>
   <ItemID>
    <SupplierPartID>xml-set</SupplierPartID>
   </ItemID>
   <PunchoutDetail>
    <Description>XSL Essentials and XML Schema Essentials
    </Description>
    <URL>http://www.wyeast.net</URL>
    <Classification domain="UNSPSC">55101509</Classification>
    <ManufacturerName xml:lang="en-US">Wiley</ManufacturerName>
    <EffectiveDate>2001-06-21</EffectiveDate>
   <SearchGroupData>
    <Name>XML book set</Name>
    <SearchDataElement name="title" value="xml schema"/>
    <SearchDataElement name="title" value="xsl"/>
   </SearchGroupData>
   </PunchoutDetail>
  </IndexItemPunchout>
 </IndexItem>
</Index>
```

The Index element provides a way to update the list of goods and services that are available via a punchout site. It must contain one or more

SupplierID and IndexItem elements. It may also have zero or one Comments, directly after SupplierID, and zero or more SearchGroup elements following that. SupplierID in this example is a DUNS number, though it could be some other value. No Comments appear in this example.

SearchGroup has two children: Exactly one instance of Name followed by one or more SearchAttribute elements. Name has already been discussed. SearchAttribute is an empty element with two attributes. The first, name, is required, but the second, type, is optional. Name contains the name of a book. The name attribute of SearchAttribute contains a searchable parameter xsl, which is of type string.

An IndexItem element contains a list of one or more items used to update or modify the index of products and services on the site. It can contain one or more of the following children: IndexItemAdd, for adding an item to the index; IndexItemDelete, to remove an item; and IndexItemPunchout, an additional punchout item for the index.

IndexItemDelete is not shown. It specifies an item to be removed from the index. It contains a single instance of ItemID, which identifies the item.

IndexItemAdd, shown in the example, is composed of three child elements with exactly one instance of each required. ItemID provides a unique identity for the item. ItemDetail gives general information about the item. IndexItemDetail gives an index-specific detail for the item.

The ItemID element must have one instance of SupplierPartID as a child. In the example, the content of ItemID is an International Standard Book Number (ISBN): 0471416207.

ItemID can also have zero or one instance of SupplierPartAuxiliaryID. A SupplierPartAuxiliaryID, when present, helps the remote Web site provide complex information to identify the item if and when it is presented to the remote site in the future. A SupplierPartAuxiliaryID can specify an auxiliary bit of information, such as a cookie, that identifies the part even more precisely when combined with the SupplierID and SupplierPartID. For example, you might use the same SupplierPartID for one item, but have a different price for the item based on packaging. If SupplierPartAuxiliaryID content is used to convey a cookie, the procurement application should pass it back in any subsequent sessions, including any purchase orders.

ItemDetail contains detailed information about an item. It has one instance of UnitPrice, one or more Description elements, one of UnitOfMeasure, one or more Classification elements, zero or one of ManufacturerPartID, ManufacturerName, and URL, plus zero or more `Extrinsic` elements at the end. The `domain` attribute of `Classification` has the value `UNSPSC`. This refers to the United Nations Standard Products and Services Classification (UN/SPSC), a set of global, universal classification codes for products and services.

`UnitPrice` contain a single instance of the `Money` element. `Money` contains parsed character data content that is the amount of the price. It has one required attribute, `currency`, which holds a three-letter currency code based on ISO 4217, such as `USD` for United States dollars, `XEU` for Euros, or `DEM` for Deutsche marks. There are two other optional attributes, `alternateAmount` and `alternateCurrency`, which provide a way to hold the price in an additional, different currency.

A `Description` is a string of text describing the item (`#PCDATA`). A `UnitOfMeasure` specifies the item's unit size based on Recommendation 20 from the United Nations Economic Commission for Europe (UN/ECE), such as EA (each), BX (box), and CT (carton).

A `Classification` element classifies the commodity grouping of item. All products and services must be associated with a standard UN/SPSC number. For example, the classification for educational and vocational textbook is `55101509`. (You can use one or more of these elements).

The `ManufacturerName` (with `xml:lang` attribute) and `URL` have obvious content. You can also include, if desired, a `ManufacturerPartID` element (not shown), which contains an ID specific to the manufacturer, such as a part number or SKU (stock keeping unit) number. This comes right before `ManufacturerName`, if used.

You can also use the `Extrinsic` element (not shown), as the last element of all (more than one, if you want), which provides a way to extend the data describing the item, beyond the elements already provided. I think of `Extrinsic` as the kitchen-sink element of cXML.

An `IndexItemDetail` element follows `ItemDetail` in the example. It contains elements to help define the index item in question. It has only one required element, which is `LeadTime`, the planned or estimated number of days necessary to physically receive the desired item. This is followed by zero or one of `ExpirationDate` and `EffectiveDate`, and zero or more of `SearchGroupData` and `TerritoryAvailable`.

An `ExpirationDate` element provides the date and time, in 8601 format, when the item will expire (zero or one). Likewise, an `EffectiveDate` gives the 8601 date and time when the item becomes effective (zero or one).

`SearchGroupData` contains data that identifies the item in a search (zero or more). It has two subelements: `Name`, which we have already discussed, and `SearchDataElement`, an empty element with two required attributes. They are `name` and `value`, both strings.

`TerritoryAvailable` is a region or territory, defined by ISO country and/or region codes, where the item is available (zero or more).

Finally, `IndexItemPunchout` dynamically connects an item to the supplier's resource for that item. Its content model is composed of two children, with exactly one instance of each, first an `ItemID` and next a `PunchoutDetail`, which, as you might guess, describes the punchout item in some detail.

The child elements of `PunchoutDetail` have already been discussed in other contexts. They are, in order: `Description` (one or more); `URL` (one); `Classification` (one or more); `ManufacturerName` (zero or one); `ManufacturerPartID` (zero or one); `ExpirationDate` (zero or one); `EffectiveDate` (zero or one); `SearchGroupData` (zero or more); and finally, `TerritoryAvailable` (zero or more).

# The Request-Response versus the One-Way Model

As you have already seen, a number of cXML transactions follow the HTTP model of request-response. For example, you send a `Profile-Request` to a cXML-ready server and you get a `ProfileResponse` in return. You can also send one-way messages.

One-way messages do not use the request-response model. They assume that you are going to send a message in one direction only, whether by HTTP or through URI-Encoding. While not openly stated in the spec, there is no reason you couldn't send cXML documents by FTP or SMTP, that is, if you don't care about processing the information with a cXML-capable server.

## URI-Encoding

URI-Encoding (or URL-Encoding) is a way to use forbidden characters as part of a URL or even in a document. Some of the characters that need encoding are spaces, commas, quotation marks, pound sign, percent sign, control characters, non-ASCII characters, and so forth. In URI-Encoding, the character is transformed to a hexadecimal number, preceded by a percent sign.

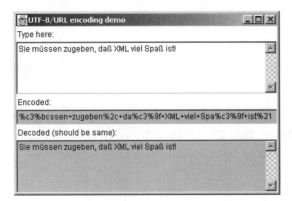

**Figure 7.1**   W3C URI-Encoding program.

To demonstrate what this encoding looks like, you can download and compile a little Java program offered by the W3C that does URI-Encoding on the fly (www.w3.org/International/O-URL-code.html). It's shown in Figure 7.1.

This German sentence contains a few letters that are not in the US-ASCII character set, such as the letter *u* with an umlaut (ü) or the double *s* or eszett (ß). It also uses spaces, a comma, and an exclamation point. Spaces are replaced with + (seen elsewhere as %20). The *ü* becomes `%c3%bx`, the comma becomes `%2c`, ß is `%c3%9f`, and ! is `%21`.

## Form Packing

The cXML specification includes a transport method called *form packing*. Earlier versions of RosettaNet (1.1) and BizTalk (1.0) both included this method of transport. Basically, you send a document as a hidden field when posting an HTML form. It enables the recipient to receive an XML document without having a listening, firewall-protected Web server, by handling it through the browser.

An HTML example with such a form follows:

```
<html>
<head>
 <title>cXML Form Packing Example</title>
<body>
 <form method="POST" action="http://testb2b.org/testb2b/stub">
  <input type="hidden" name="cXML-urlencoded"
```

```
    value="%3C?xml%20version%3D%221.0%22%20encoding%3D%22utf-
8%22?%3E%0A%3COrder/%3E%0A">
  <input type="submit" value="Submit">
  </form>
</body>
<html>
```

In this example, the `value` attribute of `input` consists of an encoded string that is, for brevity, simply an XML declaration followed by an empty instance of `Order`. This encoded string would look like this if the text were rendered normally:

```
<?xml version="1.0" encoding="utf-8"?>
<Order/>
```

The value of the `name` attribute in the first input element may also be `cXML-base64`. This allows you to send base64-encoded documents. Base64 preserves the original encoding of the document rather than using URI-Encoding and is good for preserving characters in international documents.

In a `PunchOutOrderRequest` document, for example, like the one that follows, an instance of the element `BrowserFormPost` holds a `URL` that matches the `action` attribute in the `form` element you saw in the previous HTML document.

```
<?xml version="1.0" encoding="utf-8"?>
<!DOCTYPE cXML SYSTEM
"http://xml.cXML.org/schemas/cXML/1.1.009/cXML.dtd">

<cXML payloadID="568392@testb2b.org" xml:lang="en-US"
      timestamp="2001-01-01T00:00:56-08:00">
 <Header>
  <From>
   <Credential domain="B2B Access Domain">
    <Identity>mike@wyeast.net</Identity>
   </Credential>
  </From>
  <To>
   <Credential domain="B2B Access Domain">
    <Identity>schlomo@testb2b.org</Identity>
   </Credential>
  </To>
  <Sender>
   <Credential domain="B2B Access Domain">
    <Identity>mike@wyeast.net</Identity>
    <SharedSecret>xxxxxxxxxxxx</SharedSecret>
   </Credential>
```

```
   <UserAgent>W3C Amaya 4.2</UserAgent>
  </Sender>
 </Header>
 <Request>
  <PunchOutSetupRequest operation="create">
   <BuyerCookie>5F495G832H25J69K0</BuyerCookie>
   <BrowserFormPost>
    <URL>http://testb2b.org/testb2b/stub1</URL>
   </BrowserFormPost>
   <SelectedItem>
    <ItemID>
     <SupplierPartID>0471416207</SupplierPartID>
    </ItemID>
   </SelectedItem>
  </PunchOutSetupRequest>
 </Request>
</cXML>
```

The `PunchOutSetupRequest` element has been described briefly earlier in this chapter, but I'll offer a few more details here. First, it has one required attribute, `operation`, which can have one of three values: `create`, `inspect`, or `edit`. (There is no default.) The value `create` begins a new punchout session; `edit` opens a session for editing; and `inspect` opens a session for viewing, but no changes may be made in the session.

The children of `PunchOutSetupRequest` are as follows: exactly one `BuyerCookie`, zero or more of `Extrinsic`, zero or one `BrowserForm-Post`, zero or more of `Contact`, zero or one `SupplierSetup`, zero or one `ShipTo`, zero or one `SelectedItem`, and zero or more of `ItemOut`.

## Cookies

If you don't already know, a cookie is a small bit of text that helps a Web browser identify a user or customize a Web session. This information is normally saved in a text file for future use by the browser. Cookies eliminate the need to repeatedly pass or collect identifying information securely over the Internet.

Browsers store cookies in different ways. In Windows, for example, Microsoft Internet Explorer, by default, stores cookies in separate text files under a user's home directory. Netscape stores them in one file in a more common location, and Opera stores cookies in a `.dat` file in its own main directory.

In the case of cXML, cookies help preserve state information during transactions. Cookies are required fare when a buyer issues either a

PunchOutSetupRequest or PunchOutOrderMessage, both of which have BuyerCookie as the mandatory child element. On the other hand, a supplier can also provide a cookie in the SupplierPartAuxiliaryID element, which is an optional child element of ItemID. An application can hand supplier cookies back in punchout sessions, as you can see in a purchase order example later in this chapter in the section titled *An OrderRequest Document: A Complete Example*. (It is possible, however, if not likely, for a supplier to provide information other than cookies in Supplier-PartAuxiliaryID.)

Of course, a cXML-aware Ariba application will help manage these cookies for you, but if you are going to write your own application, you will need to figure out how you will manage them in software. Java provides coding facilities for cookies in servlets (javax.servlet.http .Cookie). You can read more about cookies in section 7, "Sessions," of the *Java Servlet Specification, Version 2.2*. Cookies are also used in the Java plug-in.

Cookies are in quite common use but are not always welcome guests. You may already be aware that many Web sites are unobtrusively planting cookies on your hard drive regularly. Between well-established business partners, this may not be a problem. In fact, it may be essential for managing sessions. Cookies, however, can pose some risks and are a subtle intrusion on privacy. An interesting exercise is to run the text-based Lynx browser on a Unix system with the Cookies option set to ask user. Then visit some of your favorite Web sites and watch how many of them are pushing cookies on you.

As Extrinsic, BrowserFormPost, and Contact have already been described, SupplierSetup has been deprecated. SelectedItem contains an ItemID that has a SupplierPartID and, if desired, a SupplierPartAuxiliaryID. ShipTo has one child element, Address. All these have already been discussed as well.

> **NOTE** The ItemOut element will be explored with an example in the upcoming section titled *An OrderRequest Document: A Complete Example*.

## The PunchOutSetupResponse

A PunchOutSetupResponse has one child, StartPage, which has one child itself, URL. This URL redirects the session to a start page. (The URL in the example does not work.) As I mentioned before, there is an ASP launch page example starting on page 28 of the cXML specification that may be useful if you can use ASP.

```
<?xml version="1.0" encoding="utf-8"?>

<!DOCTYPE cXML SYSTEM
"http://xml.cXML.org/schemas/cXML/1.1.009/cXML.dtd">

<cXML payloadID="568392-2@testb2b.org" xml:lang="en-US"
      timestamp="2001-01-01T00:04:51-08:00">
 <Response>
  <Status code="200" text="OK"/>
  <PunchOutSetupResponse>
   <StartPage>
    <URL>http://testb2b.org/B2B/start.asp?7465392</URL>
   </StartPage>
  </PunchOutSetupResponse>
 </Response>
</cXML>
```

# Purchase Orders

The last step in a punchout session is to transmit one or more automated purchase orders, based on the selections made during the session. You can send and receive purchase orders outside of the punchout process if you wish. Whether part of a punchout session or not, the process and application functions are about the same.

You establish a URL where purchase orders will be sent when you set up your Web site and the accompanying hub server, such as an Ariba platform. The order is sent in a document that has an `OrderRequest` element, and a document containing an `OrderResponse` is sent in reply. The response is a must if you are following the cXML specification closely.

Purchase orders can also include attachments, which are discussed later in this chapter under, no shock here, *Attachments*.

## An OrderRequest Document: A Complete Example

Following is an example of a cXML purchase order containing an `Order-Request` element. Not only does it contain all the information necessary for a purchase order, it also includes HTTP, MIME, and attachment information. Fasten your seat belt: It's a long one.

```
POST /B2B/punch.asp HTTP/1.1
Host: www.testb2b.org
Content-type: multipart/mixed; boundary=cXML_boundary
Content-length: 709325
```

```
Accept: text/html, image/tiff, image/jpeg, image/gif *;
User-Agent: Mozilla/4.0 (compatible; MSIE 5.0; Win32)
Connection: Keep-Alive

--cXML_boundary
Content-type: text/xml; charset="utf-8"

<?xml version="1.0" encoding="utf-8" ?>
<!DOCTYPE cXML SYSTEM
"http://xml.cxml.org/schemas/cXML/1.1.009/cXML.dtd">

<cXML xml:lang="en-US" payloadID="2458390@testb2b.org" timestamp="2001-
    01-01T00:00:01-8:00">
<Header>
 <From>
  <Credential domain="B2B Order Access">
   <Identity>mike@wyeast.net</Identity>
  </Credential>
 </From>
 <To>
  <Credential domain="B2B Order Access">
   <Identity>schlomo@testb2b.org</Identity>
  </Credential>
 </To>
 <Sender>
  <Credential domain="B2B Order Access">
   <Identity>mike@wyeast.net</Identity>
   <DigitalSignature type="PK7 self-contained"
    encoding="Base64">
    T2ghIFlvdSBjYXVnaHQgbWUhIFRoaXMgaXMgYSBmYWtlIGRpZ2l0YWwgc
    2lnbmF0dXJlIHdyaXR0ZW4gaW4gYmFzZTY0Lg==
   </DigitalSignature>
  </Credential>
  <UserAgent>Opera 5.01</UserAgent>
 </Sender>
</Header>
<Request>
 <OrderRequest>
  <OrderRequestHeader orderID="G-239573-6"
   orderDate="2001-01-01T00:00:01-8:00" type="new">
   <Total>
    <Money currency="USD">38.43</Money>
   </Total>
   <ShipTo>
    <Address isoCountryCode="US">
    <Name xml:lang="en">Wy'east Communications</Name>
    <PostalAddress>
    <DeliverTo>Mike Fitzgerald</DeliverTo>
    <DeliverTo>Bibliophile</DeliverTo>
    <Street>P.O. Box 537</Street>
    <City>West Linn</City>
```

```
    <State>OR</State>
    <PostalCode>97068-0537</PostalCode>
    <Country>United States</Country>
   </PostalAddress>
   <Email>mike@wyeast.net</Email>
   <Phone name="work">
    <TelephoneNumber>
     <CountryCode isoCountryCode="US">1</CountryCode>
     <AreaOrCityCode>503</AreaOrCityCode>
     <Number>555-9999</Number>
     <Extension>456</Extension>
    </TelephoneNumber>
   </Phone>
  </Address>
 </ShipTo>
 <BillTo>
  <Address isoCountryCode="US">
   <Name xml:lang="en">Floydene Wallup</Name>
    <PostalAddress>
    <Street>P.O. Box 537</Street>
    <City>West Linn</City>
    <State>OR</State>
    <PostalCode>97068-0537</PostalCode>
    <Country>United States</Country>
   </PostalAddress>
   <Email>floydene@wyeast.net</Email>
   <Phone name="work">
    <TelephoneNumber>
     <CountryCode isoCountryCode="US">1</CountryCode>
     <AreaOrCityCode>503</AreaOrCityCode>
     <Number>555-9999</Number>
     <Extension>789</Extension>
    </TelephoneNumber>
   </Phone>
  </Address>
 </BillTo>
 <Shipping>
  <Money currency="USD">2.44</Money>
   <Description xml:lang="en-us">USPS Priority</Description>
 </Shipping>
 <Tax>
  <Money currency="USD">0</Money>
  <Description xml:lang="en">No Oregon sales tax</Description>
 </Tax>
 <Payment>
  <PCard number="5467XXXXXXXXXXXX" expiration="2004-06-01"/>
 </Payment>
</OrderRequestHeader>
<ItemOut quantity="1" >
 <ItemID>
  <SupplierPartID>0471416207</SupplierPartID>
```

```
    <SupplierPartAuxiliaryID>5X5D89903C</SupplierPartAuxiliaryID>
   </ItemID>
   <ItemDetail>
    <UnitPrice>
     <Money currency="USD">35.99</Money>
    </UnitPrice>
    <Description xml:lang="en">XSL Essentials</Description>
    <UnitOfMeasure>EA</UnitOfMeasure>
    <Classification domain="UNSPSC">55101509</Classification>
    <URL>http://testb2b.org/B2B/punch.asp</URL>
    <Extrinsic name="opt">electronic bookmark</Extrinsic>
   </ItemDetail>
   <Distribution>
    <Accounting name="expense">
     <AccountingSegment id="CC-12">
      <Name>Books</Name>
      <Description>Technical or engineering books</Description>
     </AccountingSegment>
    </Accounting>
    <Charge>
     <Money currency="USD">35.99</Money>
    </Charge>
   </Distribution>
   <Comments>
    <Attachment>
     <URL>CID:cover.tif@testb2b.org</URL>
    </Attachment>
   </Comments>
  </ItemOut>
 </OrderRequest>
</Request>
</cXML>

--cXML_boundary
Content-type: image/tiff
Content-Transfer-Encoding: base64
Content-ID: <cover.tif@testb2b.org>
```

```
SUkqAAgAAAAPAP4ABAABAAAAAAAAAAAABBAABAAAAdQEAAAEBBAABAAAAzAEAAAIBAwADAAAA
wgAAAAMBAwABAAAAAQAAAAYBAwABAAAAAgAAABEBBABCAAAA2AAAABIBAwABAAAAAQAAABUB
AwABAAAAwAAABYBBAABAAAABwAAABcBBBABCAAAA4AEAABoBBQABAAAAyAAAABsBBQABAAAA
0AAAABwBAwABAAAAAQAACgBAwABAAAAgAAAAAAAAIAAgACABgAAAAQAAAGAAAAABAAAA
6AIAAIEhAAAaQAAAs14AAEx9AADlmwAAfroAABfZAACw9wAASRYBAOI0AQB7UwEAFHIBAK2Q
AQBGrwEA380BAHjsAQ
```

```
[truncated]

--cXML_boundary--
```

Let's start from the beginning and walk through the example.

## HTTP

At the beginning of this example, in the first line, you can see the HTTP/1.1 POST method. You learned about HTTP in Chapter 3, "Transport." The document is supposedly being posted to a program on a site that will process the document and send an `OrderResponse` in reply. (The program is fictitious; at this time, it is for illustration only.)

## MIME

You also see MIME headers, which you also learned about in Chapter 3. You can use either `multipart/mixed` or `multipart/related` contents types in the headers. The example uses `multipart/mixed`. It has two parts. The first part consists of a cXML document, and the second part is an attachment. The boundary in the example is `cXML_boundary`.

## Attachments

Because cXML supports MIME, it by extension also supports attachments. When sending a purchase order or some other cXML document, you can embed an attachment to support the document, such as a graphic, a document in binary form, or even a fax.

A `Comments` element may contain an `Attachment` element that, in turn, contains a `URL` element. This element will hold a CID-prefixed URL to an identifier in a MIME `Content-ID` header. This way of referencing content in MIME, as mentioned before, is based on RFC 2111.

## OrderRequestHeader

The `OrderRequestHeader` element shows up in this example, but it has a number of other attributes and child elements, beyond those shown. The content model looks like this: One of `Total`, zero or one `ShipTo`, exactly one `BillTo`, zero or one of `Shipping`, `Tax`, and `Payment`. After that comes zero or more of `Contact`, zero or one of `Comments`, `Followup`, and `DocumentReference`, and finally zero or more of `Extrinsic`.

I'll mention `Total`, `BillTo`, `Followup`, and `DocumentReference` here as they aren't discussed elsewhere. `Total` is the overall total amount for the order, expressed in `Money`. `BillTo` contains a single `Address` element, which holds content whose meaning is, I hope, pretty apparent by now.

`Followup` is not shown in the example. When used, it gives a URL where `StatusUpdateRequest` documents must be posted to provide input to an `OrderRequest` document. A `StatusUpdateRequest` provides a means to make changes to earlier orders.

`DocumentReference` is an empty element that has one required attribute, `payloadID`, which references the `payloadID` of the earlier order. For more information on how to do a `StatusUpdateRequest`, see page 82 of the cXML specification.

## The ItemOut Element

`ItemOut` appears in both of the previous examples. Its corollary is an element called `ItemIn`, which I won't discuss except to say that it has similar content to `ItemOut` and is used by a procurement application like Ariba Buyer to add an item to a shopping cart. `ItemOut`'s attributes include `quantity`, the number of items, which is required. The remaining attributes are optional. A `lineNumber` attribute contains the ordered position of the item. A `requisitionID` is an ID for the item from the buyer's side, and `RequestedDeliveryDate` is the date that this item was requested to be delivered.

`ItemOut` contains a number of elements, most of which should be familiar to you: One `ItemID`; zero or one of `ItemDetail`, `SupplierID`, `ShipTo`, `Shipping`, and `Tax`; zero or more `Distribution` and `Contact`, and zero or one of `Comments`.

I'll talk about the elements in the `ItemOut` content model that have not already been covered, that is, `Shipping`, `Tax`, and `Distribution`.

### Shipping and Tax

`Shipping` describes the cost and means of shipping the item ordered. It contains exactly one instance each of `Money` (`2.44`) and `Description` (`USPS Priority`). You should already understand these two subelements from the descriptions given in this chapter, but I will tell you about its attributes, none of which are required, both of which deal with tracking the item when shipped, and neither of which are shown in the example.

The `trackingDomain` attribute represents the shipping provider, such as Federal Express (FedEx) and the U.S. Postal Service (USPS). The `trackingID` is the provider's ID number for the item or package in transit. (The `tracking` attribute, though still in the cXML DTD, is deprecated, so you shouldn't use it.)

Now, for a word on everyone's favorite topic: Taxes. I'll make this as short and as painless as I can. `Tax`, like `Shipping`, has two required elements, `Money` and `Description`. These are for carrying the sales and any other tax on the items. Fortunately for us Oregonians, we don't have to pay a sales tax. (But don't be jealous: We make up for it in property tax.)

### Using Your Credit Card

The elements `Payment` and `PCard` express information about a credit or debit card used to pay for an item or items. The `number` and `date` attributes, as you might guess, are required. The `number` attribute is a credit or debit card number (you won't get very far with the number in the example), and expiration is the expiration date for the card. You can optionally supply the name on the card in the name attribute. You may or may not— it's up to you—provide an instance of `PostalAddress`, with `Name`, `Street`, `City`, and the like.

### The Distribution Element

`Distribution` helps out the accounting department by allowing you to assign or divide up item costs. Only one segment is given, but it is possible to divide up an expense into several pots. This element has two required child elements: One instance each of `Accounting` and `Charge`.

`Accounting` contains either one or more `Segment` elements, an older method, or one or more of the newer, more preferred `Accounting-Segment` elements. `Accounting` also has a name attribute (optional).

`AccountingSegment` has one attribute, `id`, a unique ID that is required. It has two child elements, `Name` and `Description`, with obvious content. `Charge` contains an instance of `Money`, which holds the charge against the account segment.

## OrderResponse

A much shorter reply is sent in response to the `OrderRequest`. It comes in the form of an `OrderResponse` document. Every `OrderRequest` must be acknowledged with an `OrderResponse`. This response only confirms that an `OrderRequest` document was received in, we hope, good condition, and it does not commit the receiver to act on it.

An example of an `OrderResponse` follows:

```
<?xml version="1.0" encoding="utf-8" ?>
<!DOCTYPE cXML SYSTEM
"http://xml.cxml.org/schemas/cXML/1.1.009/cXML.dtd">

<cXML payloadID="2458390-1@testb2b.org"
timestamp="2001-01-01T00:00:30-08:00">
```

```
<Response>
 <Status code="200" text="OK"/>
</Response>
</cXML>
```

## cXML Summary

This ends our brief tour of cXML. Again, if you are going to implement cXML, you must refer to the cXML 1.1 specification for all the details. Though cXML is simpler than xCBL, cXML may be adequate for your catalog or purchase order management, even if you are not using Ariba software in your enterprise. However, using this vocabulary will be essential to you if you are interacting with Ariba platforms in your partner network.

# CHAPTER 8

# Simple Object Access Protocol

Simple Object Access Protocol (SOAP) does not fit in the family of B2B vocabularies. It's not like other B2B vocabularies you've already seen: It is a protocol. It can not only exchange documents between servers in a special wrapper called an envelope, but it can also exchange special messages that contain, for example, method calls to be executed on a remote server.

SOAP is based on the concept of the remote procedure call (RPC). The basic idea is that a program on one computer that is connected by a network can issue a procedure call to a program on another computer. The remote computer, be it down the hall or on another continent, can accept the call and hand it to a local program. The local program may issue a return value or some other response, then send back the return value or whatever to the computer that issued the call in the first place.

SOAP is ideal for trading information rapidly, especially small amounts of information or information that can change quickly. Some data suited for SOAP includes time of day, weather reports, stock quotes, commodities prices, postal codes, word or phrase translations, you name it. There are no restrictions on the size of document you can send in a SOAP message.

Think about this: Selling bits and pieces of information through a SOAP Web service at a quarter penny a request could be a lucrative business. And because it's based on standard Web technology, you can use SOAP regardless of platform—Windows, Linux, Mac, or Solaris.

Microsoft's Distributed Component Object Model (DCOM), the Object Management Group's Unix-based Common Object Request Broker Architecture (CORBA), Internet Inter-ORB Protocol (IIOP), and Sun's Remote Method Invocation (RMI) are all similar technologies with the same basic thing in mind, but that require infrastructure (software licenses usually) on both local and remote systems. SOAP is different in that it relies on two ubiquitous technologies—XML and HTTP—to accomplish the same thing, thus reducing overhead in time, money, and hassle. Any system connected to the Internet is already prepared more or less to handle HTTP and XML, making SOAP relatively easy to implement.

The main technology employed for SOAP transport now is HTTP, but SOAP specification does not mandate HTTP. You might use SMTP, FTP, or some other method, but HTTP is the most likely suspect at this stage.

In this chapter I will cover the basics of SOAP, show you how to try out a simple implementation of it, and point you in the direction of some resources for the protocol. I think the best place to start is with an example of a SOAP document.

**NOTE** The discussion on SOAP in this chapter is based on the SOAP version 1.1 specification, which is published as a Note on the W3C Web site. Please don't construe my discussion of this note as the final definition of the protocol, but rather as a look at a snapshot of a maturing technology. In other words, SOAP will probably change before it becomes an approved recommendation by W3C or any other standards body, if it ever does.

## A SOAP Example

Without any further delay, let's see what a SOAP message—contained in a SOAP envelope—looks like, without the HTTP headers. This is an example of a SOAP request message:

```
<SOAP-ENV:Envelope
xmlns:Soap="http://schemas.xmlsoap.org/soap/envelope">
 <SOAP-ENV:Header>
  <program:Info SOAP-ENV:mustUnderstand="1"
     xmlns:program="urn:eddys-stockomatic:program.xsd">
   <program:Name>Stockomatic</program:Name>
   <program:Version>0.83</program:Version>
  </program:Info>
 </SOAP-ENV:Header>
 <SOAP-ENV:Body>
  <stocks:GetQuote
    xmlns:stocks="urn:eddys-stockomatic:stocks.xsd">
   <stocks:Symbol>GTW</stocks:Symbol>
```

```
        <stocks:Time>2000-09-05T16:00:00.000-05:00</stocks:Time>
      </stocks:GetQuote>
    </SOAP-ENV:Body>
  </SOAP-ENV:Envelope>
```

The following sections will explain what's happening in this SOAP document, pretty much line by line.

## The SOAP Envelope Element

The SOAP `Envelope` is the container that holds the content of the SOAP message. The first or root element of this or any other SOAP document must always be an `Envelope` element.

### The SOAP Envelope Namespace

The root element in this example contains an XML namespace declaration (`xmlns`). The conventional namespace prefix is `SOAP-ENV`. You can use a prefix of your choice, but you should use a prefix. In some earlier XML examples, I used the default namespace, that is, with no prefix, but I recommend using prefixes with SOAP. Using prefixes will make SOAP documents easier to follow, because by nature, they contain more than one namespace.

The namespace is `http://schemas.xmlsoap.org/soap/envelope`. This identifier is unlikely to change. According to the XML Namespaces specification, you can use a URI or a URN as a unique namespace identifier. A logical assumption would be that the URI identifies a resource such as a schema that defines or describes the content that is allowed in the namespace. This is permissible but is not always the case: The namespace ID is simply supposed to distinguish the namespace as unique. The URI may point at a physical resource, such as a file that contains a schema, but this is not a requirement.

Nevertheless, SOAP bucks the trend and does what appears to be logical. If you request the URI `http://schemas.xmlsoap.org/soap/envelope` with your browser, you will see the XML schema for the SOAP envelope. (The Resource Directory Description Language, which is being developed by members of the XML-DEV mail list since January 2001, should prove to be a helpful arbitrator for resolving a namespace against a schema. You can read about it at www.openhealth.org/rddl.)

## The SOAP Header Element

The `Header` element is optional, but if you do include it, it must be the first child element after the `Envelope` element—it must come right after `Envelope`, that is, with no elements in between.

The `Header` element is defined in the SOAP schema, but the child elements of `Header` are not. A qualifying namespace URI is required for the elements that follow `Header`, which are of your choosing. I am using a Uniform Resource Name (URN) syntax with a prefix of `program`. (This URN is for illustration only; it does not identify an actual resource.) The URN syntax is simple. I repeat it here and then follow with a few words of explanation:

```
urn:eddys-stockomatic:program.xsd
```

The `urn` prefix, followed by a colon, can be either uppercase or lowercase. The next phrase is the namespace identifier (NID). Legal characters for NIDs can consist of `A-Z`, `a-z`, `0-9`, and hyphen (`-`). An NID provides a unique namespace name.

After the second colon comes the namespace-specific string (NSS). Legal characters for an NSS are also `A-Z`, `a-z`, `0-9`, plus the characters `( ) + ,
. : = @ ; $ _ ! * '` but the four characters `% / ? #` are reserved and should not be used in an NSS. Spaces are also a no-no. You can encode a reserved or forbidden character by using the hexadecimal notation. For example, you could encode `%20` for a space or `%3F` for a question mark (?).

You can use any legal string here, but I have chosen the name of the XML Schema file against which the elements qualified by the namespace could be validated. This is a nonstandard approach, but it is legal.

The elements following `Header`, `Info`, and its children `Program` and `Version`, are my choice. They embody supplemental or explicit, human-readable information. It's up to the implementers to figure out what to do with such information or to use a `Header` element at all.

### The mustUnderstand Attribute

The `mustUnderstand` attribute is defined in SOAP's schema (notice the `SOAP-ENV` namespace prefix). It can take a Boolean value, either 0 or 1. If its value is 1, the server on the receiving end must be able to understand the information contained in the `Header` element. If it does not recognize the information, the message must fail. If `mustUnderstand` is absent, the meaning `mustUnderstand="0"` (zero) is implied.

### The actor Attribute

Another attribute (not shown in any example) is the `actor` attribute, which names a recipient for the information in the `Header` element. The `Header` element, if present, does not need to be consumed by every SOAP server (hop) along a message's path. All you may care about is that the first destination server receives the content of Header, not the SOAP interme-diary servers that are just passing the document along.

If the value of actor is http://schemas.xmlsoap.org/soap/actor/next, only the very first SOAP application server that processes the message should process the Header element. This actor, then, is the only recipient of the Header, regardless of how many times the message hops between other servers. If you leave off the actor attribute, the server that winds up being the final recipient of the message is the only one that digests the contents of Header.

## The SOAP Body Element

The Body element like Header must be a direct child of Envelope, but it need not be the first immediate child if Header is present. If a Header ele-ment is not present, the Body element must be the first immediate child of Envelope. In other words, Body is first if Header isn't.

The Body element is what carries the payload of the SOAP message. In the preceding example, the Body element carries elements intended to pro-vide directives, such as method calls and parameters for those calls, to a program on the receiving server.

Child elements of Body are called *body entries*. The child element Body in this example is GetQuote. This is the name of the method you want to call in a program on the server. (Again, this program does not really exist; it is just an illustration.) GetQuote, in turn, has two children, Symbol and Time. Symbol is the short name of the stock for which you want a quote (GTW is for Gateway, Inc., by the way), and Time contains the exact date and time for which you want the quote. Symbol and Time are intended as parameters to the method call.

The GetQuote element declares the namespace using again the URN syntax as in urn:eddys-stockomatic:stocks.xsd. The NSS (tail end of the namespace) is the implementer's choice, and again I have chosen the name of a fictitious XML Schema file, admittedly nonstandard but legal.

You can assume that the method will look up a value stored in a data-base or table or some other efficient means for storing or even calculating data. Perhaps each symbol has an associated table with money values asso-ciated with a time or range of times, or maybe it is calculated on the fly. The program itself does not need to be transported across the Net, only the val-ues it produces, so you are more or less free to choose the programming language you prefer. The program itself does not have to interoperate with the Internet or with the compiled code of a different programming lan-guage. It just has to accept the call and spit out a value based on the call.

## Response Message

The whole big deal behind SOAP is that after you have issued a method call or some other instruction in a message, you should be able to expect a message in return that will satisfy your request. This is not unlike `Order-Request` and `OrderResponse` in xCBL or cXML. Here is a response message that you could very well expect from the first example:

```
<SOAP-ENV:Envelope
xmlns:Soap="http://schemas.xmlsoap.org/soap/envelope">
 <SOAP-ENV:Body>
  <stocks:getquote
    xmlns:stocks="urn:eddys-stockomatic:stocks.xsd">
   <stocks:Price stocks:currency="USD">63.97</stocks:Price>
  </stocks:getquote>
 </SOAP-ENV:Body>
</SOAP-ENV:Envelope>
```

Like the request message, the response payload is tucked inside a `Body` element. The namespace is the same as the request, as well as the namespace prefix. The `getquote` element is not intended as a method call but as an element container for the return value of the method call `GetQuote`. The change from uppercase to lowercase is subtle, but sufficient for reminding us that this is a response and not a request.

The `Price` element holds the value of $63.97 in U.S. dollars (Gateway stock has been traded in decimals since August 28, 2000). The namespace-qualified attribute `currency` is intended to have enumerated content. XML Schema allows a datatype that can represent a list (an enumeration) of valid values such as USD (U.S. dollars), EUR (Euros), GBP (British pounds), DEM (German marks), and so forth.

## The SOAP Fault Element

SOAP provides the optional `Fault` element for reporting error and status information. The `Fault` element may appear in a SOAP response if there is an error in the preceding request message. It must appear as a body entry, only once, if used at all. As defined in SOAP 1.1, there are four possible child elements for `Fault`. Following is an example of a response with a `Fault` element as a body entry:

```
<SOAP-ENV:Envelope
xmlns:Soap="http://schemas.xmlsoap.org/soap/envelope">
<SOAP-ENV:Body>
 <SOAP-ENV:Fault>
  <SOAP-ENV:faultcode>Server</SOAP-ENV:faultcode>
```

```
<SOAP-ENV:faultstring>Error. Try again.</SOAP-ENV:faultstring>
  </SOAP-ENV:Fault>
 </SOAP-ENV:Body>
</SOAP-ENV:Envelope>
```

If `Fault` appears in a SOAP response message, it must also contain the `faultcode` and `faultstring` elements. The `faultactor` and `detail` elements are necessary under other circumstances: `faultactor` must be present if one of the network hops or forwarding servers fails, and `detail` spells out that something went wrong within the `Body` element of the request.

The first child of `Fault`, `faultcode`, contains algorithmic responses concerning the error or problem, while `faultstring` is intended to provide human-readable information about the fault. The value of `fault-code` in this example is `Server`, one of four basic values for faultcode. The other possible values are `Client`, `MustUnderstand`, and `VersionMis-match`. `Server` and `Client` each name a culprit server or client that is in an error. `VersionMismatch` signifies a namespace problem for the SOAP `Envelope` element. Finally, `MustUnderstand` shows specifically that a child of `Header` was not understood. (The `faultcode` value `Must-Understand` is different from the attribute `mustUnderstand` discussed in the section titled *The mustUnderstand Attribute*.)

# SOAP and HTTP

Let's add an HTTP header to our SOAP request message, as if we were going to transport it. The HTTP method POST sends data to a fictitious program at `/SOAP/stockomatic` on the host or server `testb2b.org`. The `Content-Type` (also called a MIME or media type) is plain text in XML format with a standard Latin-1 (Western European) character set, that is, ISO-8859-1.

```
POST /SOAP/stockomatic HTTP/1.1
Host: testb2b.org
Content-Type: text/xml; charset="iso-8859-1"
SOAPAction: http://testb2b.org/SOAP/intent#GetQuote

<SOAP-ENV:Envelope
xmlns:Soap="http://schemas.xmlsoap.org/soap/envelope">
 <SOAP-ENV:Header>
  <program:Info SOAP-ENV:mustUnderstand="1"
    xmlns:program="urn:eddys-stockomatic:program.xsd">
   <program:Name>Stockomatic</program:Name>
   <program:Version>0.88</program:Version>
```

```
    </program:Info>
  </SOAP-ENV:Header>
  <SOAP-ENV:Body>
   <stocks:GetQuote
      xmlns:stocks="urn:eddys-stockomatic:stocks.xsd">
    <stocks:Symbol>GTW</stocks:Symbol>
    <stocks:Time>2000-09-05T16:00:00.000-05:00</stocks:Time>
   </stocks:GetQuote>
  </SOAP-ENV:Body>
</SOAP-ENV:Envelope>
```

The fictitious program `stockomatic` on the server ostensibly knows what to do with the SOAP message once it gets it. It accepts the method call `GetQuote` with two parameters, one for the stock `Symbol`, another, `Time`, specifying a date and time. The local program, which might be written in Java, Perl, or Java Server Pages (JSP), for example, processes the request and generates a SOAP message as output, which is embedded in an HTTP response shown in the section titled *The HTTP Response*.

`Content-Type` is an example of an entity header. An entity header provides meta information about entity bodies—entity bodies consist of the document or payload that is part of the HTTP message of which the SOAP message is an example. The HTTP version 1.1 specification provides for extension headers. Extension headers are entity headers that go beyond standard headers to allow, under certain conditions, additional information about a message. `SOAPAction` is an example of such an extension header.

## The SOAPAction Header

The `SOAPAction` header is mandatory in any HTTP SOAP request. It expects as a field value a URI that identifies the intent of the associated message. The URI may point to a resolvable or even human-readable document, or it may just serve as an identifier, not unlike a namespace URI. The preceding example shows a simple URI with no actual document associated with it.

Whatever the case, the header field can help servers or firewalls figure out if they want anything to do with the request. A server can parse the value of the `SOAPAction` header to filter messages and see if the message is from a trusted partner or a renegade.

## The HTTP Response

Following is an example of an HTTP response consistent with the previous HTTP request:

```
HTTP/1.1 200 OK
Date: Fri, 01 Sep 2000 20:01:58 GMT
Content-Type: text/xml; charset="iso-8859-1"
Content-Length: 277

<SOAP-ENV:Envelope
xmlns:Soap="http://schemas.xmlsoap.org/soap/envelope">
 <SOAP-ENV:Body>
  <stocks:getquote
    xmlns:stocks="urn:eddys-stockomatic:stocks.xsd">
   <stocks:Price stocks:currency="USD">63.97</stocks:Price>
  </stocks:getquote>
 </SOAP-ENV:Body>
</SOAP-ENV:Envelope>
```

HTTP returns its version number (`1.1`), a client-success status code (`200`), and a response message (`OK`). The `Date` header provides the date and time that the response was sent. The `Content-Type` header, as you saw in the preceding HTTP request example, indicates that the response is of type `text/xml` and uses the Latin-1 character set. Finally, a `Content-Length` header gives the number of octets or 8-bit bytes in the SOAP message (277).

## SOAP, HTTP, and Firewalls

TCP/IP relies on ports to make connections between hosts. For IP version 4, these ports are identified with integers in the range 0–65535. Often a firewall will block ports from receiving packets. Nonetheless, the default HTTP port (port 80) that SOAP uses must be left unblocked if the system is to function as a public SOAP server. This reliance on trusted protocols like HTTP makes SOAP versatile, and, in addition, an attractive choice because no new software is needed to enable SOAP messaging, unlike CORBA, DCOM, or RMI.

Because SOAP messages bypass the firewall, there is some concern that SOAP can get past a firewall with unreliable data, such as data encoded as base64, which may be an encoded binary file. Although there is not much concern about passing text files to a server, there is concern about passing data such as base64, which, if converted incidentally to a binary stream, could act as a Trojan horse. Well-written server software, however, can allay these fears.

Troubles notwithstanding, you can take a number of precautions to make sure that your SOAP content comes from a trusted source. The `SOAP-Action` header will help, as may technologies such as HTTP digest authentication (RFC 2617), IPSec, Kerberos, or combinations thereof. In the extreme, there is nothing keeping you from encrypting and digitally signing your SOAP messages, but it may cost you in compatibility and performance.

## SOAP Encoding

SOAP provides its own encoding scheme based on XML Schema. Standard SOAP encoding is provided as a simple system for describing SOAP content. If you want to use SOAP's encoding, the Envelope element must also contain a SOAP-ENV:encodingStyle attribute with a value of http://schemas.xmlsoap.org/soap/encoding/.

The SOAP encoding scheme provides an XML-Schema-based grammar for describing the data in a SOAP message. Because it supports XML Schema, SOAP messages can contain any data that can be legally described by XML Schema, such as simple types (datatypes), complex types, and so on.

One handy way to pass values to a SOAP server is with compound types in the form of structs and arrays—familiar terms to a programmer. For example, assuming that you wanted to send a set of data to a server, your SOAP data could take the form of a struct that looks similar to order.xml and in which the qualified name ord:Order acts as the accessor.

```
<ord:Order>
 <Date>2001-01-02</Date>
 <Item type="title">SOAP Essentials</Item>
 <Quantity>18</Quantity>
 <Comments></Comments>
 <ShippingMethod class="1st">USPS</ShippingMethod>
</ord:Order>
```

With structs, the accessor name provides a distinctive name that other accessors cannot share. You could send instances of this struct in a SOAP-encoded array, where the ordinal position provides distinction:

```
<SOAP-ENC:Array SOAP-ENC:arrayType="ord:Order[2]">
 <ord:Order>
  <Date>2001-01-02</Date>
  <Item type="title">SOAP By Example</Item>
  <Quantity>18</Quantity>
  <Comments>ASAP</Comments>
  <ShippingMethod class="1st">USPS</ShippingMethod>
 </ord:Order>
 <ord:Order>
  <Date>2001-01-02</Date>
  <Item type="title">Clean Up with SOAP</Item>
```

```
  <Quantity>53</Quantity>
  <Comments>None.</Comments>
  <ShippingMethod class="4th">USPS</ShippingMethod>
 </ord:Order>
</SOAP=ENC:Array>
```

This instance of SOAP-ENC:Array has two member values (ord: Order[2]). Here is an example of an array of type anyType that contains two member values, each of a different type:

```
<SOAP-ENC:Array SOAP-ENC:arrayType="xsd:anyType[2]">
 <SOAP-ENC:uriReference>
  http://testb2b.org
 </SOAP-ENC:uriReference>
 <SOAP-ENC:string>Web site</SOAP-ENC:string>
</SOAP-ENC:Array>
```

You can learn more about SOAP encoding in section 5 of the SOAP 1.1 note.

## A Working SOAP Example

A working SOAP example that uses HTML and scripting is available online at the address http://soap.develop.com/xsltwire/ client.htm. This example was created be Don Box of DevelopMentor. With it you can either add or subtract numbers by sending values and getting responses via SOAP. The example page is shown in Figure 8.1, and it is deceptively simple.

Just enter numbers in the first and second boxes, and then click either the Add or Subtract button. When you click on the Add button, a script on the page sends the values (9 and 4 by default) to the script at http://soap .develop.com/xsltwire/calculator.xslt in the following SOAP envelope:

```
<env:Envelope
 xmlns:env="http://schemas.xmlsoap.org/soap/envelope/"
 xmlns:enc="http://schemas.xmlsoap.org/soap/encoding/"
 xmlns:icalc="uuid:84124454-ff27-4c41-8f21-dff5f2aa241d">
 <env:Body>
  <icalc:Add>
   <a>9</a><b>4</b>
  </icalc:Add>
 </env:Body>
</env:Envelope>
```

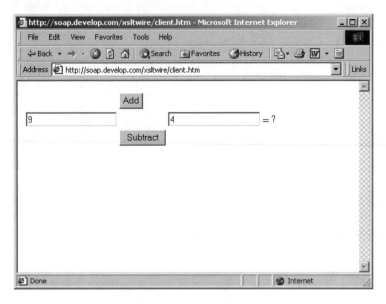

**Figure 8.1** DevelopMentor SOAP example.

If you clicked the Subtract button, the element icalc:Add would be replaced by icalc:Subtract. The namespace for icalc is a Universally Unique Identifier (UUID), a 128-bit value that is guaranteed to be unique in a Distribute Computing Environment (DCE). The Web page is updated with the sum of 13 (or dividend of 5) by passing back a value with a SOAP response message:

```
<?xml version="1.0" encoding="UTF-16"?>

<env:Envelope xmlns:env="http://schemas.xmlsoap.org/soap/envelope/">
 <env:Body>
  <icalc:AddResponse
   xmlns:icalc="uuid:84124454-ff27-4c41-8f21-dff5f2aa241d">
   <result>13</result>
  </icalc:AddResponse>
 </env:Body>
</env:Envelope>
```

If you clicked the Subtract button, the element icalc:AddResponse would be replaced by icalc:SubtractResponse and the value in result would be 5. To see this response message, you must dereference the resource that holds the response message and resulting value immediately after receiving them (`http://soap.develop.com/xsltwire/calculator.xslt`).

## An SMTP Example for SOAP

As I mentioned earlier in the chapter, SOAP 1.1 does not require that all transactions be marshaled with HTTP. Simon Fell (www.zaks.demon.co.uk) has put together an SMTP endpoint that allows you to send a SOAP message to an email address and get a SOAP response message in reply. This is part of Fell's work "Simon's SOAP Server Services for COM," which is composed of SOAP-to-COM server bindings that can invoke methods. (COM stands for Microsoft's Component Object Model.)

If you would like to check it out, just send a plain text email message to the address `soap-listener@zaks.demon.co.uk` with the following SOAP request in the body of the email message:

```
<SOAP-ENV:Envelope
 xmlns:SOAP-ENV="http://schemas.xmlsoap.org/soap/envelope/"
 xmlns:SOAP-ENC="http://schemas.xmlsoap.org/soap/encoding/"
 xmlns:xsd="http://www.w3.org/1999/XMLSchema"
SOAP-ENV:encodingStyle="http://schemas.xmlsoap.org/soap/encoding/">
 <SOAP-ENV:Body>
  <m:doubler xmlns:m="http://simon.fell.com/calc">
   <nums SOAP-ENC:arrayType="xsd:int[1]">
    <number>10</number>
   </nums>
  </m:doubler>
 </SOAP-ENV:Body>
</SOAP-ENV:Envelope>
```

The SOAP listener on the other end picks up the value 10 in the number element, doubles the value, and returns it to you in an email message. Notice that the element `number` has a SOAP encoding array type (a single member value of type `int`). This SOAP response message will look something like this:

```
<?xml version="1.0"?>
<SOAP-ENV:Envelope
xmlns:SOAP-ENV="http://schemas.xmlsoap.org/soap/envelope/"
xmlns:SOAP-ENC="http://schemas.xmlsoap.org/soap/encoding/"
```

```
xmlns:xsd="http://www.w3.org/1999/XMLSchema"
xmlns:xsi="http://www.w3.org/1999/XMLSchema-instance"
SOAP-ENV:encodingStyle="http://schemas.xmlsoap.org/soap/encoding/">
 <SOAP-ENV:Body>
  <m:doublerResponse xmlns:m="http://simon.fell.com/calc">
   <nums xsi:type="SOAP-ENC:Array"
         SOAP-ENC:arrayType="xsd:int[1]">
    <item xsi:type="xsd:int">20</item>
   </nums>
  </m:doublerResponse>
 </SOAP-ENV:Body>
</SOAP-ENV:Envelope>
```

Granted this is not a complex mathematical calculation, but it shows the basic steps of how you could use an SMTP-style SOAP interface.

## SOAP and MIME

Even though it is not part of the original W3C SOAP 1.1 note, an additional note, "SOAP Messages with Attachments," was submitted to the W3C in December 2000. This note outlines the use of MIME headers in SOAP. This will allow for the transmittal of attachments, which assumes also that you could send multipart documents (`multipart/related`) in a SOAP message. This capability is a logical addition to SOAP, and I imagine it will be incorporated into a future release of SOAP.

With the addition of MIME, a future SOAP message might look like the following example. I've added MIME to an earlier example, plus included a representation of an attachment—a one-day chart given as a TIFF image, rendered as base64.

```
POST /SOAP/stockomatic HTTP/1.1
Host: testb2b.org
Content-Type: multipart/related; boundary=testb2b; type=text/xml;
start="<2000-09-01-9785-order.xml@testb2b.org>"
Content-Length: XXX
SOAPAction: http://testb2b.org/SOAP/intent#GetQuote
Content-Description: Quote plus 1-day chart

--testb2b
Content-Type: text/xml; charset=iso-8859-01
Content-Transfoer-Encoding: 8bit
COntent-ID: <2000-09-01-9785-order.xml@testb2b.org>

<?xml version="1.0" ?>
<SOAP-ENV:Envelope
```

```
    xmlns:Soap="http://schemas.xmlsoap.org/soap/envelope">
     <SOAP-ENV:Header>
      <program:Info SOAP-ENV:mustUnderstand="1"
         xmlns:program="urn:eddys-stockomatic:program.xsd">
       <program:Name>Stockomatic</program:Name>
       <program:Version>0.88</program:Version>
      </program:Info>
     </SOAP-ENV:Header>
     <SOAP-ENV:Body>
      <stocks:GetQuote
         xmlns:stocks="urn:eddys-stockomatic:stocks.xsd">
       <stocks:Symbol>GTW</stocks:Symbol>
       <stocks:Time>2000-09-05T16:00:00.000-05:00</stocks:Time>
      </stocks:GetQuote>
     </SOAP-ENV:Body>
    </SOAP-ENV:Envelope>

    --testb2b
    Content-Type: imag/tiff
    Content-Transfoer-Encoding: base64
    COntent-ID: <2000-09-01-9785-order.xml@testb2b.org>


    XXXXXXXXXXXXXXXXXXXXXXXXXXXXXXXXXXXXXXXXXXXXXXXXXXXXXXXXXXXX
    YYYYYYYYYYYYYYYYYYYYYYYYYYYYYYYYYYYYYYYYYYYYYYYYYYYYYYYYYYY
    ZZZZZZZZZZZZZZZZZZZZZZZZZZZZZZZZZZZZZZZZZZZZZZZZZZZZZZZZZZZ
    . . .

    --testb2b--
```

## SOAP Programming Resources

Microsoft has already built a SOAP toolkit into its Visual Studio (http://msdn.microsoft.com/xml/general/toolkit_intro.asp), and it is likely that other interactive development environments (IDEs) will follow. I like Phalanx Systems' little SOAP demo written by Matt Long (www .phalanxsys.com/soap/soapbyproxy.asp). You can get a stock quote, time from the U.S. Naval Observatory, or word and phrase translations on the fly. James Snell's site is also a good starting point (www.soap-wrc.com/webservices/).

Apache offers a Java implementation of SOAP (http://xml.apache.org/soap/), as well as ZVON's IDOOXOAP (http://www.zvon.org/index .php?nav_id=34). DevelopMentor (www.develop.com/soap/) also provides free downloads of preliminary SOAP servers in Java and Perl.

## Apache SOAP Calculator Example

In order to get the Apache SOAP examples to work on your local machine, you have to install the Apache Tomcat server on it. It is available at http://jakarta.apache.org/. If you extract the ZIP archive, the documentation for installing Tomcat is in the `c:\jakarta-tomcat\docs\install` (or `/home/mike/jakarta-tomcat/docs/install` on Unix) directory.

After Tomcat is installed and your classpath is properly set, you can start the Tomcat server with this command:

```
jakarta-tomcat\bin\tomcat start
```

Then after downloading Apache SOAP, deploy a service to your local Web site with this line:

```
java org.apache.soap.server.ServiceManagerClient
http://localhost:8080/soap/servlet/rpcrouter deploy c:\soap-
2_0\samples\calculator\DeploymentDescriptor.xml
```

The deployment descriptor file contains four JavaScript functions that add, subtract, multiply, and divide, which are employed by the SOAP server. With all this running, you can submit the following command:

```
java samples.calculator.Calculator
http://localhost:8080/soap/servlet/rpcrouter
```

This brings up the a calculator dialog box, as shown in Figure 8.2.

Enter a number, then an operator, then another number. The second operator fires off a SOAP request to the server and returns a response.

> **NOTE**   As you can tell, these instructions are not trivial. I must warn you that the Apache calculator program may not work as described. It is not unlikely that the sources and instructions for this example will change between the time of writing and publication. My suggestion to you is to use this text as a guide, but rely on the latest Apache documentation for the details.

# SOAP and the Future

SOAP is the basis for a new W3C activity called the XML Protocol, or XP. XP is based on SOAP 1.1, but I will be surprised if XP doesn't take SOAP by the horns. The goal for XP is, like SOAP, to encapsulate peer-to-peer messages in XML, with perhaps a broader swathe. The W3C, for example,

**Figure 8.2** Apache SOAP calculator.

will develop XP in concert with Internet Engineering Task Force (IETF). They are also working with the OASIS folks who are developing the transport, routing, and packaging piece of ebXML. The SOAP and ebXML message envelopes do not behave or look that differently. It is going to be interesting to see if XP somehow merges their efforts together.

Microsoft appears to have gone to the bank on SOAP 1.1, having recreated BizTalk as a SOAP implementation, as if it were a fully-approved W3C recommendation. BizTalk, it seems to me, is the most highly-developed implementation of SOAP available. We'll take a look at it in Chapter 9.

# BizTalk

Microsoft enters the B2B fray with its BizTalk framework. Following a trend you have already seen, BizTalk has more similarities to than departures from the other initiatives discussed in earlier chapters. Not surprisingly, BizTalk, like its counterparts, is a framework of technologies such as XML, HTTP, and SOAP, to provide structure for business document or message exchange. In spite of being the product of a vendor-controlled consortium, BizTalk is straightforward, reasonably simple, and flexible.

BizTalk relies on a BizTalk Framework Compliant Server (BFC) to get its work done, namely BizTalk Server 2000. Now the version 2.0 draft spec does not come and say that a BFC server has to be a BizTalk Server 2000, only that it has to be BFC-compliant. BizTalk Server 2000 relies on Windows 2000 Server, SQL Server 2000, and Visio 2000, so that when you gather all the pieces, you are looking at quite a bit of disk space and a hefty price tag. Cost notwithstanding, you know BizTalk will be a player on the B2B field because if anyone knows how to play hardball, it's Microsoft. I have not found a direct discussion on how to write a compliant BFC server, but if you follow the BizTalk rules closely, you have a good chance of getting there in absence of a BFC server specification.

A BizTalk application is one that can read and write BizTalk documents and communicate with a BFC server. There is no reason why Microsoft

Internet Explorer 5.0 (or later) can't render a BizTalk document as well as any browser that supports XML can read a BizTalk document. Microsoft also provides an application called BizTalk Editor that comes bundled with the BizTalk server. You can view and edit BizTalk messages with this editor.

A word of caution: BizTalk, which calls itself an extension of SOAP, apparently relies on SOAP as if it were a solid standard, which it is not. It is likely to become some sort of a standard, if only de facto, but a W3C Note is hardly a normative standard. Nonetheless, Microsoft will no doubt support SOAP in the future, so if you have a predominantly Microsoft infrastructure, SOAP is a safe bet for you, even if the Internet community at large does not accept it.

BizTalk is not a total B2B solution, but it is probably a must if you need to interface happily with a Microsoft B2B environment. For example, while there are procedures for sending out receipts in response to BizTalk messages, there is no built-in mechanism to acknowledge receipts, such as a receipt for a receipt. In addition, there is no contingency plan in the event of a catastrophic server crash. All that said, knowing that Microsoft is in the B2B game to win gives me hope that we will see solid additions to BizTalk in the near future.

The version 2.0 draft of BizTalk is quite a bit different from the original draft that came out early in 2000. With the advent of SOAP, Microsoft decided to sacrifice backward compatibility to forward movement. In other words, SOAP wins over the original spec as the way to do things.

**NOTE** This chapter is an introduction to BizTalk. If you are serious about developing BizTalk documents, you should read the BizTalk 2.0 draft specification, available at http://msdn.microsoft.com/xml/articles/biztalk/biztalkfwv2draft.asp.

Before we go any further, let's jump head first into an example—it's the best way to get going down the road.

## A Simple BizTalk Example

This is a simple BizTalk example, without HTTP headers (you'll see those later), where you will see, yet again, `order.xml`, highlighted in bold.

```
<?xml version="1.0" ?>
<SOAP-ENV:Envelope>
```

```
      xmlns:SOAP-ENV="http://schemas.xmlsoap.org/soap/envelope/"
      xmlns:xsi="http://www.w3.org/2000/10/XMLSchema-instance">
      <SOAP-ENV:Header>
       <eps:endpoints SOAP-ENV:mustUnderstand="1"
        xmlns:eps="http://schemas.biztalk.org/btf-2-0/endpoints"
        xmlns:b2b="http://testb2b.org/b2b">
        <eps:to>
         <eps:address xsi:type="b2b:DUNS">06-853-2535</eps:address>
        </eps:to>
        <eps:from>
         <eps:address xsi:type="b2b:DUNS">86-757-8317</eps:address>
        </eps:from>
       </eps:endpoints>
       <svc:services SOAP-ENV:mustUnderstand="1">
        <svc:deliveryReceiptRequest>
         <svc:sendTo>
          <svc:address xsi:type="b2b:svcurl">
           http://www.testb2b.org/B2B/receipts
          </svc:address>
         </svc:sendTo>
         <svc:sendBy></svc:sendBy>
        </svc:deliveryReceiptRequest>
       </svc:services>
       <prop:properties SOAP-ENV:mustUnderstand="1"
        xmlns:prop="http://schemas.biztalk.org/btf-2-0/properties">
        <prop:identity>7691CD20D329B64A469FA61DDB10418F
        </prop:identity>
        <prop:sentAt>2001-01-02T12:00:00-08:00</prop:sentAt>
        <prop:expiresAt>2000-01-03T13:00:00-08:00</prop:expiresAt>
        <prop:topic>http://testb2b.org/order</prop:topic>
       </prop:properties>
      </SOAP-ENV:Header>
      <SOAP-ENV:Body>
      <order:Order order:partner="06-853-2535"
       xmlns:order="http://testb2b.org/order">
       <order:Date>2001-03-05</order:Date>
       <order:Item order:type="ISBN">0471404012</order:Item>
       <order:Quantity>22</order:Quantity>
       <order:Comments>None.</order:Comments>
       <order:ShippingMethod
        order:class="4th">USPS</order:ShippingMethod>
      </order:Order>
      </SOAP-ENV:Body>
     </SOAP-ENV:Envelope>
```

This is a minimal document that demonstrates the structure of a BizTalk message. I'll begin taking it apart piece by piece so that you can better identify what is going on.

# BizTalk Messages and Documents

Right off the bat, a BizTalk document is part of a BizTalk message. A complete BizTalk message will contain a BizTalk document but might also include HTTP 1.1 headers, MIME or S/MIME headers, or attachments. A BizTalk message is a container for BizTalk documents. BizTalk documents are SOAP messages that contain the additional elements and attributes required by BizTalk.

## The Root Element Envelope

Because a BizTalk message is also a SOAP message, the root element is the SOAP `Envelope` element, including a namespace declaration for `Envelope`, `http://schemas.xmlsoap.org/soap/envelope`. I've used the conventional prefix `SOAP-ENV` for the namespace, but you, of course, can use another prefix if you wish. This element also declares the XML Schema Instance namespace as well, that is, `http://www.w3.org/2000/10/XMLSchema-instance`, with the conventional prefix `xsi`.

### XML Schema Instance Attributes

Several attributes are defined in the XML Schema Instance namespace for direct use in XML documents, not in an XML Schema document that defines an XML document. One of those attributes is `xsi:type`, which explicitly declares an element's type for the express purpose of validation. Though the `xsi:type` attribute appears in BizTalk documents, the BizTalk spec does not mandate the use of XML Schema or any other document definition language. You can use DTDs, XML Schema, or XDR, however, if you wish. By the way, BizTalk documents may be validated against either XDR or XML Schema documents, which are documented in the BizTalk specification.

## The Header Element and BizTags

The SOAP element `Header`, if present, must immediately follow an `Envelope` element. In a BizTalk document, `Header` contains BizTags. Also called *header entries*, BizTags are child elements or subelements of `Header` elements. There are five of them: `endpoints`, `properties`, `services`, `manifest`, and `process`. BizTags are processed by the BFC server as well as the applications that interface with server.

## The mustUnderstand Attribute

Remember the `mustUnderstand` attribute from Chapter 8, "Simple Object Access Protocol"? Just as the name suggests, a BFC server—which by nature is a SOAP server—must be able to understand the contents of the SOAP `Header` element in your BizTalk document. That's what a value of 1 means. A value of 0 (zero) or an absent `mustUnderstand` attribute means that it's OK if the server does not recognize the contents of `Header`. The use of `mustUnderstand` in the `endpoints`, `properties`, and `services` elements is always mandatory.

### BizTalk Versioning

Because BizTalk follows SOAP 1.1, it uses a namespace URI to indicate what version is in use, rather than a version number. If a SOAP header does not carry a recognized namespace URI, the BFC server must spit back an error. A `mustUnderstand="1"` attribute/value pair indicates that the server must recognize the message header; if not, you get an error in your face.

## BizTalk Namespaces

As you can see, `endpoints` declares two namespaces. One, `http://schemas.biztalk.org/btf-2-0/endpoints`, is a BizTag namespace, while the other, `http://testb2b.org/b2b`, is vendor-specific. BizTalk assigns several namespaces to the five BizTags and their children, as well as the `receipt` element. Table 9.1 lists them.

The BizTags are also complex types conforming to those found in XDR or XML Schema. A complex type element contains attributes as well as other elements. A simple type element contains only character data, essentially text.

**Table 9.1**  BizTalk Namespaces

| ELEMENT | PREFIX | NAMESPACE |
| --- | --- | --- |
| endpoints | eps | http://schemas.biztalk.org/btf-2-0/endpoints |
| properties | prop | http://schemas.biztalk.org/btf-2-0/properties |
| services | svc | http://schemas.biztalk.org/btf-2-0/services |
| manifest | fst | http://schemas.biztalk.org/btf-2-0/manifest |
| process | prc | http://schemas.biztalk.org/btf-2-0/process |
| receipt | rct | http://schemas.biztalk.org/btf-2-0/receipt |

### The endpoints Element

The endpoints element contains information about the source and destination of the BizTalk document. The mandatory child elements to and from must each contain an address element. The elements inform the server and applications about the routing and delivery of BizTalk messages.

The xsi:type attributes state that both instances of the element address have a type of b2b:DUNS—that is, the vendor-specific DUNS attribute in the http://testb2b.org/b2b that is prefixed b2b. An attribute of type DUNS expects a DUNS number as a value. The xsi:type attribute is required, but it can define addresses of various types, such as the name of the organization or a URI reference to the partner's Web site.

The address element is not expected to contain only the URL for a business partner or participating entity. It is best thought of as containing an indicator or pointer to a larger record. The larger record that the address points at—such as a DUNS number—probably contains a physical address, phone and fax numbers, URLs for corporate Web sites, and so on. The BFC must be able to understand address elements and process them properly.

### The Optional services BizTag Element

The services element is an optional BizTag that requests verification of reliable delivery of a BizTalk document by means of a receipt. It must carry the mustUnderstand attribute with a value of 1.

The services element has two child elements, both of which are optional. The first, deliveryReceiptRequest, requests that the server that receives the BizTalk document must send back a delivery receipt to the server sending the document. The second, commitmentReceipt-Request, requests that a commitment receipt be sent back to the sending entity. For an explanation of delivery and commitment receipts, see *The BizTalk Receipt* section, later in this chapter.

The deliveryReceiptRequest element must have two elements as children, namely sendTo and sendBy. The sendTo element, in turn, must contain a single address element. The address element names where the delivery receipt must be sent. This could be a URI, as shown in the example, a DUNS number, or some other scheme. The absolute time by which the delivery receipt must be sent is contained in sendBy. This time instant is in ISO 8601 format.

The commitmentReceiptRequest element (not shown) must also contain the sendTo (with address) and sendBy elements.

### The properties BizTag Element

The `properties` element is a required `Header` entry element that must, in turn, contain the child elements `identity`, `sentAt`, `expiresAt`, and `topic`. These elements help to identify and ascribe properties to a business document. For reasons expressed earlier, the `properties` element includes a `mustUnderstand` attribute and a proper namespace declaration.

The `identity` element contains a string that identifies the business document in the message (see the upcoming section titled *The Body Element and Business Documents*). This could be a URI, a Universally Unique Identifier (UUID), or a simple MD5 digest of the document as is shown in the example (`7691CD20D329B64A469FA61DDB10418F`). BizTalk does not mandate the form of `identity`, only that it identifies the associated business document uniquely.

Both `sentAt` and `expiresAt` contain time instances, the first representing the time at which the properties element was created, the second representing the absolute time that the message expires or goes stale. An expired message is no longer valid and must not be processed. There should be enough elapsed time between `sentAt` and `expiresAt` to allow a reasonable amount of time for delivery. BizTalk chose an absolute rather than relative time or time-to-live (TTL) latency, but it may support TTL in later releases. Relative or TTL latency would allow a document to remain valid for a certain amount of time, based on, for example, when the document was originally sent. Absolute time, on the other hand, sets a specific time after which the document becomes invalid.

The `topic` element contains a URI reference that identifies the purpose and intent of the business document, and it has the same essential purpose as a URI used at the field body of the `SOAPAction` HTTP header.

### The process Element

One last header entry, the optional `process` element, provides a context for describing and understanding the business processes included in the business document. This is referred to as *process management*. The processes are understood by and agreed on by the partners exchanging documents. The following fragment shows you how `process` is composed:

```
<prc:process SOAP-ENV:mustUnderstand="1"
 xmlns:prc="http://schemas.biztalk.org/btf-2-0/process"
 xmlns:b2b="http://testb2b.org/b2b">
 <prc:type>urn:testb2b-orf:Orders</prc:type>
 <prc:instance>urn:testb2b-org:Orders-5719</prc:instance>
```

```
<prc:detail>
 <b2b:exceptionHandling>java2_v1.3</b2b:exceptionHandling>
</prc:detail>
</prc:process>
```

Assuming that the SOAP Envelope namespace was declared earlier, the mustUnderstand attribute indicates that "yes" (1), the server must be able to figure out what process is presenting. The type element uses a URI—in this case, a URN—to identify the business process, while instance also labels it with a URI to ascribe some unique ID. Finally, detail is an optional element that allows you to extend information in process with elements or other content of your choosing. The exceptionHandling element, defined within the fictional namespace http://testb2b.org/b2b, holds content that defines how exceptions will be handled (after the java2_v1.3 scheme).

## The Body Element and Business Documents

Any child elements of the SOAP Body element in a BizTalk document are considered the domain of the vendor or user. BizTalk documents may contain business documents in Body. Business documents are XML documents that are not defined by the BizTalk specification but are agreed on by business partners who are transacting business with BizTalk. For example, you could include xCBL or cXML documents as business documents, if you wish.

Business documents are not permitted to contain BizTags, which must be children of the SOAP Header element in order to be processed properly. Though a business document may contain a URL, hinting at an HTTP connection, the structure of these documents is independent of the transport mechanism by which the BizTalk message is sent. In other words, transport is handled at the server level, regardless of what a business document may contain or indicate.

A business document may be wrapped in a BizTalk document and message by the BFC server or by an application that talks to the server. This is up to the implementer.

In this example, you see that the familiar namespace-qualified order .xml document is the BizTalk business document. BizTalk documents can contain legal XML documents. BizTalk also supports the SOAP encoding mechanisms discussed in Chapter 8, "Simple Object Access Protocol."

# Multiple Business Documents

A Body element may contain a number of business documents. Every direct child of Body is considered by a BFC server to be a separate business document. In the previous example, the Order element is the only direct child of Body, and so Order and its children constitute the only business document in the entire BizTalk document. If there were multiple instances of Order (with children), each instance would be considered a separate business document. The content of Body is serialized; that is, it is considered an object that can be converted to a stream of bytes and then transferred across a network or written to a file. This stream can then later be reconstructed into an object again.

It is also possible to share information between business documents by means of relative URIs (fragment URIs) pointing to elements that have attributes of type ID. If such an element is a direct child of Body, you can turn it off, so to speak, so that it is not interpreted as a separate business document by using the SOAP-ENC:root attribute with a 0 value. An element with this attribute will not be a root in the serialized value graph, or in our context, it will not be a root element of a business document assembled from a Body in a BizTalk document.

The following fragment example should help to illustrate this:

```
<SOAP-ENV:Body>
 <order:Order order:partner="#partner"
  xmlns:order="http://testb2b.org/order">
  <order:Date>2001-03-05</order:Date>
  <order:Item order:type="ISBN">0471404012</order:Item>
  <order:Quantity>22</order:Quantity>
  <order:Comments>None.</order:Comments>
  <order:ShippingMethod
   order:class="4th">USPS</order:ShippingMethod>
 </order:Order>
 <order:Order order:partner="#partner"
  xmlns:order="http://testb2b.org/order">
  <order:Date>2001-03-06</order:Date>
  <order:Item order:type="ISBN">0471404012</order:Item>
  <order:Quantity>17</order:Quantity>
  <order:Comments>None.</order:Comments>
  <order:ShippingMethod
   order:class="4th">USPS</order:ShippingMethod>
 </order:Order>
 <info:Info SOAP-ENC:root="0" id="partner"
  xmlns:SOAP-ENC="http://schemas.xmlsoap.org/soap/encoding"
  xmlns:info="http://testb2b.org/info">
```

```
        <info:Duns>06-853-2535<info:Duns>
        <info:Name>Wy'east Communications</info:Name>
        <info:URL>http://wyeast.net</info:URL>
        <info:Contact>Schlomo</info:Contact>
      </info:Info>
  </SOAP-ENV:Body>
```

Introduced in this example is the element `Info` and its namespace with prefix. Its `root` attribute, with its conventional `SOAP-ENC` prefix, is taken from the SOAP encoding namespace (`http://schemas.xmlsoap.org/soap/encoding`). The `id` attribute—of type ID—with its value `partner` is referenced from the value `#partner` from the `partner` attributes in the `Order` element. The `Order` elements, child elements of `Body`, are each considered separate business documents, but `Info` is not, having the `SOAP-ENC:root` attribute as an earmark.

## The manifest Element

One meaning for the word *manifest* is a bill or list of cargo on a ship, train, or truck. Java JAR files include manifest files, such as the default `META-INF/MANIFEST.MF`, to list their contents. BizTalk likewise has the optional `manifest` element to list its cargo or payload. A BizTalk document's cargo is called the *document catalog*.

A `manifest` element, if included as a header entry, must contain one or more `reference` elements. A `reference` element, in turn, must have a `uri` attribute that points to either content included in the BizTalk document or an external document. These URIs can be URLs to a resource on the Web (`http://testb2b.org/B2B/order.xml`), a pointer to a `Content-ID` in a MIME part (such as an attachment) in the BizTalk document itself (`CID:cover.jpg`), or a fragment identifier (`#backorder`) to an attribute of type ID somewhere in the BizTalk document, as in the example in the section titled *Multiple Business Documents*.

A `reference` element must include either a `document` or an `attachment` element. An optional `description` element may also be included to provide human-readable text that describes an entity referenced by either `document` or `attachment`. BizTalk supports MIME, so the `href` attribute may reference a Content-ID or CID that is embedded in a MIME part found later in the document. This attribute may also reference a business document with a fragment identifier (like `href="#partner"`) or an external document.

The example does not include a manifest, but here is a chunk of markup to illustrate what one looks like:

```
<fst:manifest xmlns="http://schemas.biztalk.org/btf-2-0/manifest">
 <fst:reference>
  <fst:attachment href="CID:cover.jpg"/>
  <fst:description>Book cover</fst:description>
 </fst:reference>
 <fst:reference>
  <fst:document href="http://testb2b.org/B2B/order-archive.xml"/>
  <fst:description>Complete order archive.</fst:description>
 </fst:reference>
</fst:manifest>
```

> **NOTE**  BizTalk is attempting to keep the structure of `manifest` similar to elements in the XML Signature specification for future integration. This promises to be a good, standard practice—that is, to incorporate digital signatures in a standard XML wrapper. Stay tuned on this one.

## Fault Codes

BizTalk, as in SOAP, can also have a `Fault` element appear within a `Body` element (not shown). `Fault` and its child tags, such as `faultcode` and `faultstring`, make sense in reply messages, when fault information about a related request might be necessary. Fault-related elements are described in Chapter 8 in the section called *The SOAP Fault Element*.

# The BizTalk Receipt

A BizTalk receipt is a SOAP message that acknowledges receiving a previous BizTalk message. The receipt contains an `identity` element (child of `properties`) in its header entries. The content of `identity` in a receipt is based on the content of `identity` in the message received. This is given as evidence that the receipt is a reply to the previous message. The `Body` element is always empty in a receipt message. There are two kinds of receipt messages in BizTalk: The delivery receipt and the commitment receipt.

## The Delivery Receipt

A delivery receipt is sent in reply to a `deliveryReceiptRequest` element in a message that is received. A delivery receipt will contain `endpoints` and `properties` elements, and their children, as header entries. In addition, it will also contain a `deliveryReceipt` element as a header entry.

A `deliveryReceipt` must contain a single instance of both the `receivedAt` and `identity` child elements. The `receivedAt` element details the date and time when the acknowledged message was received. The identity element's content corresponds with the content of the identity element of the message being acknowledged.

The `deliveryReceipt` element and its child are highlighted in bold in the following example. The `properties` element is unique to the receipt as every BizTalk document has its own identity. The `identity` element under `deliveryReceipt` has the same content as the `identity` element in the preceding or received message. Note that the `Body` element is empty.

```
<SOAP-ENV:Envelope
 xmlns:SOAP-ENV="http://schemas.xmlsoap.org/soap/envelope/">
 <SOAP-ENV:Header>
   <prop:properties SOAP-ENV:mustUnderstand="1"
   xmlns:prop="http://schemas.biztalk.org/btf-2-0/properties">
<prop:identity>7ECB98A0E446D39C9C853AD4E1DA83DD </prop:identity>
     <prop:sentAt>2001-01-02T12:00:00-08:00</prop:sentAt>
     <prop:expiresAt>2000-01-03T13:00:00-08:00</prop:expiresAt>
     <prop:topic>http://testb2b.org/order</prop:topic>
   </prop:properties>
   <rct:deliveryReceipt xmlns:rct="http://schemas.biztalk.org/btf-2-
0/receipts" SOAP-ENV:mustUnderstand="1">
     <rct:receivedAt>2000-01-02T15:06:26-8:00</rct:receivedAt>
     <rct:identity>7691CD20D329B64A469FA61DDB10418F</rct:identity>
 </SOAP-ENV:Header>
   <SOAP-ENV:Body/>
</SOAP-ENV:Envelope>
```

BizTalk documents are expected to act responsibly. This means that if they don't do their job in a reasonable amount of time, such as beat their absolute deadline (`expiresAt`) or send back a receipt, the message should fail. If a message does not get delivered on its first try, retries are permissible as long as the message does not change in any way. If the document arrives after the time set by `sendBy` (delivery deadline) but before `expiresAt` (processing deadline), the receipt should be sent nonetheless.

Somewhere in the application, a retry attempts parameter could be set. If a message, after the maximum retry attempts, fails to be delivered by its absolute deadline, the application that interfaces with the server should cancel it, place it in something like a dead-letter box or queue, and perhaps through a different channel notify the other party of the difficulty. This behavior is at your option and is not specifically laid down in the BizTalk framework, but BizTalk provides the hooks, such as the `expiresAt` and `sendBy` elements, to make it happen.

BizTalk also assumes that, once received, the BizTalk document will be cordially stored and archived for a predetermined period by the receiving partner in a manner determined by the partners. This is referred to as *durable storage*. The exchange of documents should be *idempotent*. This means that only one copy of a delivered storage is kept, even if multiple attempts were made successfully.

## Commitment Receipts

A commitment receipt has a different mission than a delivery receipt. A commitment receipt not only acknowledges the received BizTalk document, but also provides an indication as to whether the receiving server has accepted or rejected the document. The following fragment shows the pertinent part of a commitment receipt:

```
<rct:commitmentReceipt
 xmlns:rct=http://schemas.biztalk.org/btf-2-0/receipts
 xmlns:b2b="http://testb2b.org/b2b" SOAP-ENV:mustUnderstand="1">
 <rct:decidedAt>2001-01-03T13:40:08-08:00</rct:decidedAt>
 <rct:decision>positive</rct:decision>
 <rct:identity>7691CD20D329B64A469FA61DDB10418F</rct:identity>
 <rct:commitmentCode>instantShip</rct:commitmentCode>
 <rct:commitmentDetail>
  <b2b:shipDate>2001-01-03</b2b:shipDate>
 </rct:commitmentDetail>
</rct:commitmentReceipt>
```

The `commitmentReceipt` comes in reply to a `commitmentReceipt-Request` in the original message. The `decisionAt` element provides the 8601 time instant when the received document was either accepted or rejected. The `decision` element can have one of two values, either `positive` or `negative`. This indicates whether the document was accepted (`positive`) or not (`negative`).

As before, `identity` contains the identifying content from the preceding message. (The `properties` element, with its child `identity`, though not shown, provides an ID for the receipt.) The optional elements `commitmentCode` and `commitmentDetail` supply information about the transaction, based on definitions from the `http://testb2b.org/b2b` namespace.

For more information on receipts and the reliable delivery of BizTalk documents, see Section 8 of the *BizTalk Framework 2.0: Document and Message Specification*.

# A Complete BizTalk Message:
# HTTP and MIME with Attachments

BizTalk uses the `multipart/related` MIME type. Sometimes you may want to send along additional files that support a business transaction but are not XML documents. For example, you might include photos, drawings, or support documents that are part of a product catalog; these files are usually saved in some sort of binary format such as TIFF, GIF, or Microsoft Word. Using the `manifest` header entry and MIME structures, BizTalk can handle attachments as well. Attachments are usually binary files encoded, as MIME prescribes, in base64 format.

If an attachment exists in a BizTalk document, a `manifest` element must also exist within the `Header` element. The `href` attribute of the `attachment` element references any attachments with a Content-ID (CID) URL, such as `CID:cover.jpg`.

The HTTP and MIME additions to our previous example are shown in bold:

```
POST /B2B/Submit HTTP/1.1
Host: www.testb2b.org
MIME-Version: 1.0
Content-Type: Multipart/Related;
        boundary=biztalk_boundary;
        type=text/xml;
        start="<7691CD20D329B64A469FA61DDB10418F@testb2b.org>"
Content-Length: 2991
SOAPAction: http://testb2b.org/SOAP/intent#Submit
Content-Description: Orders

--biztalk_boundary
Content-Type: text/xml; charset=UTF-8
Content-Transfer-Encoding: 8bit
Content-ID: <7691CD20D329B64A469FA61DDB10418F@testb2b.org>

<?xml version="1.0" ?>
<SOAP-ENV:Envelope>
 xmlns:SOAP-ENV="http://schemas.xmlsoap.org/soap/envelope/"
 xmlns:xsi="http://www.w3.org/2000/10/XMLSchema-instance">
 <SOAP-ENV:Header>
  <eps:endpoints SOAP-ENV:mustUnderstand="1"
   xmlns:eps="http://schemas.biztalk.org/btf-2-0/endpoints"
   xmlns:b2b="http://testb2b.org/b2b">
   <eps:to>
    <eps:address xsi:type="b2b:DUNS">06-853-2535</eps:address>
   </eps:to>
```

```
    <eps:from>
     <eps:address xsi:type="b2b:DUNS">86-757-8317</eps:address>
    </eps:from>
  <prop:properties SOAP-ENV:mustUnderstand="1"
    xmlns:prop="http://schemas.biztalk.org/btf-2-0/properties">
    <prop:identity>7691CD20D329B64A469FA61DDB10418F
    </prop:identity>
    <prop:sentAt>2001-01-02T12:00:00-08:00</prop:sentAt>
  <prop:expiresAt>2000-01-03T13:00:00-08:00</prop:expiresAt>
  <prop:topic>http://testb2b.org/order</prop:topic>
</prop:properties>
<fst:manifest xmlns:fst="http://schemas.biztalk.org/btf-2-0/manifest">
 <fst:reference>
  <fst:attachment href="CID:cover.jpg"/>
  <fst:description>Book cover</fst:description>
 </fst:reference>
 </fst:manifest>
 </SOAP-ENV:Header>
  <SOAP-ENV:Body>
  <order:Order order:partner="06-853-2535"
   xmlns:order="http://testb2b.org/order">
   <order:Date>2001-03-05</order:Date>
   <order:Item order:type="ISBN">0471404012</order:Item>
   <order:Quantity>22</order:Quantity>
   <order:Comments>None.</order:Comments>
   <order:ShippingMethod
    order:class="4th">USPS</order:ShippingMethod>
  </order:Order>
 </SOAP-ENV:Body>
</SOAP-ENV:Envelope>


--biztalk_boundary
Content-Type: image/jpeg
Content-Transfer-Encoding: base64
Content-ID: <cover.jpg>
```

```
/9j/4AAQSkZJRgABAQAAAQABAAD/2wBDAAUDBAQEAwUEBAQFBQUGBwwIBwcHBw8LCwkMEQ8SE
hEPERETFhwXExQaFRERGCEYGh0dHx8fExciJCIeJBweHx7/2wBDAQUFBQcGBw4ICA4eFBEUHh
4eHh4eHh4eHh4eHh4eHh4eHh4eHh4eHh4eHh4eHh4eHh4eHh4eHh4eHh7/wAARCAH
bAYYDASIAAhEBAxEB/8QAHwAAAQUBAQEBAQEAAAAAAAAAAECAwQFBgcICQoL/8QAtRAAAgED
AwIEAwUFBAQAAAF9AQIDAAQRBRIhMUEGE1FhByJxFDKBkaEII0KxwRVS0fAkM2JyggkKFhcYG
RolJicoKSo0NT
. . .
```

```
--biztalk_boundary--
```

The MIME headers should be familiar to you by now. The boundary delimiter `biztalk_boundary` is arbitrary—you can set it for whatever you want, as long as it is unique. The `Content-Description` header is optional. The starting MIME part has a unique identifier based on an MD5 digest for the BizTalk document.

The `manifest` element contains a reference to an attachment (`CID:cover.jpg`) that is in the second part of the MIME document. The attachment, a JPEG image, is rendered in base64.

> **NOTE**    BizTalk also supports S/MIME. For an example, see Section 10.1, *S/MIME Packaging*, in *BizTalk Framework 2.0: Document and Message Specification*. See also *S/MIME* in Chapter 4, "Security."

## Normative and Non-Normative Specifications

BizTalk 2.0 relies on a number of normative specifications, such as XML 1.0, Namespaces in XML, and ISO 8601, to name a few. Relying on these specs makes good business sense, which is good for developers as well as for Microsoft.

BizTalk also names a few non-normative specs, such as XDR and XML Schema, that it supports. While the BizTalk 2.0 specification claims to support SOAP 1.1 as a normative specification, as far as the W3C is concerned, it is just a Note made available for the sake of discussion only. W3C does not yet endorse SOAP and has no editorial control over the SOAP spec. The Note lists eight authors, half of them employed by Microsoft. Even if SOAP does not achieve recommendation status through W3C, it is likely that Microsoft will support it, or, in the future, XP, which is based on SOAP 1.1.

## BizTalk Basics

I have covered BizTalk basics in this chapter to give you an understanding of the essentials of how BizTalk works. It has not been a comprehensive treatment—I'll leave that to the BizTalk specification—but it has provided you with enough information to get well acquainted with the protocol and perhaps help you get ready to make some decisions.

BizTalk isn't for everyone, but if you are a Microsoft house, you can't ignore it. The BizTalk framework combined with BizTalk Server 2000 is one of the most complete B2B systems around, but you have to pay for it—to get all the pieces together, it could cost you in the tens of thousands of dollars. If you or your company can afford it, go for it. It will probably be worth your money.

# CHAPTER 10

# Putting It All Together

We have covered a lot of territory in these few hundred pages, from the foundation of XML, through transport and security, then on to the XML vocabularies and protocols for B2B. You have been exposed to an abundance of standards that try to govern the way we exchange information. If your head feels like it's about to burst, you are not alone. We live is a sea of information, and sometimes it is hard to stay afloat. This last chapter is dedicated to sorting and sifting through the previous chapters, drawing some conclusions, and getting you poised to make some decisions.

## Why XML?

XML is not a panacea to all the ailments of information processing, but it is an important step in the right direction. I wonder if the team that developed XML only a few years ago—Jon Bosak, James Clark, Tim Bray, Jean Paoli, Eve Maler, and the rest—really knew what they were creating. What started out as an extensible way to define documents for the Web turned out to be a global, standard, universal language for describing data. Sometimes you set out on a trip and wind up in a different place than you planned. Sometimes this is a very good thing.

When hype reaches a certain level, which it certainly has in the case of XML, reality can get a bit distorted. My wife once mused whether *XML* didn't stand for "Excess Male Leisure." With the amount of spare time I have dedicated to XML in recent months, I wonder if she isn't on to something. Am I spending my time, leisure and otherwise, chasing something worthwhile and real, or is it just marketing gone mad?

I have done some homework on the topic, and my conclusion is that XML is real.

XML is the best thing we have going yet, and I don't have the least bit of reluctance in recommending it to you whole-heartedly. If you are using computers to store and share information, XML should be the basis for the structure of that information. You can go to the bank on that. And when you get there, you won't have to withdraw any money because, in its unvarnished form, XML won't cost you a thin dime.

Even though XML is a sure bet, that doesn't mean it's without its problems. To my knowledge, unparsed entities—that is, including non-XML data in an XML document such as JPEG or GIF image—have never worked satisfactorily, at least not with a browser. Namespaces are a highly contentious issue, and some say they are just a mess, though XML-DEV's RDDL may come to the rescue. Supporting specifications, such as XLink, have been tiresomely slow in coming and controversial once they arrive, to say the least. I needn't go on with the list, but I will say this: I don't really care about XML's problems. I am going to use it anyway. I believe the problems will work themselves out over time.

To me, one of the best things about XML is that it is a wide-open frontier land. It is not owned by a big, clutching, secretive, power-hungry behemoth of a corporation. It is managed by a consortium (the W3C), but it's there for anyone to claim and use.

# XML Vocabularies and Protocols

If XML is such a good investment, where do you buy stock? In the second part of this book, I covered a number of the front-running XML vocabularies and protocols for B2B: ebXML, xCBL, cXML, SOAP, and BizTalk. There are others, too, such as RosettaNet for the IT, semiconductor, and electronic components world, Extensible Business Reporting Language (XBRL) for exchanging financial and other business reports and data, and BizTalk's XLang.

**NOTE** You can read more about RosettaNet and other vocabularies on the companion Web site, www.wiley.com/compbooks/fitzgerald.

I will spend a little time going over these vocabularies and postulating about their utility and future.

## ebXML

It's not all there yet, but I think ebXML will win big. Because of its association with OASIS and UN/CEFACT, it's being developed on relatively neutral ground, and this gives me confidence that it won't be overly influenced to lean toward a peculiar corporate worldview. UN/CEFACT's overt awareness of the global needs of small- and medium-sized businesses gives me the feeling that ebXML is looking out for the little guy, not just big corporate interests, though the big hitters are heavily involved, too.

Besides that, ebXML is broad in its scope. It will define not only a messaging protocol, not unlike SOAP, but also core business components and processes, a registry, and collaborative partner arrangements as well. An integrated security strategy is not yet spelled out, but I have no doubt that it will be.

If any business is contemplating its B2B strategy, it will be a good idea to keep a close watch on what is happening on www.ebxml.org.

## xCBL

Commerce One has done a good job with xCBL. With nearly 600 elements, you can create a large range of XML B2B documents, by my count the largest range of any of the XML collections out there. Auction documents are a strength, especially when compared to its competition, as are its security measures. Already at version 3.0, it is fairly mature and stable. If you are interacting with any Commerce One infrastructure on your supply chain, then xCBL is a natural choice.

Its support of the SOX and XDR schema languages narrows its scope somewhat, but, of course, xCBL documents can be validated against plain, old DTDs, as any legal, valid XML must. I am sure Commerce One will throw its support behind XML Schema as well, once it becomes a W3C recommendation, which probably will happen in the first half of 2001. It might get along fine without them, but xCBL does not (yet) use namespaces as specified by the W3C; however, given the controversy swirling about namespaces, that is not a serious detriment—yet.

Commerce One offers xCBL freely to all takers, which is generous enough, but you must take into account that xCBL is not under neutral control and corporations survive not on the principles of greater good but on the principle of what is practical and profitable. If xCBL were not tied in with Commerce One's product offerings, it would never have seen the light of day.

## cXML

Ariba's cXML, like xCBL, is mature and has had a few years to spread itself around. It is offered freely for the taking. Its innovative catalog management and punchout site facilities make it stand out among its peers. I like how the *cXML User's Guide* offers sample ASP programs to help you set up pages that support cXML.

But cXML is under vendor control. If you want to see something in the specification change, you may have a tough time finding a forum for your voice. If you plan to use Ariba products anywhere along the line, cXML will be important to you. Like xCBL, Ariba does not use W3C namespaces, but I figure they will be supported when the namespace specification untangles some of its knots.

## RosettaNet

Even though it is not covered by a chapter is this book, I would like to say a few things about RosettaNet. It is a very strong offering, especially for those in the semiconductor or electronic component business. Many big players are behind it, including Intel, IBM, Cisco, Lucent Technologies, Motorola, NEC, and Toshiba. They have developed an innovative way to document and support business processes with their Partner Interface Process (called PIP for short). RosettaNet's specifications and supporting documents are well thought out and of high quality.

RosettaNet appears to labor as a vendor-neutral consortium, but the barrier of entry can be up to $25,000 a year for solution partners. I have followed RosettaNet closely for a number of months, and it was because the final version 2.0 draft of the RosettaNet Implementation Framework was not published until early January 2001 that a chapter failed to make it into this book.

The strengths and weaknesses of ebXML and RosettaNet seem well matched at this particular moment. If the two were to somehow join forces or at least cooperate in some way, the world would be a better place because of it. For example, ebXML is attempting broad global reach, whereas RosettaNet seems to appeal to the top dogs. Blending their approach would do much to strengthen the overall B2B effort. Rosetta-Net's orderly documentation of business practices and processes through PIPs seems to be an area where it could bolster ebXML.

## SOAP

SOAP provides a neat, orderly way to wrap up XML documents and method calls and send them zipping all over the Internet. It is not an XML vocabulary per se, but it is an important protocol for enveloping and transporting data. Microsoft is one of its chief proponents—a proponent that is perhaps a little too ardent. In the BizTalk specification, SOAP is listed as a normative specification even though it is still only a W3C note.

SOAP is fun and will be an important protocol for enveloping B2B documents, but XML Protocol (XP) is hot on its heels. As I mentioned in Chapter 8, XP is an activity sponsored by the W3C and is based on SOAP 1.1. It stands a chance of overtaking SOAP, but probably not for a couple of years. Until then, SOAP will likely make gains in popularity. SOAP, in one form or another, is here to stay, though it had better make room for XP.

By the way, if you didn't catch this earlier, the ebXML messaging envelope is remarkably similar to the SOAP envelope.

## BizTalk

To put it plainly, the BizTalk protocol is Microsoft's enhanced implementation of SOAP. It relies on the SOAP envelope but offers many enhancements. BizTalk relies on BizTalk Framework 2.0 Compliant servers in order to do its work. I know of only one so far, and that is Microsoft's BizTalk Server 2000, which costs approximately $5000 for a single license and about $25,000 for an enterprise license. You can write your own BFC server, I guess, but I think Microsoft would rather do the work for you and take your money.

Microsoft really has done a good job, though. BizTalk is suitable for many purposes, including heavy-duty B2B operations. Especially if you are a Microsoft operation, I would strongly consider implementing BizTalk.

# Standards

Without my mentioning it, I am sure that you have noticed that the XML vocabularies and protocols discussed in this book almost uniformly sup-

**Table 10.1**  Standard Support

| TECHNOLOGY | EBXML | XCBL | ROSETTANET | CXML | BIZTALK | SOAP |
|---|---|---|---|---|---|---|
| XML | X | X | X | X | X | X |
| DTD | X | X | X | X | X | X |
| XDR | | X | X | X | X | X |
| XML Schema SOX | X | X | X | | X | X |
| HTTP | X | X | X | X | X | X |
| SMTP | X | X | X | X | X | X |
| FTP | X | X | X | X | X | X |
| MIME | X | | X | X | X | X |
| S/MIME | | | X | | X | |
| Security* | X | X | X | X | X | |
| SOAP | | X | | X | X | X |

\* Directly implements some form of security, such as encryption, digital signatures, etc. XML Signature could be applied conceivably to any XML document.

port the same standards. Table 10.1 is a comparison chart that shows what standards these technologies support, either directly or by association. What I mean by association is that, even though a specification may not spell out support for a standard, nothing technically would hinder its use.

In addition to these standards, you have most likely gathered that, wherever possible, the B2B vocabularies use an established standard to express dates and times (ISO 8601), codes for countries (ISO 3166), product classifications (UN/SPSC), and on and on. This is not only good practice but also essential for exchanging consistent, reliable documents.

# Building Applications

Looking back over the chapters, I see that I introduced a number of simple Java programs to perform certain tasks, and I offer one last program in this chapter, `GetOrderLog.java`. This program is demonstrated in the section called *Logging and Tracking*.

Table 10.2 recaps the Java programs in this book. For convenience, all these programs are stored in the program archive available on the book's

**Table 10.2** Java Programs

| NAME | CHAPTER | PURPOSE |
|------|---------|---------|
| `Get.java` | 3 | With HTTP GET, gets a specified file from `testb2b.org`. |
| `GetAny.java` | 3 | With HTTP GET, gets a specified URL and saves it locally with a unique filename. |
| `GetOrder.java` | 3 | With HTTP GET, gets a known file, `order.xml`, from `testb2b.org` and saves it locally with a unique filename. |
| `Put.java` | 3 | With HTTP PUT, puts a known file, `order.xml`, on `http://localhost/B2B`. |
| `SendSMTP.java` | 3 | Generates a copy of `order.xml` from command-line input and sends it to an email address given as an argument. |
| `GetKeys.java` | 4 | Generates DSA keys and prints them to standard output. |
| `SignOrder.java` | 4 | Gets keys and digitally signs `order.xml`. |
| `VerifyOrder.java` | 4 | Verifies the digital signature of `order.xml`. |
| `GetOrderLog.java` | 10 | Logs text printed to standard output in a local log file. |
| `OrderWriter.java` | 10 | Creates and locally saves an XML document based on `order.xml` (no listing given). |

companion Web site, with the class files archived in `testb2b.jar`. All these programs are license-free and free for the taking.

The Java programs in this book will allow you to transport B2B documents via HTTP with either the GET or PUT methods. You saw a way to send a document to an email address and to enter content in a document as you would fill out a form. You also saw how to get public and private keys, digitally sign a document, and then verify the digital signature of a document. Now you will see how to log activities in a file.

## Logging and Tracking

One useful feature you will want to include in a B2B application is logging and tracking. You will want to keep a log or logs of what your programs do and keep track of the files you are managing. You can get a start with the final Java program in the book, `GetOrderLog.java`.

The program first performs a GET method on a B2B document found at
`http://testb2b.org/B2B/order.xml` and then saves the file locally
with a unique filename. It then saves any text printed to the standard output
and error streams to a local, daily log file.

```java
/*
//
// GetOrderLog.java
//
// Gets order.xml from testb2b.org
// Logs stdout to log.txt
//
*/

import java.net.*;
import java.io.*;
import java.util.*;
import java.text.*;


class GetOrderLog {

 public static void main(String[] args) {

  // Start off with a clean slate

  InputStream input = null;
  OutputStream output = null;

  // Random number for unique filename

  Random rn = new Random();

  // Formatted date for unique filename
  // Date format conforms to ISO 8601 and XML Schema date

  DateFormat today = new SimpleDateFormat("yyyy-MM-dd");

  // Form unique filename

  String ufn = new String(today.format(new Date()) + "-" +
rn.nextInt(10000) + "-order.xml");

  try {

  // Capture output into log file

  Logger.start(today.format(new Date()) + "-log.txt");

  // Open URL, input stream, file output stream
```

```
    URL url = new URL("http://testb2b.org/B2B/order.xml");
    input = url.openStream();
    output = new FileOutputStream(ufn);

    // Buffer for download

    byte[] buffer = new byte[1024];
    int readbytes;
    while((readbytes = input.read(buffer)) != -1)
      output.write(buffer, 0, readbytes);
    System.out.println("\nWrote file: " + ufn);

    // Close input

    input.close();

    }

    // Handle exceptions

    catch (Exception err) {

     System.err.println(err);

    }

    finally {

    // Stop logging output and restore settings

    Logger.stop();

      }
    }
}

class Logger extends PrintStream {
 static OutputStream log;
 static PrintStream oldso;
 static PrintStream oldse;

 Logger(PrintStream prt) {
     super(prt);
 }

 // Copy stdout and stderr to a file

 public static void start(String fos) throws IOException {

 // Save old settings
```

```
oldso = System.out;
oldse = System.err;

// Create and open log

log = new PrintStream(new BufferedOutputStream(new
FileOutputStream(fos)));

// Redirect output

System.setOut(new Logger(System.out));
System.setErr(new Logger(System.err));
}

// Restore settings

public static void stop() {

  System.setOut(oldso);
  System.setErr(oldse);

  try {
   log.close();
  } catch (Exception ex) {
     e.printStackTrace();
    }
}

// Overload PrintStream methods

public void write(int pswm) {
try {
 log.write(pswm);
} catch (Exception x) {
   x.printStackTrace();
   setError();
  }
super.write(pswm);
}

public void write(byte buffer[], int offset, int length) {
  try {
   log.write(buffer, offset, length);
  } catch (Exception ex) {
    ex.printStackTrace();
    setError();
   }
   super.write(buffer, offset, length);
 }
}
```

If you read Chapter 3, "Transport," I hope you are familiar with the program `GetOrder.java`. I am not going to reexplain that part of the program here, but I will touch on the new material. This is a fairly simple logging program. If you want to expand your logging capabilities, try IBM alphaWorks' Logging Toolkit for Java (JLog) (http://alphaworks.ibm.com/tech/loggingtoolkit4j).

### What's Going on in GetOrderLog.java?

The first difference, you will notice, is an invocation of the `start()` method from the `Logger` class. This method creates a file called *log.txt* prefixed with today's date and a random number. After all the downloading business is through, the program invokes the `stop()` method from `Logger`. The program is done writing text to the log file, and this method seals off the file, so to speak. It also restores any previous settings.

Following this, the `Logger` class is defined. `Logger` extends `PrintStream`, which means it adds functionality to it. `Logger` writes output not only to standard output but also to the log file. The current settings for `System.out` and `System.err` are tucked away—in `oldso` and `oldse`—so that they can be restored later.

An output file stream is created for the log file, and the `setOut` and `setErr` methods replace the old output streams with the new ones. Finally, it is necessary to override two `write()` methods in `PrintStream` so that they will write the text to both the log file and the print stream.

## A Minimal B2B Application

Now you have the tools and resources necessary to build a working B2B application. Here is a minimal list of the facilities you will need to create a simple yet robust system.

**Choose an XML vocabulary for your B2B system or, for extra fun, write your own.** You can use one of the vocabularies described in earlier chapters or, if you are so inclined, you can write your own vocabulary, as I did for `order.xml`. If you are going to need to interoperate with a variety of vendors or partners, you probably will want to use an established vocabulary rather than your own. On the other hand, perhaps you are working in an area of business that does not have its own markup language. Nothing is stopping you from forming a consortium and creating a suitable markup language. Go for it. Be a pioneer. (You'll do well if you define your vocabulary in a DTD and XML schema, if you write one.)

**Create B2B documents in XML, with an ordinary text editor or with a specialized XML editor such as Altova's XML Spy or SoftQuad's XMetal.** You can also use the method shown in `OrderWriter.java` that automatically creates the markup for you. All you have to do is add the content to the elements and attributes when prompted. This may take a while for longer documents, but it will be a nice way to create documents consistently and quickly. Plus, with proper quality evaluation, such a program will lessen the need for document validation because your markup is no longer arbitrary. The content, however, remains arbitrary and should be checked. I'll leave that to the reader as an exercise!

**Choose a naming scheme for your documents.** You could use the naming scheme introduced in the `GetOrder.java` program, which prepends an ISO 8601 date and a random number to a filename. The main thing is that you want the filenames to be unique and easily trackable. A date helps you track the files—and sort them as well— and a random number guarantees uniqueness.

**Before moving the files, if privacy and security are important to you, you can sign your files on one end of the transaction.** You'd do this with code similar to `SignOrder.java`, and then you'd verify signatures on the opposite end with something like `VerifyOrder.java`. Another simple means of security is to use PGP in script batch form or by using a PGP SDK.

**Once your documents are created, you are ready to transport them to or from your trading partners, over the Internet.** Select the Web site where you will do business. Choose the best transport mechanism for your needs. You might prefer to just use a browser to request or download files or use one of the Java programs, such as `GetOrder.java`, to GET a file or `Put.java` to PUT a file on a server. Probably the simplest way to move files is to use FTP in a script or batch file so that you can automate file movement with an `at` or `cron` command, or with some other task scheduler. You could easily move the file nightly or hourly, depending on the volume of documents you manage. You can even incorporate PGP into an FTP script, combining a couple of steps into one. You may also want to use WebDAV. SSH and SCP also provide secure means of transport.

**In many instances, a reply message is necessary to confirm that a message has been sent successfully and arrived safely.** This is also part of a safety mechanism, so that recipients of a document cannot later repudiate it by denying it ever came. Most of the B2B document exchange schemes require this. Think of it in terms of an auto-reply to an email message. Most modern mail clients allow you to set up an automated reply or an autoresponder message, in response to a message from a given email address. If you use SMTP to move your messages, you can use that mechanism. Otherwise, in the case of HTTP, you can use PHP, ASP, JavaScript, or Java servlets to help you automate a response. With some FTP clients, you can log your sessions, which could be part of a reply-confirmation sequence.

**The person who receives the documents must take responsibility for them, gleaning such information as is necessary to enact business.** This step could be as simple as a `grep` or `find` command that is part of a script or batch command and that redirects output to a file. You could also use XSLT. Or you can create an elaborate parsing program that reads a file and extracts the desired data.

**Logging, tracking, and storing files.** You should also keep logs of your activities, as demonstrated in `GetOrderLog.java`, as these are important documents for nonrepudiation of transactions both sent and received. In addition, it is important to set up a consistent directory structure for storing business documents and logs. For example, you might store copies of documents sent after this model:

```
c:\AcmeAlliedInc\sent\2001-01-01\2001-01-01-7788-order.xml
```

or:

```
/usr/AcmeAlliedInc/sent/2001-01-01/2001-01-01-7788-order.xml
```

Likewise you can store copies of documents received using this model:

```
c:\AcmeAlliedInc\received\2001-01-01\2001-01-01-6375-order.xml
```

or:

```
/usr/AcmeAlliedInc/received/2001-01-01/2001-01-01-6375-order.xml
```

## This Is Only the Start

The programs in this book are only the beginning of what I hope will become a large collection of programs, all freely available, to help you and others build B2B applications. So far, this book has just given you the resources, the pieces of the puzzle, but it does not put the puzzle together for you. I wish I could have done more, but why should I hog all the fun?

Some of you would have preferred to get these programs only after a graphical user interface was added, such as with the Java Swing classes. Where appropriate, these programs could add built-in XML parsing and validation. And what about writing the programs in C++ and even C as well? Maybe even in COBOL? All this will come with time perhaps.

Look at it this way: If I wrote a single, monolithic B2B application, I might not have time to write this book. I might be inviting you to an IPO party for my company that sells B2B applications.

I have a better idea. You write the application and invite me to your IPO party.

# Notes

## Chapter 1: Getting Down to Business-to-Business

| PAGE | REFERENCE |
|------|-----------|
| 1 | **War of 1812:** Don Nardo, *The War of 1812* (San Diego: Lucent, 2000), 25–27. Robert V. Remini, *The Battle of New Orleans: Andrew Jackson and America's First Military Victory* (New York: Penguin, 1999), 169–183. |
| 5 | **EDI:** Walter Houser et al., "EDI Meets the Internet," RFC 1865, January 1996 (www.ietf.org/rfc/rfc1865.txt). |
| 5 | **OBI:** www.openbuy. |
| 7 | **Pony Express:** www.ponyexpress.org/history.htm; www.usps.com; Raymond W. Settle and Mary Lund Settle, *Saddles and Spurs, The Pony Express Saga* (Harrisburg, Penn.: Stackpole, 1955). |
| 7 | **Western Union:** www.westernunion.com. |
| 7 | **Telegraph:** See also Tom Standage's *The Victorian Internet: The Remarkable Story of the Telegraph and the Nineteenth Century's On-Line Pioneers.*(New York: Walker and Co., 1998). |
| 7 | **First electronic commerce transaction:** www.firstdata.com/Pages/Doing_Biz/DW/2110-DW.jsp. |
| 8 | **Internet was born:** www.isoc.org/internet-history/brief.html; see also http://millennium.cs.ucla.edu/LK/Inet/birth.html. |
| 8 | **ARPANet:** Advanced Research Projects Agency Network. ARPA, established by a U.S. Department of Defense directive in 1958, became the Defense Advanced Research Projects Agency in 1972. See www.arpa.gov. |

9    **Goldman Sachs:** *B2B: Just How Big Is the Opportunity?* www.gs
     .com/hightech/research/b2b-opp.pdf.

12   **ROI:** webMethods, "The Model for B2B Integration: Dell Com-
     puter Corporation and webMethods." www.webMethods.com.

# Chapter 2: The XML Foundation

PAGE    REFERENCE

15   **XML:** www.w3.org/TR/REC-xml.html.

15   **XML's impact:** www.softwareag.com/xml/Books/XML%20
     Shockwave.pdf.

18   **"Information Management: A Proposal":** www.w3.org/History/
     1989/proposal.html.

19   **Jon Bosak:** http://java.sun.com/xml/birth_of_xml.html.

19   **James Clark:** www.jclark.com.

21   **HTML Working Group:** www.w3.org/MarkUp/xhtml-
     roadmap/.

22   **IANA:** ftp://ftp.isi.edu/in-notes/iana/assignments/character-
     sets.

23   **Dun & Bradstreet:** www.dnb.com.

26   **ISO 8601 format:** ISO/IEC 8601:1988 Data elements and inter-
     change formats—Information interchange—Representation of
     dates and times: www.iso.ch/cate/d15903.html or www.iso
     .ch/markete/8601.pdf.

29   **10646:** ISO/IEC 10646-1:1993 Information technology—Univer-
     sal Multiple-Octet Coded Character Set (UCS)—Part 1. Architec-
     ture and Basic Multilingual Plane: www.iso.ch/cate/d18741
     .html. An earlier, related ISO standard is ISO/IEC 646:1991
     Information technology—ISO 7-bit coded character set for infor-
     mation interchange: www.iso.ch/cate/d4777.html.

29   **Unicode:** www.unicode.org; for supported characters, see
     Appendix B, "Character Classes," in www.w3.org/TR/REC-xml.

29   **XML namespaces:** www.w3.org/TR/REC-xml-names/. You
     can find hints about namespaces in www.w3.org/TR/REC-xml
     .html, but the bulk of the work was left for a later time. The

namespaces recommendation appeared in January 1999, 11 months after XML 1.0.

30  **XML Schema:** The primer-tutorial is at www.w3.org/TR/xmlschema-0; the structure specification is at www.w3.org/TR/xmlschema-1; www.w3.org/TR/xmlschema-2 is the datatypes specification.

35  **Regular expressions:** www.w3.org/TR/xmlschema-0/ #regex Appendix.

36  **CSS:** www.w3.org./TR/css2/.

39  **XLST recommendation:** www.w3.org/TR/xslt.

40  **Michael Kay's Saxon XSLT processor:** http://users.iclway.co .uk/mhkay/saxon/.

40  **XPath:** www.w3.org/TR/xpath.

40  **XSLT processors:** www.w3.org/style/XSL/#software.

40  **Xalan XSLT processor:** http://xml.apache.org/xalan-j/ index .html.

41  **Sun's Java classpath documentation:** http://java.sun.com/ j2se/1.3/docs/tooldocs/solaris/classpath.html, http://java.sun .com/j2se/1.3/docs/tooldocs/win32/classpath.html, and http:// java.sun.com/j2se/1.3/docs/tooldocs/findingclasses.html.

47  **FOP:** http://xml.apache.org/fop.

47  **FOP documentation:** Look in the docs directory in the top directory of your FOP installation; for example, C:/fop-0_14_0/ docs.

50  **XLink and XPointer:** www.w3.org/TR/xlink and www.w3.org/ TR/xptr.

51  **Document Object Model or DOM:** www.w3.org/DOM/.

51  **SAXCount.java and DOMCount.java:** http://xml.apache .org/xerces-j/domcount.html (Java distribution).

54  **Resource Description Framework:** www.w3.org/RDF/.

54  **XML Query:** www.w3.org/XML/Query.html.

54  **XForms:** www.w3.org/MarkUp/Forms.

54  **XBase:** www.w3.org/TR/xmlbase.

54  **XInclude:** www.w3.org/TR/xinclude.

54  **XML Signature:** www.w3.org/Signature/.

54    **XML Infoset:** www.w3.org/TR/XML-infoset.

54    **Cononical XML:** www.w3.org/TR/XML-c14n.

# Chapter 3: Transport

PAGE    REFERENCE

56    **IP:** www.ietf.org/rfc/rfc0791.txt.

57    **IP addresses:** Jon Postel, "Assigned Numbers," RFC 820, January 1983 (www.ietf.org/rfc/rfc0820.txt).

57    **IPv6:** www.ipv6.org. There are many specifications related to IPv6; see www.ipv6.org/specs.html.

58    **Layers:** The traditional, seven-layer ISO Open Systems Interconnect (OSI) reference model is organized as follows: (1) physical; (2) data-link; (3) network; (4) transport; (5) session; (6) presentation; and (7) application. IP falls under the network layer while TCP falls under transport.

58    **TCP:** www.ietf.org/rfc/rfc0793.txt and www.ietf.org/rfc/rfc1180.txt.

58    **HTTP:** www.ietf.org/rfc/rfc1945.txt and www.ietf.org/rfc/rfc2616.txt; see also www.w3.org/Protocols/HTTP/HTTP2.html.

61    **URI:** T. Berners-Lee et al., "Uniform Resource Identifiers (URI): Generic Syntax," RFC 2396, August 1998 (www.ietf.org/rfc/rfc2396.txt).

63    **Java and XML:** http://java.sun.com/xml/ncfocus.html.

64    **Download the JDK:** http://java.sun.com/j2se/1.3/.

64    **Java Developer's Connection (JDC):** http://java.sun.com/jdc.

65    **Linux path variable how-to:** www.linuxdoc.org/HOWTO/mini/Path.html.

66    **Sun's Java classpath documentation:** http://java.sun.com/j2se/1.3/docs/tooldocs/solaris/classpath.html, http://java.sun.com/j2se/1.3/docs/tooldocs/win32/classpath.html, and http://java.sun.com/j2se/1.3/docs/tooldocs/findingclasses.html.

68    **Get.java:** This and other programs inspired by programs from www.davidflanagan.com.

77     **mod_put:** www.apacheweek.com/features/put.

78     **Web-based Distributed Authoring and Versioning (WebDAV):** www.webdav.org; see also Y. Goland et al., "HTTP Extensions for Distributed Authoring—WebDAV," RFC 2518, February 1999, (www.ietf.org/rfc/rfc2518.txt).

78     **Dreamweaver:** www.macromedia.com/software/ dreamweaver/.

78     **Go Live:** www.adobe.com/products/golive/main.html.

79     **Status codes:** Roy T. Fielding et al., "Hypertext Transfer Protocol—HTTP/1.1," RFC 2616, June 1999, 5771 (www.ietf.org/rfc/ rfc2616.txt).

81     **FTP:** J. Postel and J. Reynolds, "File Transfer Protocol (FTP)," STD 9, RFC 959, October 1985. (www.ietf.org/rfc/rfc959.txt).

88     **MIME:** Nathaniel S. Borenstein and Ned Freed, "MIME (Multipurpose Internet Mail Extensions) Part One: Mechanisms for Specifying and Describing the Format of Internet Message Bodies," RFC 2045, November 1996 (www.ietf.org/rfc/rfc2045.txt).

88     **base64:** Base64 encoding was introduced early in 1993 in John Linn, "Privacy Enhancement for Internet Electronic Mail: Part I: Message Encryption and Authentication Procedures," RFC 1421, February 1993 (www.ietf.org/rfc/rfc1421.txt), 13. It was called "printable encoding" in this RFC.

88     **Standard for Internet text messages:** David H. Crocker, ed., "Standard for the Format of ARPA Internet Text Messages," STD 11, RFC 822, August 13, 1982 (www.ietf.org/rfc/ rfc0822 .txt).

88     **SMTP:** Jonathan B. Postel, "Simple Mail Transfer Protocol," RFC 821, August 1982 (www.ietf.org/rfc/rfc0821.txt).

88     **RFC 733:** David H. Crocker et al., "Standard for the Format of ARPA Network Text Messages," RFC 733, November 21, 1977 (www.ietf.org/rfc/rfc0733.txt).

90     **New top-level domains:** www.icann.org/announcements/icann-pr16nov00.htm.

90     **at sign (@):** RFC 733, 8.

90     **Domain Name System:** P. Mockapetris, "Domain Names—Concepts and Facilities," RFC 1035, November 1987 (www .ietf.org/rfc/rfc1034.txt) and P. Mockapetris, "Domain Names—

Implementation and Specification," RFC 1035, November 1987 (www.ietf.org/rfc/rfc1035.txt). See a list of related RFCs at www.dns.net/dnsrd/rfc/.

90   **Network Solutions, Inc.:** www.networksolutions.com.

93   **POP3:** J. Myers and M. Rose, "Post Office Protocol—Version 3," RFC 1939, May 1996 (www.ietf.org/rfc/rfc1939.txt).

93   **Sendmail:** www.sendmail.org.

94   **IMAP4:** M. Crispin, "Internet Message Access Protocol—Version 4 rev. 1," RFC 2060, December 1996 (www.ietf.org/rfc2060.txt).

96   **MD5:** Ronald L. Rivest, "The MD5 Message-Digest Algorithm," RFC 1321, April 1992 (www.ietf.org/rfc/rfc1321.txt).

99   **Received field:** RFC 822, 20.

100   **Content-type header field:** M.A. Sirbu, "Content-type header field for Internet messages," RFC 1049, March 1, 1988 (www.ietf.org/rfc/rfc1049.txt).

100   **Content types:** ftp://ftp.isi.edu/in-notes/iana/assignments/media-types/.

102   **Quoted-printable encoding:** RFC 2045, 19–23.

104   **Azalea Software:** www.azalea.com/freebies.html; see also John Walker's code at www.fourmilab.ch/webtools/base64/.

107   **Multipart/related type:** E. Levinson, "The MIME Multipart/Related Content-type," RFC 2387, August 1998 (www.ietf.org/rfc/rfc2387.txt).

112   **JavaMail:** http://java.sun.com/products/javamail/.

# Chapter 4: Security

PAGE   REFERENCE

113   **Security measures:** For general information on Internet security, see R. Shirley, "Internet Security Glossary," RFC 2828, May 2000 (www.ietf.org/rfc/rfc2828.txt). See also Simon Singh's popular *The Code Book: The Science of Secrecy from Ancient Egypt to Quantum Cryptography* (New York: Anchor, 1999). It is as entertaining as it is educational. I highly recommend it. Another good overall reference for cryptography is RSA Security's *Frequently*

*Asked Questions about Today's Cryptography*, version 4.1 (May 2000), available at ftp://ftp.rsasecurity.com/pub/labsfaq/rsalabs_faq41.pdf.

117    **RSA:** www.rsasecurity.com.

117    **Ron Rivest:** http://theory.lcs.mit.edu/~rivest/.

117    **DSA and DSS:** Digital Signature Standard (DSS), which supports DSA, is available at http://csrc.nist.gov/fips/fips186-2.pdf. DSA is also defined in *ANSI X9.30.1-1997: Public-Key Cryptography for the Financial Services Industry—Part 1: The Digital Signature Algorithm (DSA)*, American Bankers Association, 1997.

119    **SHA-1:** http://csrc.nist.gov./fips/fip180-1.pdf.

120    **Certificate authorities (CA):** World Internet Security (www.wisekey.com), Entrust (www.entrust.com), Verisign (www.verisign.com), GlobalSign (www.globalsign.com), Thawte (www.thawte.com), Baltimore Technologies (www.baltimore.com).

123    **MD4:** Ronald L. Rivest, "The MD4 Message-Digest Algorithm," RFC 1320, April 1992 (www.ietf.org/rfc/rfc1320.txt).

123    **RIPEMD-160:** www.esat.kuleuven.ac.be/~bosselae/ripemd160.html.

123    **John Walker's MD5 program:** www.fourmilab.ch/md5/; to see what Autodesk, purveyors of AutoCAD, is all about: www.autodesk.com.

125    **java.security.*:** http://java.sun.com/j2se/1.3/docs/api/java/security/package-summary.html.

125    **SignOrder.java:** http://javasun.com/docs/books/tutorial/security1.2/apisign/gensig.html.

128    **VerifyOrder.java:** http://java.sun.com/docs/books/tutorial/security1.2/apisign/versig.html.

130    **java.security.spec.*:** http://java.sun.com/j2se/1.3/docs/api/java/security/spec/package-summary.html.

130    **policytool:** http://java.sun.com/docs/books/tutorial/security1.2/toolsign/index.html.

132    **Apache authentication:** http://apachetoday.com/news_story.php3?ltsn=2000-07-19-002-01-NW-LF-SW.

133    **NCSA HTTPd:** http://hoohoo.ncsa.uiuc.edu/.

133     **Apache digest authentication:** www.apache.org/docs/mod/ mod_digest.html.

134     **RFC 2617:** J. Franks et al., "HTTP Authentication: Basic and Digest Access Authentication," RFC 2617, June 1999 (www.ietf .org/rfc/rfc2617.txt).

134     **DES:** www.itl.nist.gov/fipspubs/fip46-2.htm.

136     **Other means of authentication:** PAM (www.kernel.org/pub/ linux/libs/pam/), Kerberos network authentication protocol (http://web.mit.edu/kerberos/www/ and www.cs.cornell.edu/ Courses/cs513/2000SP/L25.kerberos.paper.html), RSA Security, Inc. (www.rsasecurity.com), Secure Access Control Technologies, Inc. (www.sacman.com), Apache user authentication (www.apacheweek.com/features/userauth), NCSA Mosaic user authentication (http://hoohoo.ncsa.uiuc.edu/docs/tutorials/ user.html).

137     **Kerberos:** J. Kohl and C. Neuman, "The Kerberos Network Authentication Service (V5)," RFC 1510, September 1993 (www.ietf.org/rfc/rfc1510.txt). See also T. Ts'o, "Telnet Authentication: Kerberos Version 5," RFC 2942, September 2000 (www.ietf.org/rfc/rfc2942.txt); http://web.mit.edu/kerberos/ www/; www.isi.edu/gost/info/kerberos/; and to come up to speed quickly, see Brian Tung's Kerberos tutorial at www .isi.edu/gost/brian/security/kerberos.html.

137     **S/MIME:** B. Ramsdell, "S/MIME Version 3 Message Specification," RFC 2633, June 1999 (www.ietf.org/rfc/rfc2633.txt).

139     **XSS:** www.alphaworks.ibm.com/tech/xmlsecuritysuite.

139     **keytool documentation:** http://java.sun.com/products/jdk/1.3/ docs/tooldocs/win32/keytool.html or http://java.sun.com/ products/jdk/1.3/docs/tooldocs/solaris/keytool.html.

144     **Canonical XML:** http://www.w3.org/TR/2000/ WD-xml-c14n- 20000710.

144     **X.509:** *ITU-T X.509 Information technology—Open Systems Interconnection—The Directory: Public-key and attribute certificate frameworks,* available at www.itu.int/itudoc/itu-t/rec/x/x500up/ index.html. There is usually a charge for ITU documents.

146     **IPSec:** www.ietf.org/html.charters/ipsec-charter.html contains a list of IPSec-related RFCs and Internet drafts; see also www.ipsec.com.

146     **SSH IPSec Express:** www.ssh.com/products/ipsec/.

146     **SSH:** Some free SSH distributions include SSH Secure Shell from www.ssh.com; FiSSH from MIT at http://pgpdist .mit.edu/FiSSH/index.html. For IETF activity on SSH, see www.ietf.org/html.charters/secsh-charter.html. See also www .lns.mit.edu/compfac/ssh.html and www.ssh.com/tech/archive/ secsh.html.

146     **IDEA:** International Digital Encryption Algorithm. Was developed at the Swiss Federal Institute of Technology for Ascom, a Swiss telecommunications firm, which owns the patents for it.

146     **Triple-DES:** ANSI X9.52-1998. Triple Data Encryption Algorithm Modes of Operation.

147     **PGP from MIT:** http://web.mit.edu/network/pgp.html; Open PGP information is available at www.ietf.org/html.charters/ openpgp-charter.html.

148     **ZIP file:** www.pkware.com, www.winzip.com.

153     **PGP from international sources:** www.pgpi.org (freeware) and www.pgpinternational.com (Network Associates) are examples.

153     **Network Associates C++ PGP SDK:** www.pgp.com/products/ sdk/default.asp; for other C/C++ resources, see www.pgpi .org/products/sdk/c++/.

153     **Cryptix international OpenPGP Java implementation:** www .cryptix.org/products/openpgp/index.html; for other resources in Java, COM, and Visual Basic, see www.pgpi.org/products/ sdk/other/.

153     **SSL:** http://home.netscape.com/eng/ssl3/draft302.txt.

153     **TLS:** T. Dierks and C. Allen, "The TLS Protocol Version 1.0," RFC 2246, January 1999 (www.ietf.org/rfc/rfc2246.txt).

154     **TLS versus IPSec:** www.ssh.com/tech/techie/article11101999 .html.

154     **JSSE:** Java Secure Socket Extension, available at http://java .sun.com/products/jsse/.

154     **Firewalls:** See Yahoo's fairly long of list of firewall-related products at http://dir.yahoo.com/Business_and_Economy/Business_ to_Business/Computers/Security_and_Encryption/Software/ Firewalls/.

155    **Carnegie Mellon University:** www.cmu.edu.

155    **CERT:** www.cert.org.

155    **X.500:** *ITU-T X.500 Information Technology—Open Systems Inter-connection—The Directory: Overview of Concepts, Models, and Services*, available at www.itu.int/itudoc/itu-t/rec/x/x500up/index.html.

155    **OSI:** *ISO/IEC 7498-1:1994 Information Technology—Open Systems Interconnection—Basic Reference Model: The Basic Model.* There are many documents related to OSI available from the International Standards Organization site, www.iso.ch. There is usually a charge for ISO documents.

156    **LDAP:** G. Good, "The LDAP Data Interchange Format (LDIF)—Technical Specification," RFC 2849, June 2000 (www.ietf.org/rfc/rfc2849.txt). See also www.openldap.org.

157    **DSML:** www.dsml.org.

157    **JNDI:** http://java.sun.com/products/jndi/index.html.

158    **UDDI:** www.uddi.org.

# Chapter 5: ebXML

PAGE    DESCRIPTION

163    **ebXML:** www.ebxml.org.

163    **OASIS:** www.oasis-open.org.

163    **UN/CEFACT:** www.unece.org/cefact.

164    **UN/EDIFACT:** www.unece.org/trade/untdid/welcome.htm.

165    **Requirements:** www.ebxml.org/specdrafts/ReqSpecv1-0.pdf.

165    **Technical architecture:** www.ebxml.org/specdrafts/ ebXML_TA_v0.9.pdf.

165    **Transport:** www.ebxml.org/project_teams/transport/ebXML_Message_Service_Specification_v-0.8_001110.pdf.

165    **Business processes:** www.ebxml.org/project_teams/business_process/wip/metamodel/ebxml Collaboration Modeling Meta-model.zip.

165    **Core components:** www.ebxml.org/project_teams/core_components/ Latest/CC-papers_2000_12_18.zip.

166 **Open-EDI:** *ISO/IEC 14662:1997 Information technology—Open-edi reference model* [Geneva]: International Organization for Standardization, 1997.

166 **IBM's tpaML:** www-106.ibm.com/developerworks/library/tpaml.html. See also www.oasis-open.org/cover/tpa.html.

166 **ISO 3166:** *ISO 3166-1:1997 (E). Codes for the representation of names of countries and their subdivisions—Part 1: Country codes* [Geneva]: International Organization for Standardization, 1997.

166 **UN/SPSC:** www.unspsc.org.

172 **RFC 2376:** E. Whitehead and M. Murata, "XML Media Types," RFC 2376, July 1998 (www.ietf.org/rfc/rfc2376.txt).

175 **RFC 2392:** E. Levinson, "Content-ID and Message-ID Uniform Resource Locators," RFC 2392, August 1998 (www.ietf.org/rfc/2392.txt).

# Chapter 6: xCBL

| PAGE | REFERENCE |
| --- | --- |
| 181 | **xCBL:** www.xcbl.org. |
| 181 | **EDIFACT:** www.unece.org/trade/untdid/welcome.htm. |
| 181 | **X12:** www.x12.org. |
| 181 | **XDR:** www.ltg.ed.ac.uk/~ht/XMLData-Reduced.htm. |
| 181 | **MarketSet:** http://commerceone.com/solutions/emarketplace/marketset.html. |
| 182 | **XML namespaces:** www.w3.org/TR/REC-xml-names. |
| 183 | **SOX:** www.xcbl.org/sox/sox.html. |
| 184 | **XML Schema:** www.w3.org/TR/xmlschema-0 (primer), www.w3.org/tr/xmlschema-1 (structures), and www.w3.org/tr/xmlschema-2 (datatypes). |
| 185 | **XDK:** www.xcbl.org/xdk/xdk.html. |
| 186 | **James Clark's xp and xt:** www.jclark.com. |
| 186 | **SAX:** www.megginson.com/SAX/. |
| 195 | **UN/ECE Recommendation 20:** www.unece.org/cefact/rec/rec20en.htm. |

196    **Commerce One Auction Services:** www.commerceone.com/solutions/business/auction.html.

## Chapter 7: cXML

PAGE    REFERENCE

203    **Ariba:** www.ariba.com.

203    **cXML:** www.cxml.org.

203    **cXML license:** www.cxml.org/home/license.asp.htm.

203    **BizTalk and cXML:** www.ariba.com/pdf/cXMLBizTalk.990913
       .pdf.

207    **Dates and times:** *ISO 8601:1988. Representations of dates and times.*
       [Geneva]: International Organization for Standardization, 1988.
       www.iso.ch/markete/8601.pdf.

208    **RFC 1766:** H. Alvestrand, "Tags for the Identification of Lan-
       guages," March 1995, RFC 1766 (www.ietf.org/rfc/rfc1766.txt).
       See also section 2.12, "Language Identification," in the XML spec
       (www.w3.org/TR/REC-xml#sec-lang-tag).

208    **Language codes:** *ISO 639:1988 (E). Code for the representation of names
       of languages.* [Geneva]: International Organization for Standard-
       ization, 1988.

208    **User-Agent:** See section 14.43, "User-Agent," from R. Fielding et
       al. "Hypertext Transfer Protocol—HTTP/1.1," RFC 2616, June
       1999 (www.ietf.org/rfc/rfc2616.txt).

208    **PKCS #7:** B. Kaliski, "PKCS # 7: Cryptographic Message Syntax
       Version 1.5," RFC 2315, March 1998 (www.ietf.org/rfc/
       rfc2315.txt).

214    **UN/SPSC:** www.unspsc.org. The United Nations and Dun &
       Bradstreet have merged their efforts to come up with a universal
       numbering scheme for over 8000 products and services.

214    **CIF:** Catalog Interchange Format v2.1, www.ariba.com/pdf/
       cif2_1spec.pdf.

217    **Country codes:** *ISO 3166-1:1997 (E). Codes for the representation of
       names of countries and their subdivisions—Part 1: Country codes*
       [Geneva]: International Organization for Standardization, 1997.

217    **RFC 2111:** E. Levinson, "Content-ID and Message-ID Uniform Resource Locators," RFC 2111, March 1997 (www.ietf.org/rfc/rfc2111.txt).

223    **Currency codes:** *ISO 4217: 1995. Codes for the representation of currencies and funds* [Geneva]: International Organization for Standardization, 1995.

223    **Recommendation 20:** www.unece.org/etrades/codesindex.htm.

227    **Opera:** www.opera.com.

227    **Java servlet Cookie class:** http://java.sun.com/products/servlet/2.1/api/javax.servlet.http.Cookie.html; see also section 7 of the *Java Servlet Specification, Version 2.2*, available at ftp://ftp.java.sun.com/pub/servlet/22final-182874/servlet2_2-spec.pdf.

227    **Java plug-in:** http://java.sun.com/products/plugin/1.3/docs/cookie.html.

# Chapter 8: Simple Object Access Protocol

PAGE    REFERENCE

237    **SOAP:** www.soapxml.org.

238    **W3C SOAP 1.1 note:** www.w3.org/TR/SOAP.

239    **Namespaces in XML recommendation:** www.w3.org/TR/REC-xml-names.

239    **URN:** www.ietf.org/rfc/rfc2141.txt.

242    **Gateway traded in decimals:** www.nyse.com/pdfs/decimaltradeimp.pdf.

243    **HTTP version 1.1:** www.ietf.org/rfc/rfc2616.txt.

244    **HTTP extension headers:** RFC 1945, Section 7.1.

247    **Don Box demo:** http://soap.develop.com/xsltwire/client.htm.

249    **Simon Fell's SMTP SOAP endpoint:** www.zaks.demon.co.uk/com/soap.html.

250    **SOAP with Attachments:** www.w3.org/TR/SOAP-attachments; see also earlier work by Barton, John J., Satish Thatte, Henrik Frystyk Nielsen, *SOAP Messages with Attachments*, October 16, 2000 (www.hpl.hp.com/personal/John_Barton/HTTP-A/

SOAPAttachments16OCT00.htm). See also http://msdn.microsoft .com/xml/general/soapattachspec.asp.

251    **James Snell's resource page:** www.soap-wrc.com/webservices/.

251    **Microsoft SOAP toolkit:** http://msdn.microsoft.com/xml/ general/toolkit_intro.asp.

251    **Apache SOAP:** http://xml.apache.org/soap.

251    **DevelopMentor free downloads:** www.develop.com/soap.

251    **Matt Long SOAP demo:** www.phalanxsys.com/soap/ soapbyproxy.asp.

251    **IDOOXOAP:** www.zvon.org/index.php?nav_id=34.

253    **XML Protocol:** www.w3.org/2000/xp/; see also www.w3.org/ 2000/xp/Activity.html for an overview statement.

# Chapter 9: BizTalk

PAGE    REFERENCE

255    While the Biztalk.org Web site doesn't appear to be a subdomain of the Microsoft site, the domain name was registered by Microsoft: www.networksolutions.com/cgi- bin/whois/whois? STRING= biztalk.org.

255    **BizTalk:** www.biztalk.org.

255    **BizTalk Server 2000:** www.microsoft.com/biztalk/.

256    **BizTalk 2.0 draft specification:** www.microsoft.com/biztalk/ techinfo/BuzTalkFramework20.doc.

259    **SOAP 1.1:** www.w3.org/tr/SOAP.

260    **ISO 8601 format:** *ISO/IEC 8601:1988 Data elements and interchange formats—Information interchange—Representation of dates and times*: www.iso.ch/cate/d15903.html or www.iso.ch/markete/ 8601.pdf. See especially section 5.4, "Combinations of date and time of the day representations," on page 7.

263    **URIs:** T. Berners-Lee et al., "Uniform Resource Identifiers (URI): Generic Syntax," RFC 2396, August 1998 (www.ietf.org/rfc/ rfc2396.txt). See especially section 4, "URI References," on page 15.

268    **Multipart/related MIME type:** E. Levinson, "The MIME Multi-part/Related Content-type," RFC 2387, August 1998 (www.ietf.org/rfc/rfc2387.txt).

# Chapter 10: Putting It All Together

PAGE    REFERENCE

272    **RosettaNet:** www.rosettanet.org.

272    **XBRL:** www.xbrl.org.

277    **Logging:** This program was inspired by a logging program found at http://developer.java.sun.com/developer/TechTips/1999/tt1021.html; see also http://alphaworks.ibm.com/tech/loggingtoolkit4j for information on JLog, the IBM alphaWorks Logging Toolkit for Java.

282    **XML Spy:** www.xmlspy.com.

282    **XMetal:** www.softquad.com.

# Index